Scraping a Living

A Life of a Violinist

by

Peter Mountain

Bloomington, IN   Milton Keynes, UK
authorHOUSE®

AuthorHouse™
1663 Liberty Drive, Suite 200
Bloomington, IN 47403
www.authorhouse.com
Phone: 1-800-839-8640

AuthorHouse™ UK Ltd.
500 Avebury Boulevard
Central Milton Keynes, MK9 2BE
www.authorhouse.co.uk
Phone: 08001974150

First published by AuthorHouse 3/20/2007

ISBN: 978-1-4259-8390-1 (sc)

Printed in the United States of America
Bloomington, Indiana

This book is printed on acid-free paper.

Dedication

To my dear wife Muriel (Angela Dale), in memory of her help and inspiration, and with thanks for a lifetime of musical collaboration.

Also, dedication to the memory of Emanuel Hurwitz, great violinist, great musician and friend over sixty years who sadly died in his 87th year as this book was going to press.

Acknowledgements

First and foremost I want to thank Donald Gunn, my daughter Alison's partner, for his detailed and painstaking editing of the entire book, and also for his invaluable advice on all aspects of style and appropriateness. I accept all his emendations with much gratitude, and it is only in the rarest instances that I have stubbornly stuck to my own less correct phraseology in the belief that despite its fault it expresses more truly what I really meant. So, I unreservedly accept responsibility for any mistakes, omissions or inaccuracies that the book may contain. I am also very grateful to Alison for proof-reading Donald's final version.

My thanks to Alan Fearon, a great friend and great musician, for reading the manuscript and for his encouragement. I am grateful for his suggestion of the Selective Appendix giving more details of persons mentioned in the book. But I apologize for the fact that to give a true appreciation of all the people I have talked about, this section could have been extended indefinitely.

In this connection, I apologize to the many colleagues, friends, relatives and acquaintances whom I have either not mentioned at all, or mentioned inadequately. As one gets older, the memories of yesterday or even yester hour become more and more unreliable, but memories of long ago emerge stronger than ever. The temptation to add every new reminiscence is very strong, but at some stage one has to call a halt. Maybe reserve some other past thoughts for future scribblings!

Glossop 2006

SCRAPING A LIVING by PETER MOUNTAIN

The story of a typical professional musician's life and work in Britain, from just before the last war up to the present.

Peter Mountain was born in Shipley, West Yorkshire in 1923 into a family of musicians. He was taught music by both parents and won a scholarship to the Royal Academy of Music when he was sixteen. He studied the violin with Rowsby Woof and played under the baton of Sir Henry Wood, arriving in London the day after the beginning of the German Blitz. During the latter part of hostilities and post-war he played in the Staff Band of the Royal Marines, and was among the first British troops to enter Paris. He also led a Symphony Orchestra sent to accompany Mountbatten on his re-entry into Singapore after the end of the Japanese war. During this tour of duty he played the Tschaikovsky Violin Concerto in Bangkok to an audience that included the King of Siam.

He later went on to study with the eminent Russian pedagogue Sascha Lasserson. He was a member of the Boyd Neel String Orchestra and the original Philharmonia Orchestra. From 1955 to 1966 he was leader of the Royal Liverpool Philharmonic Orchestra. Later posts include Concertmaster of the BBC Training Orchestra, Head of Strings at the Royal Scottish Academy of Music and Drama, and guest leaderships of many orchestras, including the London Philharmonic Orchestra, the BBC Scottish Orchestra and the Northern Sinfonia.

He has played concertos with many orchestras and led his own string quartet and other chamber ensembles, including a long-term sonata ensemble with his wife, the pianist Angela Dale. He has worked widely as an examiner and adjudicator; and as a coach for many Youth Orchestras, including the National Youth Orchestra and the Scottish National Youth Ochestra. He has served on the Board of the Scottish Arts Council, and was also Chairman of the Scottish Society of Composers. He has been awarded Fellowships by the

Royal Academy of Music and the Royal Scottish Academy of Music and Drama, and an honorary Doctorate of Literature by Bradford University in reognition of his work in musical education.

CONTENTS

BOOK 4

Introduction

Some reminiscences delight in reminding us of how lucky we are today. Others (as in Schubert's song "Die Alte") bemoan these "schlechte Zeite" (wicked times) and long for the good old days. As is usually the case, the truth lies somewhere in between. I am trying to follow the advice, as told by the late great comedian Dave Allen, of the Irish father to his son - "My bhoy, in this great journey of life, you must always strive to follow the strait and narrow path, betwixt right and wrong."

It's true that things were different in many ways when I was young, but in others they were very similar. It was better, and it was worse. Prophets of doom about the future of "serious" music are no more right today than they ever were. Conditions for musicians may not be ideal, but when are they likely to be?

They are certainly an improvement on the past that I remember. A young lad learning an instrument back then was definitely looked upon as a bit odd. I used to hide round street corners to avoid the shame of being seen walking home from school with a violin case. Kids nowadays are far less likely to be subjected to the kind of mockery we used to suffer, partly no doubt because it's been reclassified as bullying, and can be dealt with accordingly!

My earliest orchestral experience was Bingley Grammar School Orchestra. It had ten members, including the conductor. There were two violinists, myself and Herbert Whone, my junior by one year. Bert not only became a fine player, but also shines as an artist, photographer and writer. His book "The Simplicity of Playing the Violin" has become a best-seller in the musical world, although as I have pointed out to him, I personally never found it all that simple!

These days, in addition to basic orchestras in most schools, for any child showing ability there are youth orchestras at every level of proficiency, and the best national youth ensembles stand comparison with professional orchestras.

On the other hand, I remember a childhood where for anyone musical, there were ample opportunities to play at church concerts, bazaars, and local music festivals, without the distraction of the myriad other activities available today. In those prehistoric times, there was obviously no TV to devour spare time. For a musical family, home chamber music was a regular reality, which it seldom is now, even amongst professional musicians, who are more likely to be busy doing "gigs" or taking the children to karate. Life then was more relaxed, and there was more time to talk about music. Not that the art of musical conversation is by any means entirely dead, particularly when musicians from different generations get together. If you have music in you I'm afraid it's an incurable disease, and one that makes hypochondriacs of all of us!

The time from just before World War Two to the end of the century was a lively and interesting period in British musical life. It was a hard time for many players, who up to the 30s had earned a living playing for silent cinema, but with the advent of the "talkies" were suddenly unemployed. Many switched careers and took up other trades, but the ones who stayed in music, and were the respected elders of the profession by the time I started out, reaped the benefit of their rigorous upbringing in the cinemas. They were superb sight-readers, and even more importantly, the need to match what they were playing to the mood of what was happening on screen had instilled in them a deep appreciation of the meaning of music. Music isn't just playing in tune and making a beautiful sound. Throughout my life, what I have looked for in music is meaning, and the divine spark that you find every now and then, amongst so much that is merely excellent and admirable.

During my career as a violinist and musician I have been able to observe the evolution of British musical life from ground level. I have been lucky enough to meet and make music with many of the great names of this period. My impression is that while musical talent has never been so widespread at the highest level, among both ensemble players and soloists, we perhaps do not, in the early years of the 21st century, have quite as many people as we used to with true individuality and original flair. The general standard is higher, but there are fewer noticeable peaks to marvel at.

My career as a professional musician in the Britain of the mid and late 20th century was a typical one, involving orchestral playing, chamber music, some degree of solo performance, teaching and musical administration. I hope in reviewing it here that I can offer an insight into this rich and diverse world, and that I may be forgiven if I make occasional detours into any personal observations and hobby–horses that I feel obliged to unload upon the reader!

BOOK 1

Chapter 1 - Early Days

I was born in Shipley, in the West Riding of Yorkshire, on 3rd October 1923. This date should probably have been quite a bit earlier, as I weighed in at an unusual 13 pounds and still have the scars of the forceps on the side of my head to prove it.

The family name, Mountain, always excites curiosity, but a glance at most telephone directories will show that it is not so uncommon. It may be of Huguenot origin. Many of the Huguenots went to Dublin, and you can find the name Montaigne surviving on some old Dublin tombstones. The anglicisation to Mountain probably came later.

Henry Mountain was a Dublin music publisher in the 18th century, and his son John (or Joseph) Mountain was a violinist who crossed the Irish Sea to become the first leader of an orchestra in Liverpool. One notable performance was in the hall in Concert Street, off Bold Street, for the visit of Paganini. He later went to London, played at Covent Garden, and married a singer who became known as Mrs. Mountain:

Mountain [née Wilkinson], Rosemond [Rosoman]

(b London, c1768; d Hammersmith, 3 July 1841). English soprano and actress. She sang in a children's company trained by Charles Dibdin and then worked in the provinces before her Covent Garden début in 1786. She was a sweet singer and a handsome woman who was shown to advantage in 'vocal parts of a genteel and sentimental nature' (Oxberry). She married the violinist John Mountain in 1787 and they often worked together. From 1798 to 1800 she studied with Rauzzini while working in Bath and Bristol. On her return to London the Monthly Mirror described her as 'clearly the best singer now upon the boards'. When Nancy Storace retired in 1808 Mountain took over her roles; she herself left the stage in 1815.

OLIVE BALDWIN, THELMA WILSON: 'Mountain, Rosemond', Grove Music Online ed. L. Macy

Her portrait exists in the Royal College of Music , and John Mountain is mentioned in "Mendelssohn and his Friends in Kensington" (Letters from Fanny and Sophy Horsley edited by Rosamund Gotch), a fascinating picture of London's cultural and social life between 1833 and 1836. He is remembered as a regular visitor coming to play violin sonatas, and is referred to as "dear old Mountain!"

My paternal grandfather was from a Bingley family of sound Methodist stock, and by trade a wool valuer. His second wife, Naomi Hill, came originally from Haworth, and her father knew the Brontës. The coincidence in names goes further than Hill and Mountain - my mother's maiden name was Wood, and my wife was a Dale. Not only that, my father was at one time engaged to Dorothy Wood, a violinist, but broke it off and eventually married a different Dorothy Wood, a pianist.

Grandma Naomi deserves special mention. She was the eldest of a large family, and led a hard early life. When her mother died, Naomi was left to look after her younger siblings. All the children had Biblical names. One sister, Hepzibah, lived in nearby Morton, and we used to visit her. She seemed much older than Grandma, but was in fact three years younger. Grandma remembered the Crimean War, and had started working in the local mill at the age of 10. She gave birth to my father when she was at least 42, and far outlived Grandpa, becoming the oldest inhabitant of Bingley.

She had an unbending work ethic – even in her 90s she would walk the three miles to our house in Shipley, and demand to be allowed to help. This, to my mother's annoyance, often meant finding old, worn out garments or sheets, and using valuable new material to cover them with patches. She had fixed ideas about health and diet. I remember one recurring pronouncement – "I'd rather drink a glass of beer than eat a sausage!" This despite the fact that she was the strictest of teetotallers! Her Yorkshire accent was a joy to my ears – I especially appreciated her use of the phrase "I amn't" as an abbreviation for "I am not". Much more correct than "aren't" or "ain't".

I have particular reason to remember Grandma, because she undoubtedly saved my life. When I came into the world weighing

13 pounds, the doctor put me to one side and concentrated on saving my unfortunate mother. Grandma took charge of me, and according to family accounts stayed up for a fortnight with hardly any sleep, watching over my precarious state. It was the kind of thing that was typical of her – although a touch eccentric, she was full of character and compassion.

My parents were from a comfortably off middle class background, with interests in the arts. My father, Harry Mountain, was a keen amateur violinist. Grandpa Frederick Mountain, after spending years working for a relative pittance as chief buyer for Lister's Mill in Bradford, had been persuaded by Naomi, who had a keen business brain, to set up on his own. He purchased a small wool-sorting warehouse in Bingley, where the Magistrates' Court now stands, and I have early memories of being taken over from Shipley and being allowed to play there. The warehouse had a distinctive smell of raw wool, and there was a crane outside which was used for moving the bales up and down between the three storeys. Dad took his older half-brother Frank into partnership, and the business prospered. We had a car, a great rarity in those days, and Grandpa was able to buy for Dad, from Balmforth's Violin Shop in Leeds, a top-class Italian violin, made in Brescia in 1733 by Pietro Ruggerius. More of this anon.

My mother Dorothy was the daughter of Benjamin Wood, a wool merchant in Bradford and like my other grandparents, a devout Methodist. He built the three substantial late 19th century houses in Shipley known as Victoria Grove, bringing up his family in one of them. Mum had three older brothers and a twin sister. The boys all left home to marry, and the flu epidemic of 1919 carried off Mum's mother and sister, so when she married Harry in 1922, they had to set up house in Victoria Grove to look after Grandpa. This was the house I grew up in, and the focus of all my early memories. Particularly vivid is the recollection of a concert at the Princess Hall in Bingley in 1934 – Dad was the leader of the Bingley Orchestral Society - when the death of Elgar was announced.

I started piano at five years of age and violin at seven, and was soon allowed into the orchestra and other domestic music making. Lessons with Mum were always loving and encouraging; but with Dad rather more tempestuous. He had studied in Huddersfield with Arthur Willie Kaye, who was a pupil of Sevcik and produced several generations of such fine violinists as Laurence Turner, Jessie Hinchliffe and Jane Marcus. To my father, Kaye's word on the importance of stance, bow action and left hand discipline carried the weight of divine authority. Lessons often ended in tears, with Mum coming in to pour oil on stormy waters! Nevertheless, it was to the violin that I turned. I was a reasonably proficient second study pianist at the Academy, but I have always regretted not working harder to develop better technique and facility on that instrument.

Sadly, our prosperity didn't last. Grandpa Mountain's death in 1928 and the slump of 1929 marked a turn in our fortunes. We were suddenly bankrupt. I have a clear memory of crying bitterly, aged 6, when men came to take the car away.

Out of necessity, Mum and Dad turned to their great love, music. They took intensive lessons, passed exams and set themselves up as music teachers. Through hard work and persistence, this proved remarkably successful. The secret, they soon found, was that building up a clientèle depended very little on advertising, and much more on word of mouth. They both discovered a natural ability as teachers, and a real affinity with their pupils. Although they talked "shop" quite a lot, it was always about how their individual students were responding - I can't remember either of them once expressing any weariness or disillusionment at the prospect of another long day of lessons.

My sister Kathleen and I absorbed this way of being, and I hope carried it on into later life. We were brought up to be professional in our music, outward looking and dependable. Having said that, Mum and Dad were two very different personalities. Mum was warm, loving, unflappable and ever reliable. She had a keen sense of humour and awareness of personal foibles. Unlike Grandpa and other branches of the family, she had little time for what she saw as the blinkered attitude of the local religious community, and although Kath and I did go to Sunday School, we were encouraged to adopt the same sceptical approach. Mum didn't favour the head-on apostasy of Uncle Frank, who was a science teacher in Halifax but never became a headmaster because his conscience wouldn't permit him to take morning prayers. Instead, her gentle mockery of the clergy would show itself in little favourite anecdotes, like the one about the dour Yorkshire-man working in his allotment. Along comes the Vicar, who observing the sumptuous array of flowers and vegetables says benignly, "My man, you and God have done a marvellous job of work on this plot of land!" "Aye" comes the reply. "Ye should 'a' seen it when God 'ad it!"

Mum was a boon to local amateur music making, partly because she had the knack of picking up the basics of a variety of instruments, including the violin, viola, flute, and, rather bizarrely, the French Horn. Even more importantly, she had good organisational abilities and was excellent at conducting small orchestral ensembles. She got us through stacks of Charles Woodhouse string arrangements of pieces by the likes of Stamitz, Abel, J C Bach, Avison and Vivaldi - all tremendous fun for young players. Bradford Corporation, to its credit, supported her in a regular weekly orchestral session at Belle Vue School for many years before and after the war.

Dad was a completely different kettle of fish. Whatever he did, he did with zest, always convinced he was completely right. To the world at large he came over as entertaining and lively – Jessie Hinchcliffe, who studied with him in Huddersfield under Arthur Willie Kaye and visited our house frequently when I was a toddler, used to call him Handsome Harry. (Jessie was a very attractive girl and I think she quite fancied Dad!) To his nearest and dearest, it was a slightly different story. He had favourite topics of conversation which, once started on, he would pursue interminably. My wife Muriel, when she first arrived on the scene as my girl-friend, soon found out that if she mentioned anything about musical performance to him, he would end up giving her a violin lesson – not much use to her as a pianist!

There was a lengthy list of things that must not on any account be mentioned to Pa, as they would send him off on one of his tirades. Elgar was one of his dislikes. He thought the music bombastic and chauvinistic – he judged it all by Land of Hope and Glory. Another pet hate was Menuhin. He had heard the young violinist in a Manchester recital, and while impressed by his prodigious talent, had recognized a fundamental weakness in his bowing action. It wasn't until much later that lesser mortals identified this as the cause of technical problems for the mature artist.

Although we had to admit that many of his quirky ideas contained a grain of truth, his obsessive insistence on his own point of view always compelled us to argue with him. In later years when I was in Liverpool, he came over from Yorkshire to spend a few days with us. I warned my son Paul, then aged 11 and already a bit of a stirrer, not on any account to mention Menuhin or Elgar to Grandpa. On the way back from picking Dad up from Lime Street Station, Paul, in the back seat, piped up innocently: "Oh Grandpa, Dad's just bought a recording of Yehudi Menuhin playing the Elgar Violin Concerto". The resulting diatribe must have gone on for at least half an hour.

Dad taught me from the beginning until I went up to the Royal Academy when I was 16. It was a classic example of the inadvisability of parents instructing children, because he always expected too much from me and was intolerant of any failings. This eventually resulted in a tendency on my part to automatically take issue with anything he said – and yet, time and again I have found myself, with my own students, echoing the precepts he drummed relentlessly into me in those early years. He was quietly suspicious of my Academy teaching from Rowsby Woof, but I was glad that he never voiced the same feelings about my later teacher, the great Sascha Lasserson.

He was fiercely proud of my successes, and I always treasured the rare compliments I received from him. But he always reserved the right to point out any lapses from the perfection that he craved. In 1975 he was terminally ill from cancer, and I was using every available excuse to come up to Yorkshire from Bristol, where I was working with the BBC Training Orchestra, knowing that each time I saw him might be the last. In the summer, I called in to see him en route to Glasgow to audition for the post of Head of Strings at the Royal Scottish Academy of Music and Drama. He wished me well, and I went on my way. A few days later, I rang Kath to say that I had been offered the job. She went to see Dad, who by then was in hospital and quite close to the end. During a lucid interval, she said "Dad, I've just heard from Peter – he's got the job in Glasgow!"

"Oh, has he? Hmm. I'm a bit surprised."

"Oh? Why do you say that?"

"Well, his bowing isn't good enough!"

He was almost right – bowing is one of the most important things in string playing, and it is *never* good enough. But of course, the most important thing of all is really intonation - playing perfectly in tune.

This relentlessly musical background did sometimes make us feel a little different from other local families. Endless streams of youngsters arrived for lessons at Victoria Grove, 116 Bradford Road, every afternoon and evening, with my own lessons and Kath's on violin and piano squeezed into any gaps. Weekend evenings often included chamber music parties with musical friends, and there were also the Pupils' Concerts, first in our front room at home, and later at the Connaught Rooms in Bradford. Associated Board Exams were held every term at home, and we entertained visiting musical celebrities who came to play, or more often to sing, with the Bingley Orchestra. For some reason I have particular memories of the soprano Olive Groves and the baritone Keith Faulkner, an impressive but kindly presence who was later to be Principal of the Royal College of Music, London.

As soon as I showed some promise I was taken regularly to concerts in Bradford. To the city's great shame, the St. George's Hall, where my parents had seen and heard so many great artists early in the century, was used between the wars as a Gaumont British cinema, and the venue for the monthly visits of the Hallé and for celebrity recitals was the far less adequate Eastbrook Hall, normally used as a Methodist meeting place. My earliest memory of that venue is from 1930, when aged 7 and just starting the violin, I heard Fritz Kreisler for the only time in my life. The actual playing I can barely recall, although my collection now includes nearly all Kreisler's recordings, but what left a clear impression was the commanding stance of the man and the power of his personality.

I was a season ticket holder for the Hallé concerts, which provided an invaluable introduction to a high quality classical and romantic repertoire. These were pre-Barbirolli days, and the regular conductor then was Beecham, at the height of his powers. He could always be relied upon for a wittily phrased impromptu after-concert speech, berating either the management or the Corporation (but never the Orchestra) for some real or imagined omission. On one occasion his podium was furnished with unexpectedly high side rails, upon which his more generous gestures were seen to impact during the concert. He complained bitterly that he was "not accustomed to conducting in a child's play-pen"!

One advantage the Eastbrook Hall had for Beecham was that the artists' entrance was at the top of an impressive flight of stairs, leading directly down across the stage to the conductor's position. Sir Thomas used to make the grandest of entrances, like some divine Apollo from Elysium descending from on high, prompting the awestruck question from a small girl at one concert, "Oh mummy, is it God?" On one rare occasion when Beecham was not present, Sir Henry Wood conducted in his place, and scuttled down and up the staircase with most unseemly haste - not at all what the discerning Bradford concert-goers were used to!

The leader of the Hallé was Alfred Barker, who had a formidable technique and I believe had previously held a post as violinist at the Imperial Russian court in St Petersburg. Leading the seconds was a youthful Leonard Hirsch, whom I knew later as leader of the Philharmonia, and later still as a colleague in directing the BBC Training Orchestra. Haydn Rogerson was an impressive principal cello - at that time first names like Haydn and Handel were quite common, testifying to the lively tradition of choral music in the North of England. The Hallé boasted a number of fine players, many of whom had been recruited during the previous regime of Sir Hamilton Harty. I very much regret never having seen Harty conduct in the flesh. A good friend of mine, Ambrose Gauntlett, one-time first cellist of the BBC Symphony Orchestra, used to say that the greatest orchestral leader he ever played with was Albert Sammons, and the greatest conductor was Hamilton Harty. The reissues of Harty's recordings that are increasingly becoming available make exciting listening.

My education proceeded along fairly predictable lines, with a scholarship to Bingley Grammar School, where Dad had been before me, and appearances at local Music Festivals and the usual Associated Board Exams. I was examined by Ernest Read, who recommended that I should go to London to play to him and to Rowsby Woof, leading violin professor at the Royal Academy of Music. I was also heard by Charles Hooper, Director of Music for the then West Riding County Council, which operated an enlightened policy of support for young musicians, and was awarded a scholarship which covered a large part of my expenses when I duly took my place at the Academy. I was grateful for this opportunity, and remain conscious of the fact that help available to talented young people in whatever discipline is still all too often dependent on an accident of domicile. Then, as now, some local authorities were very much less generous than others.

Chapter 2 - RAM and the Blitz

Sunday, September 8th, 1940. A significant day for me. I was 16 years old and leaving home to start violin studies at the Royal Academy of Music, London. And a significant day for Britain - the London Blitz had started the afternoon before with fierce aerial bombing of the Capital, which was to last continuously until the following May.

We were not to know this, of course. The so-called "phoney" war had been going on since the previous September, but had limited effect on day-to-day life in the more northern counties like Yorkshire. The Dunkirk evacuation that summer was presented in the media as a kind of triumph, and the general atmosphere was quite up-beat. We had heard about the air raids on London, but it had not succeeded in dampening my excitement at the prospect of making a full commitment to a life of music.

That spring, my parents had stipulated that if I was successful in an application for a scholarship from West Riding Education Committee, I could leave school before doing "Highers" (now A Levels), and embark on a career as a musician. Otherwise I would stay on at school, go to University or get a job, and have my violin playing as a hobby. Now the die was cast. I had been accepted as a student by Rowsby Woof, the most reputable violin teacher in the country, and I was not going to let anyone divert me from this – not even Hitler!

Both my parents walked me down to Shipley station for the 7.45am through train to Kings Cross, not, I am sure, without some misgivings. A carefully packed suitcase and my fiddle were all I needed. I was to stay with family friends, Harry Steel and his wife Marjory, in Hendon. Harry was a professional bassoonist, originally from Bingley and a school friend of my father's. Marjory played the violin, having been taught by my father, so it was a very congenial household and there were no worries for my safety and comfort. The next day I would start at the Academy. We made our fond farewells, and I was off. Shortly afterwards, back at home, Mum and Dad heard on the BBC news that a number of schools and academies would not be opening the next day due to enemy action. One of them was the RAM.

I was quite unaware of this on Monday morning. It may seem strange in a time when we take instant communication for granted, but neither my parents nor the Steels had a telephone, and neither Harry nor Marjory had heard the broadcast on the radio. So I duly took the Northern Line tube to Warren Street and walked along Marylebone Road, only to be blocked by police barriers just before I reached the Academy. An unexploded bomb had landed in York Gate, behind the building. There was nothing to be done but go back to Hendon.

The house was far enough from the centre of London not to suffer from the bombing, but near enough for us to hear another night of severe attacks. On Tuesday I set off to see the only person connected to the Academy whose address I knew – Ernest Read, who had invited me to his home to play for him the previous summer. He had a fine spacious house on Marlborough Hill, St John's Wood, with an exquisite music studio in the garden complete with two grand pianos and an extensive library. But sadly, it had been a casualty of the air raids of the previous night. A bomb had struck it directly, shattering the main house and completely destroying the air-raid shelter under the studio. By incredible good fortune, Ernest had decided the day before the raid that the bombing, particularly severe in that area, was too great a risk, and had taken his family out of London. As I appeared, he had just returned to find his beautiful home in ruins. Almost hysterical with grief, he hardly recognized me, but gave me a dustpan and brush to help clear up. Not knowing what to say, and feeling quite frustrated and useless, I left him to his thoughts.

It has now passed into legend how quickly the people of London adapted to life in real wartime. Less than a fortnight later the Academy re-opened, and I began the first of three years' study. Memories of that time are very mixed. Although it was unreal and often frightening to be part of the London Blitz, and there were many nights of broken sleep, I also have recollections of a more or less normal student life. My walk along Euston Road to the RAM on clear winter mornings was often enlivened by the sight of vapour trails intertwining high in the sky, as the Battle of Britain was fought out before our very eyes.

Fire-watching was an activity that everyone was involved in. Incendiary bombs were a significant part of the German offensive, and in the first few weeks they caused immense damage. People soon realised, however, that if tackled promptly enough with a bucket of sand and a stirrup pump, the fires could very often be put out. So it was customary to sacrifice some sleep to form part of a rota. Often this had unexpected social benefits – impromptu parties were common, and everyone got to know their neighbours much better!

In the second term, when I moved to student digs in Marlborough Place, St John's Wood, our fire-watching group met at the home of Christmas Humphreys, Senior Prosecuting Counsel at the Old Bailey and also founder of the British Buddhist Society, now the largest Buddhist organisation outside Asia. The house was full of Eastern artefacts - jade vases and figurines, intricately carved teak furniture and beautiful porcelain. Christmas and his wife Puck were both lively conversationalists, and as young students our horizons were considerably broadened by their company -Puck's real china tea was a typically exotic experience!

Christmas Humphreys was later involved in several famous cases. In 1955 he was prosecuting counsel at the trial of Ruth Ellis, the last woman in Britain to be hanged for murder. I have often wondered how he was able to reconcile his Buddhist principles with the advocacy of capital punishment.

The other, more normal side of life began with the slightly delayed start of the Autumn Term at the RAM. I arrived on a Monday morning for my interview with Mrs Rawlins, a formidable presence who rejoiced in the title of Lady Superintendent. The solemnity of the occasion was leavened by some comic relief courtesy of the Academy cat, which came stalking disdainfully along the corridor as I sat waiting nervously outside the office. Ignoring me completely, it jumped up onto one of the buckets of sand that were already stationed here and there in case of an incendiary attack. It then proceeded to relieve itself, and carefully and daintily buried the faeces in the sand before strolling off. There has always been a distinctive smell about the Academy that I can still detect whenever I revisit. I can't help wondering how much of it is ascribable to that cat and its descendants.

There was also a brief interview with Sir Stanley Marchant, the Principal, always a rather remote if benign figure that I can't remember much about. Looking back through the mists of time I recall someone not unlike (in appearance and manner) to the Conservative Prime Minister John Major. Easier to connect with was the Warden, Benjamin Dale, a fine composer whose works have been recently re-discovered. He was a friendly, towering presence, and was very fond of my girl friend, Muriel Dale, calling her his unofficial niece!

I began my bi-weekly violin lessons with Rowsby Woof. Lean, abounding in nervous energy, with grizzled hair and forbidding steel-rimmed glasses; he was a rather frightening character on first acquaintance. His unorthodox ways, however, ensured that his students remembered what he said. Those early sessions with him still stay with me vividly. My father (my only teacher until then) had always insisted on developing a strong, firm left hand finger action, maybe too much so, and I recall Rowsby snarling at me as he tried to impart better left hand fluency - "don't *stamp* about so much, boy!" But we all enjoyed our lessons, and generally met afterwards in the canteen to exchange stories about his eccentricities and oddities!

In retrospect we were quite an impressive collection of string players, who would remain lifelong colleagues and associates. We included Colin Sauer, Felix Kok, Ernest Scott, Patrick Halling, William Armon, Granville Jones (later a precociously young leader of the LSO whose career was tragically cut short by a car accident), the viola player Rosemary Green and many others. My own experience has convinced me that you learn at least as much from your fellow students at a place like the Academy as you do from your teachers, and I was lucky to have such stimulating company during those war years. Colin Sauer was the first friend I had at the Academy, and in my first term I was often invited out to his home in Ilford for a welcome Sunday dinner. We used to spend the afternoon in the front room with a wind-up gramophone, drooling over 78 rpm records of Jascha

Heifetz playing Saint-Saëns' Introduction and Rondo Capriccioso, Havanaise, Bazzini Ronde des Lutins and other salon pieces. Heifetz may be out of fashion now, but his incomparable sound will always bring a unique thrill to me.

The Academy schedule was not very arduous, and it was up to the individual student to use the time productively for instrumental practice. Chamber music was encouraged, with weekly classes given by Herbert Withers, well known for his editions of the great classical quartets. Bertie, as he was affectionately known, bore some resemblance to Casals, and was himself a cellist. He had a very pronounced lisp, and was always calling for "abtholute pianithimo!" The temptation to imitate him was too hard to resist, and none of us did. This sometimes had unfortunate consequences. When one student received a phone call to arrange changes in a rehearsal schedule, he assumed it was one of us playing a practical joke, and refused to believe it was in fact Bertie. Red faces all round!

The aural training classes with Ernest Read were good fun and very popular. Both my girl friend Muriel and I were star performers here, and Ernest always insisted that Muriel had a key rôle in the choir that he conducted, because although she didn't have a great voice, she was an excellent sight reader and could keep time. Ernest gave us some fascinating insights into musical life at the start of the 20th century when he was a student. In those days, he said, Academy students were actively discouraged from taking an interest in the music of Brahms, who was seen as dull, academic and boring. The future of music was thought to lie with Joseph Svendsen, now almost forgotten apart from his short Romance for violin, a rather old-fashioned salon piece. Ernest believed in using for our exercises not dry-as-dust theory book samples, but real live music. One favourite of his was Anitra's Dance from Grieg's Peer Gynt, which is quite tricky to write down from dictation. Ernest is still recognised today as a key figure in the development of ear training, so essential for any serious musician.

My harmony and counterpoint tutor was Mr J. A. Sowerbutts, who taught three days a week in a little room on the fourth floor. His principal occupation was organist of Guildford Cathedral. He was a quiet, distinguished–looking gentleman, who treated my rather pathetic offerings with benign forbearance. I remember him as the possessor of an elegant gold propelling pencil, with which he would delicately encircle my consecutive fifths and other abominations, and append gentle admonitions like "Would we do that? I don't think we would!" I also remember one day when he waxed eloquent on the astounding display of contrapuntal dexterity by Mozart in the coda of the last movement of the Jupiter Symphony. It awakened a passion for that masterpiece which has never left me.

I recall with great affection my piano lessons with Edgar Carr, whom I still regard as a paragon for the teaching profession. As a second study pupil I should not have taken up too much of his attention, and he recognized that my main interest was the violin, but was able to coax me along to a point where I managed a reasonably proficient performance of Chopin's Fantasie-Impromptu Op 66 at an Academy fortnightly concert. He and I shared an interest in photography, a topic of conversation I used more than once to cover up the fact that I hadn't done enough practice. I used to go occasionally to his house in Muswell Hill for lessons. He had a little dog who had the run of the place, but would come rushing into the room whenever you tinkled on the highest notes, and cock his ear ecstatically under the Steinway!

Towards the end of my student days, as the war progressed, numbers at the Academy began to decline, but traditional activities were maintained, with various concerts and prizes. Competition adjudicators were then, as now, always distinguished musicians. I remember one prize for which the test piece was three movements of the Bach Partita for Solo Violin in B minor, and the judge was Eda Kersey, a name now almost entirely forgotten. Her recording of the Bax Violin Concerto conducted by Boult is still available. She was almost entirely self taught, encouraged by her father, who took her to hear professional violinists play at every available opportunity. Sadly, she died shortly after the war. I was struck by her powerful personality, and the thought-provoking comments she made about our playing. A few years later, Muriel, my sonata partner and wife to be, would accompany her in a recital, which I was unfortunately unable to attend. Muriel often spoke of it as a great occasion.

I came second in that prize - Colin Sauer was first. He was always my great rival and, I'm afraid, generally surpassed me. I think it's fair to say that he was Woof's favourite pupil of that generation - he was the only one who could be slightly cheeky to Rowsby and get away with it. His playing had a sense of perfection, which can be clearly heard in the many recordings he later made as leader of the Dartington Quartet. In 1942 we were both members of an ensemble which entered for the annual McEwen Quartet prize. The test piece was as usual by Sir John McEwen, former Principal of the RAM, and was entitled Biscay Quartet No.6. Colin led, I was second fiddle, and Lawrence Leonard (later a conductor) played cello. Only one other ensemble entered, led by Felix Kok. The names of their second violin and cello escape me, but there was only one viola player in the Academy considered good enough to tackle this work, so she played in both quartets. Virginia Irvine-Fortescue was a spectacular red-haired girl from South Africa, who produced a gloriously rich sound to match her glorious looks and aristocratic name. Obviously, she had to rehearse with both groups, but Colin insisted that we had several rehearsals without Virginia, to make sure Felix's quartet wouldn't find out exactly what we were doing - we suspected there was a bit of a "thing" going on between Felix and Virginia. Be that as it may, the stratagem worked - we won!

Possibly the most remarkable musician studying with us at that time was the pianist Ronald Smith. He formed an outstanding sonata partnership with Colin, and a party trick of theirs was to improvise a modern sonata. They could keep this up for hours, combining the most outrageous effects with a convincing sense of form and ensemble. It was true improvisation - every time completely different, and very funny. But Ronald's real strength was as a soloist and concerto player of the most testing piano repertoire. His many recordings demonstrate a hugely impressive technique that has invited comparison with Horowitz. Latterly he developed an extensive interest in Alkan, the 19th century virtuoso pianist and composer, upon whom his writings are now considered authoritative.

Ronald had an enviable ability to practise with complete concentration. His defective eyesight obliged him to play always from memory, and his practising was ruthless in its efficiency. He could look at a new score, count the pages, and know almost instantly how many pages he would have to master each day to be ready for a performance on a precisely-calculated date. I remember being with Ronald in the Green Room of the Liverpool Philharmonic Hall when he was playing the Liszt E flat concerto with us. Outside the door, we could hear one of the orchestral violinists dashing recklessly through the more bravura sections of the Mendelssohn Concerto. Ron listened to this with growing incredulity before bursting out "Idiot, he's played it four times through, wrong every time! How the blazes can he *hope* to get any better?"

Dennis Brain, the great horn player, had left the Academy before I arrived, but he was in the RAF band at Uxbridge, and often appeared in the Academy canteen at lunchtime, where his characteristic stentorian laugh was a regular feature. I knew Dennis better later, when we played together with the Philharmonia. After I left in 1955 to lead the Liverpool Philharmonic, he came up to give a concert with his Quintet at the Rodewald Chamber Concerts in the Philharmonic Hall. A few weeks later he was dead, killed in a car crash just a few miles from his home. He was a keen driver, and almost always insisted on driving home after concerts. This time he was driving back from Edinburgh, never the easiest of journeys in those pre-motorway days. How sad that he so nearly made it, and what a career he should have had.

Someone else I just missed at the Academy, but have been privileged to have as a lifelong friend ever since, was the violinist Emanuel Hurwitz, known to everyone as Manny. What an artist! I never actually had lessons from Manny, yet through playing with him, talking to him, watching him, just being in his company, my life has been immeasurably enriched. Along with an intuitive feel for the essentials of playing and sensitive musicianship, he has an encyclopaedic knowledge of violins and bows - their values and their different qualities. He also has the ability to encapsulate an idea or concept in an inspired epigram, not unlike Groucho Marx, but if anything more subtle. More of Manny later.

19

Muriel and I began our sonata partnership at the Academy, and found an immediate rapport in ensemble which was to last throughout our lives together. She was awarded the Macfarren Gold Medal as the outstanding pianist of her year, but it was always ensemble music that she loved most. She was an ideal partner in violin sonatas, and had an unerring instinct for rhythm and balance between the instruments. She was always quick to point out that the keyboard part in nearly all these works is much more difficult than the violin, and with some reluctance I have to say I agree with her! In our last year before I went into the Marines, we gave a joint recital in the Academy's Dukes Hall, and Mum and Dad and Muriel's mother came down to London to hear it. The recital was a great success, and I can still recall the excitement of the day. Both Muriel and I were already earning quite good money here and there, and we felt terribly important taking the whole party out afterwards in the blackout for a slap-up meal at the Hong Kong restaurant in Shaftsbury Avenue.

Like many famous teachers, Rowsby Woof was given a good start by having one well-known pupil, Jean Pougnet, who was then at the height of his fame, having led the London Philharmonic Orchestra, the BBC Salon Orchestra and various chamber ensembles. Pougnet recorded many violin concertos, including a particularly memorable version of the Delius Violin Concerto with the LPO and Beecham, which entirely suited his meticulous and serene playing. With Pougnet, technical perfection perhaps came before the depth of expression we hear from the greatest players, but his performances were always a delight. The later years of his life made a sad story. A keen advocate of DIY, he injured tendons in his left arm in the course of one of his projects, and was unable to play for several years. Eventually he made a remarkable recovery, and returned to playing, but almost immediately was diagnosed with cancer. I remember seeing him sitting in the BBC Maida Vale Canteen shortly before he died, reduced by the disease to a shadow of the man he had once been.

I had only one chance to work closely with Pougnet. Early in the 50s as a freelance player in London, I was at home in our first-floor flat in King Henry's Road (between Swiss Cottage and Chalk

Farm), busily decorating the kitchen. The phone went - could I please go immediately to the BBC Maida Vale Studios? There was a recording due to be made of the programme "Music in Miniature" - immensely popular at the time – in which a group of chamber musicians performed a non-stop selection of varied and contrasting movements. This particular week the group included three of our top string players: Pougnet, Anthony (known as Charlie) Pini, one of our finest cellists, and Frederick Riddle, a formidable violist known in the profession as "God", who had once been asked to autograph a bible when he was leading the RPO violas by one of the braver members of the orchestra. They were to be joined by Louis Kentner, brother-in-law of Yehudi Menuhin and his co-dedicatee of Walton's Violin Sonata. An impressive company by anyone's standards. The programme consisted mainly of string trios, piano solos and piano quartets, but Basil Douglas, the producer and originator of the series, had also included a movement from the Schumann Piano Quintet, requiring a second violin, which somebody had forgotten to book. So here I was, thrown in at the deep end, with nothing more than a brief run-through by way of a rehearsal.

Fortunately all went well. Charlie Pini always presented the façade of a hard-boiled professional musician - unimpressed by everything and cynical to a degree. I had done my bit and was sitting nearby as the rest of them dispatched the first movement of Mozart's Piano Quartet K478.

"Fantastic," I whispered, overawed.

"Huh," said Charlie, "nothing to it. All bloody scales and arpeggios! Don't know what people make such a fuss about. Bloody rubbish!"

I can't remember what I replied, but I felt suitably put in my place.

But back to the early student days. The Academy Orchestra was of course a major focus of my attention. My earliest memory is of listening to a performance by the strings (before I had been admitted to the ensemble) of Elgar's Introduction and Allegro. It was an overwhelming experience. I have heard and performed this work many times since, and it is still one of the most striking string pieces in the repertoire, but to an impressionable youth only just turned 17, it was something never to be forgotten. It certainly altered my ideas of Elgar as inherited from my Dad!

Sir Henry Wood was the conductor of the Academy First Orchestra, but at the beginning of the Blitz, he had been evacuated from London, and rehearsals were taken by Ernest Read. Perhaps surprisingly, although he was in charge of the Academy Conductors' Course and founder of the Ernest Read Youth Orchestra (which I was later to lead and coach for a time), Ernest was not himself a great conductor. That first term we played the Brahms Tragic Overture, and despite his best efforts, accompanied by a tremendous rattling of cuff-links, he simply could not get the first two abrupt chords together. Towards the end of term, Sir Henry returned to London and took his first rehearsal at the Academy. He stood up, raised his arms, thundered one word: "*STRUCK!*", brought his baton down with two almighty swipes, and the chords were spot on together. He probably had that word marked in his score! He marked everything in blue pencil, which usually made for economical use of time, but occasionally he got it wrong. Many of his pronouncements, made in his unmistakeable cockney accent, passed into legend.

"Trumpets, you're sharp!"

"We 'aven't got there yet, Sir Henry."

"Well, yer will be when yer get there!"

"Come on cellos, vermilion tone; squirt it out!" was another of his favourites, and "None of yer Scotch effects!" was always his response to inadvertent touching of the open strings by careless bowing in the violins.

We were lucky to have such a fine orchestral trainer as a regular weekly visitor for the Senior Orchestra. "Timber", as he was affectionately known, held a unique place in British musical history. He may not have been especially sensitive or perceptive as a conductor; and indeed some performances could be described as rather stodgy and four-square. But it is worth remembering that his unremitting hard work produced the Henry Wood Promenade Concerts, now generally recognised as the world's most prestigious music festival. Some critics have suggested that for one man and one orchestra to play six concerts a week for six weeks was ridiculous, and compromised the end product by cutting back on rehearsal time. The fact is that if he hadn't done it, and his fine players hadn't supported him, the "Proms" as we know them today – which I think of as the Wimbledon of music, but lasting longer - would not exist.

When I arrived in London, I was unaware (and so was everyone else) that the previous summer had witnessed the very last Prom Season at the Queen's Hall. This beautiful building, just next to the BBC Broadcasting House in Langham Place, was the capital's most important venue for large-scale orchestral and choral concerts. In my impoverished state, I couldn't afford to attend these regularly, but the RAM did occasionally offer free or reduced tickets for students, one of which came my way in February 1941 - a balcony seat for a Sunday afternoon concert with the LPO, conducted, as it happened, by Sir Henry himself.

The piano concerto played that day by, I think, Lev Pouishnoff, was the Tschaikovsky B flat. Never having heard it before (hard to believe now) I avidly read its description in the programme notes - a hackneyed work, beginning with a bombastic theme that never recurs later, criticised by Anton Rubinstein, and much more in a similar vein. My expectations were low, but needless to say, I was completely bowled over by it, and have never believed critics or programme notes writers since!

The entire concert was a memorable experience - the first time I had heard a top-class London orchestra, and in a superb acoustical setting. The programme ended with Stravinsky's Firebird. In the midst of the brilliance of Katchai's Dance, with all hell breaking loose in the orchestra, from my seat high up in the balcony I suddenly spotted a stately black cat, tail held high, walking serenely down the centre aisle of the stalls. It entered the small enclosure directly below the vigorously gesticulating figure of Sir Henry, stopped, curled up and with the utmost nonchalance, fell fast asleep. Cats seem to be a recurring motif in these recollections!

Those are my only memories of the Queen's Hall. Only a few weeks later, on May 10th, the worst night of the Blitz, its near neighbour Broadcasting House was hit and damaged by a firebomb during a news bulletin being read by Bruce Belfrage, who carried on broadcasting although covered in debris from the explosion. Later the same night the Queen's Hall itself was completely gutted by fire-bombs. The LPO, which at that time was making extensive use of the hall, lost a considerable number of instruments. The newspapers later published a large photograph of Sir Henry standing, a tragic figure, among the ruins.

The following day, a Monday, we students had the thrill of hearing the LPO rehearse in the Duke's Hall at the Academy, with some instruments borrowed from us. The orchestra's leader at that time was Thomas Matthews. I was privileged to know Tommy later when I played as an extra with the Royal Philharmonic Orchestra, and I remember him leading an outstanding performance of Richard Strauss's Also Sprach Zarathustra at the Festival Hall, conducted by Josef Krips, when the demanding violin solos were better than I have ever heard since.

Chapter 3 - Muriel

November 14th 1940 brought the by now customary air-raid siren and the sound of bombers passing high over Hendon. But this time there were no ominous thuds of explosions, and we offered up heartfelt prayers for whoever was the target that night. It turned out of course to be Coventry. The city had already suffered some strategic strikes, aimed specifically at engine plants on the outskirts, but this was different. On November 12th the RAF had bombed Munich, birthplace of the Nazi Party, and Hitler had ordered this raid entirely as an act of retribution. 500 bombers, in continuous waves throughout the night from early evening until about 5 am, delivered shattering punishment to what had been one of the most beautiful medieval cities in Europe.

Coventry was the childhood home of Muriel Dale, a talented pianist four years older than me who had gained a scholarship to the RAM and commenced studies with Professor Victor Booth a year before the declaration of war. Believing that London had become too dangerous, Muriel's parents brought her back to the assumed safety of Coventry, where she did a little teaching and took a job in the Trustee Savings Bank. To keep her musical education ticking over, she began lessons with Alan Stevenson, the organist at Coventry Cathedral. On the night of November 14, she went into the organ loft to do a couple of hours' practice, and finished just before 7pm, leaving behind a pair of favourite practice organ slippers and taking home the Cathedral keys. The next morning the keys were all that was left of that venerable and historic building. It was a bleak time for the Dale family. Their home city was in ruins, the front door of their own house had been blown off by a bomb, and Muriel's father was terminally ill from cancer.

At that point Muriel's mother, weighing up the comparative risks and aware that the scholarship was in danger of lapsing, decided to allow her to come back to London. Not long after Christmas that year she and I both moved into the same student digs at 43 Marlborough Place, St. John's Wood, an area where we were both to be based for the next fifteen years.

A novel could easily be written about life in that extraordinary establishment. It was run by Mrs Daisy Tresehar, a retired actress and an absolute martinet. Mostly we were music students, with a sprinkling of assorted odd bods from various backgrounds. There was Paul, glasses, fair hair, plump, and with a vaguely Mid-European accent, who we were convinced was a spy. Tamara Coates, a striking-looking girl, was the daughter of Albert Coates, a half-Russian conductor who worked occasionally in England. His Tschaikovsky recordings with the British National Orchestra, made in London early in the war years, have recently been re-issued, and are worth a place in anyone's collection. The orchestra included the young Dennis Brain, and was led by David MacCallum, father of the film star and greatly admired by Kreisler.

Other notable lodgers were Rosina Buckman, famous *diva* with the original Beecham Opera Society, and her husband, the tenor Maurice d'Oisly, who also worked with Beecham. Both were teaching singing at the Academy. Maurice was a jovial character, full of stories about Beecham's provincial tours in the twenties with his own British National Opera. Beecham was notoriously rude about and intolerant of singers. When informed that the leading tenor would not be at a rehearsal because of illness, his riposte was - "Nothing trivial I trust?"

Mrs Doris Davison was Daisy's second in command. She worked as an assistant and secretary at Denham film studios for Ernest Irving, composer of many Ealing film sound tracks, and an excellent conductor of his own and other composers' film scores. In those days film conducting was a highly exacting activity. The movie was projected onto a large screen behind a full symphony orchestra, and innumerable takes were needed to achieve correct synchronisation. The composer was always in attendance, and was often required to add or subtract a couple of bars on the spot. Irving was admired by many British composers, including Sir William Walton, who dedicated his String Quartet to him in 1947. I am at a loss, incidentally, to understand why this fine work is so neglected. The BBC recording I made with my quartet in Liverpool in 1958 still stands up well, and we also played a couple of performances in Bristol with the Academy of the BBC of the version arranged by Walton himself for string orchestra with solo string quartet.

Doris used to tell us hilarious stories about the day's events at the film studios. My favourite was the one about a Paganini biopic starring Stewart Grainger, who was completely unmusical and not remotely capable of pretending to play the violin. In an attempt to achieve a degree of verisimilitude, they bound his arms tightly behind his back, and had the sound track recorded by Menuhin. David MacCallum crouched behind Grainger to do the left hand, and another violinist, Peter Tass, almost tied himself in knots trying to synchronise the bowing.

There were a half dozen or so other music students at number 43. Daisy ruled us with a rod of iron. Our ration books were commandeered, and we subsisted on the most meagre diet, while from Daisy's quarters, which we were never allowed to enter, there regularly issued the tantalising odour of eggs and bacon. As a treat we were given a monthly jar of watery jam, so unappetising that on one occasion I couldn't face mine, and left it in the wardrobe. Eventually it fermented into what seemed to my uneducated palate a quite acceptable dessert wine, so a few of us had a little party one evening, and, not yet accustomed to alcohol, got quite merry on it!

Muriel and I quickly became friends and more. I admired her playing, and she would come often to my lessons. If I felt I hadn't done enough practice, I would always get her to play for me, and Woof, who fancied himself as a pianist and accompanist, would spend the lesson showing off in front of her. He was actually a very competent accompanist, and often played in public for his best students, including memorable recitals with Felix Kok and Rosemary Green in the Duke's Hall. In his youth he had done a lot of playing with Hamilton Harty, who had taught him various tricks. One of these involved the introduction to the last movement of Lalo's Symphony Espagnole, which I was studying at the time. The idea was to keep the upper part of rhythmic fifths in octave jumps going continuously when the lower parts come in, as they do in the orchestra, rather than stopping as in the piano reduction. Any pianists reading this will know how difficult that is!

Some people find it confusing when I talk about Muriel. Although she was born Muriel Dale, her skills as an accompanist and sight-reader soon brought her a lot of work for the precursor of the Arts Council, the Council for the Encouragement of Music and the Arts (CEMA). This included Music Club recitals, factory and troop concerts, and impromptu recitals to Ack-Ack batteries with a variety of distinguished artists, to which she would travel with a battered upright piano strapped onto the back of a lorry. At that time there was a well-known contralto called Muriel Gale, and the organisers thought this might cause confusion, so my Muriel, as the younger, had to change. Someone said "you look a bit of an Angela," and that was that.

When we started out as a sonata-recital duo, it was as Peter Mountain and Angela Dale, and remained so thereafter. When we married in 1945, the confusion deepened. We typically received at least four different tax returns – Muriel was receiving pay cheques in every possible permutation of the names, including Mrs and Miss, all at the same address! The Inland Revenue obviously suspected me of running a small harem!

Two years have gone by since my dear Muriel died, on April 2nd 2004, just eight days before her 85th birthday. She had a long, productive life, with three loving children, a widely recognised and admired talent, and a sunny nature that sparkled in congenial company. The remembrance of all this makes me smile, and yet, the grief still comes in waves - not so intense or frequent now, but triggered by specific events.

Today I wept a little. Driving back from a visit to my sister Kath, I passed through Pateley Moor in North Yorkshire, where a mile long ruler-straight stretch makes a knife-cut across the heather. It was a route we travelled together often, but every time we came upon that view, Muriel would remark on its beauty as if it were a first-time discovery. It became a family joke, but it was always a special place, just for us. And today I drove it for the first time alone.

We were together for over sixty years, so this whole account, from the war years onwards, is as much of Muriel as of me. It was music that brought us together, and music that strengthened the bond between us. This isn't to say we never disagreed – we did, on both a personal and professional level – but gradually we came to realise that our relationship worked best when we relied on instinct and natural feeling; doing things rather than talking about them. Rather than drive each other into a theoretical corner, we would try just to "play it again, Sam", and more often than not the differences would disappear as if by magic.

Muriel's highest praise for another musician was that he or she was a "natural", and she herself undoubtedly fitted that description, to the highest degree. Her rhythm was impeccable, her touch crystal clear, and she always stressed the overriding importance of pedalling. Her own sensitive use of the pedal was what made her so good to work with in ensemble, both with instrumentalists and, especially, with singers. I sometimes think she would have preferred me to be a singer, such was the pleasure she took from working in *lieder* recitals!

Her skill with the pedal also meant that she was somehow able to make the most unpromising instrument sound reasonable. This was something I am sure she learned from her wartime troop and factory concerts, and the joint post-war music club recitals we did in village halls with the most ancient and battered upright pianos. I remember many an occasion when, instead of rehearsing the César Franck sonata or Beethoven's Kreutzer, I had to spend half an hour flat in my back with spanner and screwdriver trying to repair a faulty pedal mechanism.

Muriel was always modest about her own prowess, and only occasionally played concertos, although she did perform the Mozart D minor K466 with Sir Henry at the Academy. She made an early decision that bringing up her family would take priority over a successful solo career, and if truth be told, her real love was chamber music. She also loved being with people, and although she would practise unstintingly for concerts and broadcasts, the constant travelling and isolation that went with being a concert soloist were in the end not for her.

A contemporary of Muriel's in the early Coventry days was Denis Matthews, who was brought up in nearby Leamington Spa. They frequently met as competitors at Midland music festivals, and she often came first to his second. This was galling to the young Wunderkind, who expected to sweep all before him. He is reported as saying "It's no use, I'll have to get her out of the way and marry her." Sorry Denis – you didn't win that one either!

After two years at the Academy, I was due for conscription. In view of my status as a student, I was granted a year's postponement, appearing in front of a genial magistrate who was sympathetic despite claiming to be completely tone deaf. His wife, he said, had to nudge him to stand up if the National Anthem was played - to him it was just another disturbance. He probably agreed with Doctor Johnson's description of music as the least objectionable of noises. (As a violinist I appreciate another of Johnson's aphorisms: after attending a violin concert, he was assured that the performance was very difficult. "Difficult, Sir," he roared. "Difficult? I wish it were impossible!")

In June 1943 my year's grace ran out, and I enlisted in the Royal Marines.

Chapter 4 – The Royal Marines

During my last Academy Term, I had met the daughter of Colonel Ricketts, Director of Music for the Plymouth Division of the Royal Marines. For the benefit of those not *au fait* with military band lore, Ricketts's pen name was K J Alford, composer of the Marines' signature tune march A Life on the Ocean Wave, but even more famously Colonel Bogey, possibly the best known military march ever written, and certainly the most profitable. Many people now know it as the theme tune of the 1958 film Bridge over the River Kwai, and think it was written by Malcolm Arnold. Not so - he merely used it as a basis for his film music.

Ricketts became known as the English Souza, and his output in the military band genre was phenomenal. Through my acquaintance with his daughter, I learned that he was looking for a violinist to lead his Royal Marines Plymouth Division orchestra. The timing was perfect. I would have to sign on for twelve years, but that didn't matter - after the war I would be able to buy my discharge, and in the meantime I would have kept my playing in trim without any damage to hands and fingers. My parents and Muriel urged me to leap at this golden opportunity, so I did.

It was the silliest thing I have ever agreed to. Never sign up to anything you're not prepared to see through. Within a year, Ricketts retired, and six months later he died! I was left with his successor, Lieutenant Stoner, a most unsympathetic character who showed no inclination whatsoever to release me from my contractual obligations. I stayed in the Marines until December 1947, while all my musical contemporaries were busy developing their post-war careers. It was only through the intervention of the Labour MP for Plymouth, H.M.Medland, who heard me playing Monti's Czardas in the Officers' Mess, that questions were asked in Parliament, and suddenly I was out. Enough to make me a confirmed Socialist for all time, and I still have a copy of the release letter in my scrapbook!

But I'm getting ahead of myself, and I would never suggest that my unexpectedly lengthy tour of duty with the Marines was all on the debit side. Looking back from this distant perspective, it was an experience that both changed and enriched my life.

The first weeks in Stonehouse Barracks, Plymouth, sleeping in a dormitory for 24 on a rock hard mattress on an iron hard bed, were a revelation. The conversation was liberally interlarded with the f word, which I had never heard before, and I had no idea what it meant. My more streetwise fellow inmates, some of whom were 14 or 15 year old drummer boys, used it with consummate artistry. I was particularly impressed by the way they even interspersed it in mid word, as when I was accused while polishing my boots of being "too conchy-f***ing-entious". For a relatively sheltered character like me, suddenly thrust into an alien military environment, it was something of a culture shock.

On the other hand, I received nothing but kindness and friendship from everyone who actually played in the Royal Marine Band. These were mostly self-taught musicians who had grown up under the umbrella of the Plymouth division band, setting up home and establishing mini-careers in the area. Their duties included day-to-day functions at the Barracks, factory concert tours, Remembrance Day appearances at the Cenotaph, performances on seaside bandstands and so on. They also did "gigs" for weddings and other private social occasions.

I have met my fair share of "characters" throughout my career, but in this respect the Plymouth Division was in a class of its own. "Gary" Cooper was a gifted tenor trombonist, whose *recitativo* from the final section of Ricketts' Carmen Fantasy was a dramatic tour de force. It was captured in a recording by His Masters Voice which received a record of the month award from the Gramophone. Harry Eden, whose hospitality, friendship and encouragement were a constant boon, was a flautist and piccolo player noted for his barn-storming Flight of the Bumblebee on the piccolo. He was also a fine tenor sax player, and did gigs at local dance halls, regular events in a town filled with troops and a magnet for girls from all over Devon and Cornwall. He was a handsome man, with a little of the Tyrone Power about him. Although happily married, he enjoyed chatting up the talent at the dance halls. As an attractive blonde floated past the bandstand one night, Harry took the sax out of his mouth, winked outrageously and said "Hey baby, would you like to hear the story of my life?"

"No thanks," she replied. "I can see it written on your face!"

The Band Sergeant at that time was Bill Banning, a trumpet player of the old school, a Kneller Hall product who got his results by sheer force. When he played the Post-Horn Galop, which always brought the house down, he went completely red in the face and a huge vein stood out on his forehead. By the look of him, he could have dropped down dead any minute. While my playing was generally praised by members of the band, Bill was harder to please. One morning he took me aside in the band- room and hissed - "Intonation not too good last night, Peter! Don't get careless!" It came as a bit of a shock and certainly made me buck my ideas up!

Ex Band Sergeant Albert Dolbear was another good friend. An older man, and the proud possessor of a superb Vuillaume cello, he quickly persuaded me to join him and Harry Balaam, an accomplished pianist who played euphonium in the band, to form the Palm Court Trio, which performed in the Lockyer Hotel in the centre of Plymouth. The money from this and from playing at dances went on trips to London to see Muriel, and on lessons with Frederick Grinke, who became my teacher when Rowsby Woof died, and went on to lead the Boyd Neel Orchestra. Grinke, one of Woof's most eminent pupils, was himself in the Royal Air Force Band at Uxbridge during the war.

The most colourful personality of all was undoubtedly Colonel Ricketts himself. It was said that due to his financial success as a composer of military music, his salary as a colonel before the War was not enough to pay his income tax. And yet he lived a spartan existence, in one bare room at the top of the clock tower in Stonehouse Barracks. He was notoriously careful with money. One afternoon I was called to his room to discuss various matters concerning the orchestra and its programmes. It transpired his Radio Times hadn't been delivered, so he summoned his batman and sent him to get a copy from Plymouth, a walk of two miles there and back.

In the meantime, the Radio Times appeared, and on his return the unfortunate batman was sent off again to get the tuppence back!

Ricketts rehearsed long and hard, trying out every variation and nuance on the band in his quest to perfect his orchestrations, and causing in the process considerable resentment. The players felt he had made his fortune by means of their hard work There were regular BBC broadcasts, which I had heard on numerous occasions and had been a major influence in my decision to join up. I had been impressed not only by the excellence of the playing, but also by the Toscanini-like precision of ensemble and rhythm that Ricketts drew from the Band.

Earlier in life, he had been bandmaster in a Scottish regiment, and had apparently gained a reputation as a great showman, when conducting on piers and grandstands, on the strength of flamboyant gestures which caused his kilt to swirl up in a manner provocative and fascinating to the ladies. He was known ever afterwards as "Kicker" Ricketts, although no one dared to say it to his face. All the Plymouth Division, not just the musicians but everyone held him in awe. In fact, some of the less erudite were prone to exaggerating his contribution to his feasts of musical excellence. One Drill Sergeant was heard to say, after hearing the Band's rousing rendition of Tschaikovsky's 1812 Overture, that it was the best piece old Joe Ricketts ever wrote!

Life as a bandsman, while less onerous than for many wartime servicemen, was still subject to a degree of military discipline. Parades were at 8 am prompt, and you had to be fully turned out, smart, buttons and boots clean, ready for inspection. I could actually play the clarinet, having learned it as a boy in Bradford, but I never let on, so in the marching band I was given the cymbals. This was a highly skilled job, as you had no sheet music and there were various beats you had to know to miss - if you didn't it could mean disaster.

On freezing cold winter mornings the first job of the trumpet players was to rush down early to the band-room and put their instruments out on the window-ledge. At 7.55 this would lead to the following exchange with the Drum Major:

"Drum Major, sir!"

"Yes, what is it, what is it?"

"Can't go on parade, sir."

"And why not, why not?"

"Valves frozen, sir!"

With any luck we got away with it!

Every Sunday we were detailed for String Band hymn playing in the barracks Chapel. Prayers on these occasions always contained the exhortation "Dear Lord, please help and protect all members of the Royal Marines, particularly those of the Plymouth Division." (The inference being that members of Portsmouth and Chatham Divisions could look after themselves!) The latest batches of raw recruits were marched in to a refrain of "Caps off! Leffrightleffrightleffright!" One Sunday some unfortunate young lad didn't hear the first command, and ended up sitting in the front pew with his beret still firmly on his head. The eagle-eyed Sergeant spotted this, and in the reverent silence before the service began, tiptoed along the pew behind, bent down and hissed in his ear: "It is customary – In the house of the Lord – To remove your hat. - CUNT!"

In the summer we often had the odd week playing on bandstands at various seaside resorts. If there was a piano for Harry Balaam to accompany on, my contribution was a couple of selections of violin solos, and on these occasions I would ask for special permission to remove my hat. Not for religious reasons, but because the hard peak of the dress uniform cap stopped me getting to the heel of the bow. This was an unprecedented privilege, granted with the utmost reluctance!

We were obliged by contract to carry on playing as long as any audience was present. The concerts were in the open air, and a rainy evening usually meant we would be free to go to the pub. Now and again, however, there would be one miserable couple huddled under an umbrella in the front row, determined to get their money's worth.

The muttered curses and black looks they got from the band can be imagined.

As the war took its course, the North Africa campaign marked a long awaited turn for the better in the Allies' prospects. Russia was bearing the brunt of the German offensive, although in the UK we did have to cope with "doodle-bugs" and later with rocket bombs, mainly directed at London. Plymouth, having suffered its share of bombs before I arrived there, was now a place of relative safety, but I was worried for Muriel, who was still in the thick of it. Then on June 6th, 1944 came news of D Day.

It had been a well kept secret as far as most of us was concerned, although we had for some months suspected something was in the air following news of Stalin's growing impatience with the Western Allies. Before long we were seeing newsreels of the immense Mulberry Harbour, appearing as if by magic off the coast of Normandy. The initial assaults were straight onto the beaches, with fierce fighting and heavy casualties despite the element of surprise. Within a day the long sections of the Harbour were in place, and continued to unload supplies for the next ten months. A storm on June 19th almost completely destroyed the American Omaha landing place a little further up the coast, but Mulberry Harbour was not too badly hit, and on June 25th our Marine Band was sent across to land at Mulberry Port B, close to the town of Arromanches.

My memories of this time are confused. I remember parades with the regular troops through towns and villages devastated by bomb damage, and spending some time billeted on a farm, sleeping on the hay in a barn. We enjoyed generous hospitality from the locals, and as the only one in the Band with a smattering of school French, it fell to me to make diplomatic translations of the conversation as our boys got increasingly animated, fuelled by liberal draughts of Calvados!

Eventually our esteemed head honcho, Lieutenant Stoner, had the hare-brained scheme of taking things into his own hands and getting the Band to Paris. He managed to commandeer a couple of lorries, piled us all in, and we lurched off along the bumpy crater-ridden road towards the French capital.

And so it was that after a long, long day we entered Paris as the vanguard of the liberating British forces. The Americans had arrived a couple of days before, meeting nominal resistance following Hitler's failure to carry out his threat to destroy everything in the retreat. We received a tumultuous welcome, "Beating the Retreat" in fine style down the Champs d'Elysée with German snipers (so we were told) still hiding up the trees nearby.

Although there was no electricity or running water, there was plenty of wine, and the celebrations that evening were monumental, but within a couple of days we were back on the road to the Channel ports. I don't remember much about the actual journey, but it was a warship of some kind that got us back to Blighty. We gave an impromptu concert for the crew on the way back, and nearly got into real trouble. Someone said "Go on, Peter, do your Air-Raid Siren trick". This was a quite convincing imitation I used to do on the violin, sliding up and down in thirds from G and B flat to B natural and D. So I hid round the back and did it during a lull in the proceedings. The captain was in the front row of the audience – he went white as a sheet, jumped up and rushed out to the bridge. Not the most distinguished moment of my wartime career - I expected at least a court martial, but someone must have smoothed things over!

VE Day, May 8th 1945, saw the band in the midst of one of its factory tours, around Bridgend, in South Wales. We played our part in the celebrations, which I have no doubt were just as boisterous and chaotic as anything to be seen in Trafalgar Square. There was a joyous sense of relief you could reach out and touch.

But my most memorable time with the Marines was yet to come. On August 6th the first atomic bomb was dropped on Hiroshima, and the second on Nagasaki on August 9th. On August 15th Japan surrendered, and the world celebrated VJ Day.

Chapter 5 - Brenners

When I was moved to Plymouth in 1943, Muriel was left to the tender mercies of Daisy Tresehar and Doris Davison. By this time, however, she was no longer a student, and was able to be more assertive in her dealings with Daisy. She was still at the RAM as a sub-professor, teaching second-study pianists and Junior School students on Saturday mornings, and was soon to become a fully-fledged Professor. Despite an increasingly busy schedule of solo and accompanying work, she was also developing a flourishing private teaching practice in the Hampstead area.

It was through this teaching that Muriel met Friedl and Truda Brenner, who were to have a major influence on both our lives. Friedl and Truda were Jewish refugees from Berlin, who had come to London shortly before the war. It was Truda who first contacted Muriel - she was a keen amateur pianist, and had asked the Academy to recommend someone to teach her privately.

Muriel was duly dispatched to the Brenners' home at 66 Belsize Park Gardens, and was immediately adopted as part of the family. As a minor Wunderkind in Coventry, Muriel's time had been devoted entirely to piano practice. She had never been expected to participate in domestic chores; and to her, the kitchen was unknown territory. Truda however had other ideas, and she was soon introduced to the best traditions of continental cuisine It was thanks to Truda that Muriel blossomed into the accomplished cook I came to know in future years!

It wasn't long before Muriel was regularly staying the night at the Brenners', and the next logical step was to throw off the shackles of 43 Marlborough Place and move in permanently, sharing a spacious self-contained upper maisonette with the couple's two children, John and Margrit. Truda was quick to assure Muriel that I would also be welcome in her home: "Have you got a boyfriend dear? Well, bring him along my love." And so my next leave was duly spent as a further addition to this delightful family.

Friedl became, I can unhesitatingly say, one of the greatest influences of my young days. He was the epitome of the cultural life of Berlin between the wars. He introduced Muriel and me to many new ideas, not only in music, but also in painting, philosophy, architecture - everything that was life enhancing. He was a fashion designer by profession, and ran a successful business, "Nabré Mantles", with offices in Great Marlborough Street, next to the Palladium. His partner, Ernest Nassau, was the business brain, and Friedl the artistic director. Friedl (and later his daughter Margrit, who inherited his artistic flair) would travel regularly to fashion shows in Paris and other cultural centres, and bring back sketches and ideas for the Nabré Collection.

Although Friedl was a devotee of all the arts, he particularly loved music. In Berlin he had been a regular concert-goer in the heyday of Furtwängler and Otto Klemperer, who in his youth had been a champion of the *avant-garde* at the Kroll Theatre. In his spacious living room at Belsize Park Gardens Friedl had installed a state-of-the-art audio system, with a massive amplifier and speaker (only one - no stereo then!). He had also amassed a stunning collection of 78rpm shellac records. The ritual of listening to them was in a curious way enhanced by the ceremony of turning the discs over every four minutes, and the need to solemnly sharpen the thorn fibre needles after each side was played. (CDs, DVDs, MDs, iPods – pah!). To Muriel and me, it was an introduction to not only a vast musical repertoire that had hitherto been largely unknown to us, but also to many of the great performers of the early 20th Century. The Bach Brandenburgs by the Busch Chamber Players, with Rudolf Serkin on piano and Aubrey Brain (father of Dennis) on horn; Bach Suites; late Beethoven by the Budapest and Lener quartets; Schubert's String Quintet); the Bach Passions and the B minor Mass - the list is endless, encompassing all the greatest of the classical European musical repertoire, an essential foundation for anyone making a career in music. And all of course chopped up into 4 minute segments! Modern audio techniques have of course ensured that more and more of these invaluable records of past performances are available in scratch-free uninterrupted versions, and any present-day performer worth his salt will regard these archives as a source of both instruction and enjoyment.

Friedl longed to be able to play an instrument. I gave him violin lessons, but he would never become a competent violinist, having left it far too late in starting. Despite this, his innate love of beauty meant that he always managed to produce an appealing and sensitive sound, as far as his technique would allow.

With their customary wholeheartedness, the Brenners embraced the British way of life. Later, when they became friends of my family, they travelled regularly to Yorkshire for farm holidays in the Dales. Friedl loved the countryside there, and painted and sketched it often. He was also passionately devoted to cricket!

By the time the war in Europe ended, Muriel and I had been officially engaged for nearly a year, and we decided that this would be a good time to make honest citizens of each other. We were married on July 2nd 1945 at the Congregational Church in Haverstock Hill, Hampstead, with me in full Marines uniform and Muriel in an attractive suit and hat (under protest - she always hated hats!) Friedl was best man, and a select band of parents, relatives, musicians and friends joined us and were photographed at the nearby Rosslyn Hotel. The only important absentee was my sister, Kath, who never forgave Dad for not letting her come to her brother's wedding. She was detailed to stay in Shipley to look after our large menagerie of dog, cat, chickens and goats. The marriage was consummated in the De Vere Hotel in Kensington, followed by a week at New Milton, on the South Coast, at the height of the strawberry season.

Within a few weeks of my return to Plymouth, the war with Japan was also over. We began to hear rumours that the Marine Band was to be sent on a mysterious mission to the Far East, and before long the rumours became fact. The Marines had been given the task of escorting Lord Louis Mountbatten, head of South East Asia Command, from his wartime headquarters in Kandy in Ceylon (now Sri Lanka) back to Singapore, which had been surrendered to the Japanese after Pearl Harbour. Preparations were immediately made to assemble a combined band of the Plymouth, Portsmouth and Chatham Divisional

Bands, capable of handling a full range of celebratory parades during daylight hours, and of performing in the evenings as a full Symphony Orchestra, which I was appointed to lead. The orchestra included a considerable sprinkling of professional musicians like myself, and the standard of playing was quite impressive.

After a week of rehearsals and kitting up, we embarked on a troopship for the long journey East.

Chapter 6 - Far East Tour

The vessel which was to be our home for the next three weeks had been a luxury liner in peacetime, but little evidence of this remained. – we were crammed in like sardines. After a rough crossing of the Bay of Biscay we passed by Gibraltar, but in the foggy conditions I wasn't able to form much of an impression of this famous British outpost. Malta, the George Cross Island, was also shrouded in mist when we called in for refuelling. There was no opportunity to get ashore before we were off across the Mediterranean towards North Africa.

We stopped again at Port Said, and for the first time felt we were truly in the East. We were surrounded by a multitude of small boats piloted by noisy hawkers and full to the brim with the merchandise they were intent on selling us. I remember being struck not only by the heat, but by the distinctive scent of the Orient, which thereafter never left us for the entire trip. In more recent visits this has seemed nowhere near as strong - maybe my sense of smell is failing as I grow older, or perhaps people just wash more these days!

The Suez Canal was an unforgettable experience, but our subsequent journey down the Red Sea was overpoweringly hot, day and night. It was during this leg of our voyage that we heard an announcement on the radio of the death of Béla Bartók, in Washington USA. As a music student, I had become an enthusiastic admirer of Bartók, especially the quartets, and I felt a keen sense of loss. At the same time, it occurred to me that I was possibly the only person on board who actually knew who Bartók was!

When we finally arrived in Ceylon, the Band was billeted in Mount Lavinia, about 15 miles south of the capital Colombo, in a little cluster of primitive buildings by the sea. We were quite comfortable, apart from regular invasions by hordes of ants, and there was one major crisis when a large cobra was discovered in the kitchen and we all fled the building with the utmost speed. The local snake charmer was called in, and with a forked stick and a blanket efficiently bundled the interloper into a basket before departing to hearty cheers. What he did with it we had no idea. He probably removed the unfortunate creature's fangs and used it as part of his act in the Colombo bazaar.

Throughout our time in the Far East, we had surprisingly little inconvenience from local fauna. Contrary to our fears, the annoyance from insects was no greater, if indeed as much, as back home in Britain. We took our malaria pills and watched out for mosquitoes in the evening, but there was nothing to compare, for example, with the ferocious attentions of the notorious Scottish midge. The worst we had to endure was a couple of scorpions in a camp at Kandy.

There was one amusing incident, however, during a classical concert in Madras (now Chennai). We were halfway through the last movement of Tschaikovsky's 5th Symphony when a mongoose got onto the stage and spent several minutes scampering around the floor among the members of the orchestra. The mongoose, the *Rikki-tikki-tavi* of Rudyard Kipling's "Jungle Book", is highly regarded in India for its prowess at hunting and killing poisonous snakes, but it was regarded by us at the time as an oversized brown rat in the wrong place at the wrong time. Its passage through the ranks could be clearly detected from the audience by the distracted waving of fiddle bows and the clattering of upset music stands. Somehow we managed to keep going - I thought we all deserved medals for devotion to duty in the face of adversity!

Across the bay from our first billet in Ceylon lay the Mount Lavinia Hotel, a structure of Colonial origins used at that time as the Officers' Mess. In later years I was able to revisit many of my old Far Eastern haunts with Muriel, and in 1998 we stayed at the hotel, by then restored to its former glories. But attempts to discover our old camp across the bay were fruitless – palm-shaded countryside dotted with tiny farm buildings had been completely built over, and a scene I remembered as idyllic now had a crowded and tawdry feel. The Indian Ocean, at that time not yet touched by the shadow of the tsunami of December 26 2004, still looked the same, with giant waves, ideal for surfing, crashing on to the shore. My surfing days are now of course long since over! Back then, we used to bathe at night by moonlight, marvelling at the phosphorescent glow created by our arm movements in the water.

In October and November, Mountbatten did a tour of Southern India, from a base in Madras, and the Band of course accompanied him. Our main duty on that tour was ceremonial parades, and my abiding memory is of the heat, intense compared to the pleasant temperatures of Ceylon. We also had our first unsettling experience of India's mass poverty. A lot of our travelling was by rail, and the stations were always a heaving mass of humanity, living, eating (when there was any food) and sleeping on the platforms. It was common to see women with babies deformed by disease and malnutrition holding them up in the blazing sun, begging for "baksheesh".

We were glad to get back to the comparative comfort of Mount Lavinia, and our diet of fresh pineapples and coconuts, courtesy of the robust local youngsters who threw stones to knock them down from the palms. Their mastery of this skill was astonishing – we great burly foreigners couldn't get anywhere near to matching them in force and accuracy. No wonder they beat us at cricket!

The time arrived to transport the cumbersome infrastructure of South East Asia Command to Singapore, and we were taken in early December to Kandy for the ceremonies to mark the start of the process. Kandy was a delightful town, with a beautiful lake as its centrepiece, and something of the atmosphere of a Victorian spa. It contains an important shrine containing the Tooth of the Buddha, and the Temple monks took part in our parades. When Muriel and I revisited in recent times, the building had been badly damaged by a terrorist explosion, and we were able to see only a part of it.

Kandy was a day's journey by lorry from the coast, with a spectacular climb high into the tea-growing areas. I remember our little convoy crawling along tortuous mountain roads, with precipitous drops to one side, and thunderstorms and lightning coming up at us from below. We stayed at a beautiful hill-station called Diyatalawa, and waking in the early morning felt like the freshest of early English spring days - bracing, with just a touch of frost. The scenery could have been straight from Welsh Snowdonia, albeit on an altogether vaster scale.

Back at the coast, we were able to celebrate Christmas at what we had come to look on as our home. On Christmas Eve we returned to the huts after a moonlight swim to find, as often happened, that there had been a power cut and we were without light. Suddenly we heard the noise of drums, gongs, flutes and chanting, and along the road came a procession of saffron-robed Buddhist monks, surrounding what looked like a gaudily coloured palanquin. On looking closer we could see that inside this impressve structure of cloths, ribbons and sacred scrolls was the aged Abbot of the local religious order, being slowly and solemnly pushed along in a decrepit old Ausin Seven!

Chapter 7 - Singapore and Onwards

By now we had already been allotted our own exclusive sea transport, a battered tank landing craft. It was ideal for our purpose. The larger instruments were stored in the hold, the equivalent of the car-bay in a modern cross-channel ferry. There was ample living space, and the flat top deck was used either for impromptu football matches, or, if the weather was calm, for orchestral rehearsals. On December 29th we set sail for Singapore.

I revisited this unique city very recently en route to Australia to visit my first great grandson, and while it is obviously very different now, with glistening new sky-scrapers and busy traffic, much of the old atmosphere has been retained. The population, then as now, is predominantly Chinese, and it is not for nothing that they are known as the entrepreneurs of the East. When we arrived, the foundations of post-war prosperity were already being laid. The Japanese were clearly seen as the vanquished. There were still many prisoners being used as forced labour, and driven through the city in crowded lorries. They were instructed to stand and salute any Allied soldiers, of whatever rank, which included us Bandsmen, the lowest of the low. They did this with unquestioning obedience, and protocol obliged us to respond in kind. My rank in the Marines was Musician, a title I felt proud of until I discovered that it was merely the exact equivalent of Private. Any promotion I might earn, which I never did, would lift me to the giddy heights of Lance-Corporal!

Many notable buildings of that era still survive today, including the famous Raffles Hotel and, of more personal interest to me, the Victoria Halls. Singapore has recently built a state-of-the-art concert hall and cultural centre on the waterfront, known as the Esplanade, but the Victoria Halls still survive nearby, in pleasant green surroundings, and are regularly used. They consist of a twin construction, in (as one would expect) Victorian style, with a theatre to the left and a concert hall to the right, joined by an enclosed courtyard. It was here that on the evening after the parades to celebrate Mountbatten's arrival, we performed a full Symphony Concert, at which I played the first movement of the Tschaikovsky Violin Concerto.

The altogether more momentous concert given in the same hall the following night has a fascinating historical background. Early in the 1930s, Wilhelm Furtwängler took the unprecedented step of appointing the eighteen year old violinist Szymon Goldberg as leader of the Berlin Philharmonic Orchestra. Goldberg was, of course, to become one of the most eminent violinists of the 20th century. When the Nazis came to power, Furtwängler was forced to dispose of the young Goldberg and a number of other Jewish members of the orchestra, who then apparently, whether by coincidence or design, all made their way to the island of Sumatra.

After Pearl Harbour they were captured by the Japanese and imprisoned in Changi Jail (the site of Singapore's modern international airport) where in the following years they no doubt suffered hardships we can only imagine. At the time of his capture Goldberg was in possession of a magnificent Stradivari violin. Knowing that the Japanese prison guards would probably destroy it, almost unbelievably he managed to take it to pieces and hide it in the rafters of the prison building, from where he was able to retrieve it after liberation and have it rebuilt as his concert instrument.

That evening he gave a recital aimed at re-launching himself on an international career. I didn't get the chance to ask him if he was playing on the Strad, but it was an impressive performance, and certainly the playing of a truly great violinist. The only programme item I can clearly remember was the Chausson Poème. Years later I met Goldberg when I was leading the Liverpool Philharmonic Orchestra and he came to play the Sibelius Concerto. I would have cherished the opportunity to talk to him about that time, but he was not the most approachable of characters, and sadly it was not to be.

Mountbatten had to fly the flag throughout the liberated territories, and soon we were back in our TLC, wallowing up the Gulf of Siam to Bangkok. We encountered extremes of weather on that journey, including one terrifying storm, which for me had the redeeming feature of establishing that I am not too bad a sailor. As one of the few not prostrated by seasickness, I found myself floundering around in a greasy galley, trying to act as cook – though not that many of us were interested in food. The effects of the storm were intensified by the unwieldy, flat-bottomed design of the landing craft - it reared up on every great wave and smacked down on the water with a deafening series of bangs. We were told that the first tank landing craft were of a rigid construction, and in stormy conditions were liable to break in two. Later models were made more flexible, which achieved the desired purpose, but if you went up on deck in any kind of rough weather, it was pretty scary to see the flat length of the deck perceptibly bending in rhythm with the waves.

A day later, we were in tropical sun and a flat calm, ideal conditions for football, with the captain quite happy to turn the ship around if the ball went overboard! Ideal also, of course, for rehearsals. I particularly remember playing the Beethoven Concerto in very skimpy bathing trunks - a surreal spectacle, and, I imagine, a pretty surreal sound too! Our eventual arrival in Bangkok was equally bizarre. We berthed not in the harbour, which was not yet operational, but on a palm-lined sandy beach a few miles away, as if we were an assault party. The sight of our landing craft grounding on the shore, letting down the bows and spewing forth a succession of musical instruments, was well worthy of Salvador Dali!

Bangkok today, as many Western holiday-makers discover, is a vibrant mass of towering high-rise buildings; a spreading metropolis with a traffic problem as bad as any worldwide. Then, it was nothing more than a sleepy, medium-sized Oriental capital, with an attractive canal system that earned it the predictable sobriquet of The Venice of the East. A number of superb temples, notably the Wat Phra Kaeo, the Grand Palace and the Wat Pho, containing a massive golden reclining Buddha, are still there, very much as I remember them.

We stayed for nearly a fortnight, and apart from the odd parade and two orchestral concerts in the local cinema, were more or less free to be tourists. We saw Thai boxing - not the demonstration bouts now shown to visitors, but the real thing, preceded by prayers, accompanied by wild music from some kind of reed instrument, and entailing three means of attack - a whirling kick, a bare-fist punch at shorter range, and a devastating close-in elbow jab, often to the back of the neck!

The whole band was entertained one evening by what appeared to be the entire Siamese government, up to but not including the King, who did however come to one of our concerts - I must be one of the few violinists to have played the Tchaikovsky Concerto for a Siamese Monarch. (As far as I can recollect, he was assassinated shortly afterwards!). At the party, there was exquisite dancing, to a colourful musical accompaniment, by local girls with incredible costumes and impossibly long fingernails. Some of us sat at a table with a jovial character who was either Prime Minister or Foreign Secretary, I can't remember which. He very kindly offered us cigarettes - Woodbines, smuggled off a British ship on the black market! Our Band Master said "Put those away Sir, have a decent one!" – and offered him a full-size Players!

Siam, later of course Thailand, was not conquered by the Japanese during the war, and Bangkok became a popular place for GIs fighting the Pacific campaign to go on leave. As a result there were hordes of pretty girls all engaged in the oldest profession, putting on dancing shows in the bars, just as they do today. As a newly married young man, I felt no need of their services – honestly Muriel! – and the warnings we were given about the dangers of promiscuous sex were purely theoretical, but I wouldn't care to guarantee that all of our brave boys were equally abstemious.

In general, I found the Thais perhaps the most attractive and friendly people I came across in the Far East. They were also remarkably honest. I remember going exploring with some friends in Bangkok, and carelessly leaving in a shop we had just visited an expensive pair of mini Zeiss binoculars. We were only five minutes down the road when the proprietor came running breathlessly after us to restore them to me. (I still have them today.) That wouldn't have happened in Singapore!

We returned to Singapore in mid-February 1946, in time for the Chinese New Year celebrations; an important event for the city's 70% Chinese population. Then almost immediately we were off to

Rangoon for another round of parades and concerts. I don't remember much about our Burmese trip, except for one episode. It was ordained that the Band should split up into small concert parties and give performances for isolated camps of guerillas in the jungle - a bit like the concert party in TV's It Ain't Half Hot Mum. My group was given a ship's piano, so that Harry Balaam and I could play for these culture-starved jungle commandos. For the benefit of those not in the know, a ship's piano is a mini-instrument, smaller than a regular upright, but making up for its lack of bulk by being packed full of lead weights to keep it stable in a rolling vessel. It is inordinately heavy, and needs ten strong men to lift it an inch off the floor! We were expected to load this object onto lorries, unload it, carry it into concert venues, lift it onto platforms, whatever the powers that be required. Our immediate reaction, in the inimitable vernacular of the Marines, was "F*** that for a lark!!!" We managed to ruin the wretched thing within two or three days. The drill was to get it two-thirds of the way off the lorry, and then on the command OK let go and jump clear, leaving the long-suffering instrument to thud four feet down onto the sun-baked Burmese soil. Before very long, it was completely unplayable - every single key was stuck solid – and it was left in a secluded jungle glade to be reclaimed by Mother Nature. Muriel would have been appalled. After that, in view of the unanimous opinion that solo Bach on the violin would not go down too well with our audiences, my role was restricted to the occasional cymbal clash and putting up the music stands for the others!

After Burma, our next port of call was Calcutta. Mountbatten was eventually to be appointed the last Governor-General of India, and was joined there by Lady Edwina Mountbatten, in preparation for the hand-over of power which was to take place a year later on August 15th 1957. Mountbatten stayed on for a year after that to help Nehru deal with the blood-soaked aftermath of independence, thereby helping to cement (presumably unknowingly) an ardent loving relationship between Nehru and Lady Edwina. When we arrived in Calcutta we had to play at a reception, and were able to get a good look at the lady in question. She was certainly an extremely attractive woman, and one could only admire Nehru's taste!

It was in Calcutta that my time with the Band was rudely interrupted. A crowd of us had gone out of the camp for a meal in a nearby restaurant, and the last I can remember was eating an ice-cream. Apparently I passed out and had to be carried back to camp and straight to hospital, where I stayed unconscious for about a week, by which time the Band had left for Delhi. The cause, it turned out, was a particularly virulent form of quinsy called *Vincent's Angina*, in which a membrane grows across the throat, resulting if untreated in suffocation. Fortunately for me, penicillin was just then becoming available. I slowly regained consciousness to find that I was receiving injections twice a day from an enormous syringe, which seemed more suitable for a horse than a human being. I also had to suck penicillin tablets, which resembled a foul-tasting dry sticky toffee. I hated it, but it did the trick. The man in the next bed kept my spirits up with such comforting remarks as "Eee mate, I thought you were a goner when they brought you in! Never 'eard such moanin' an' groanin'".

I heard later that Muriel had received a telegram which read "Your husband is dangerously ill", but I was soon able to send another wire, saying, à la Mark Twain, that reports of my imminent death had been greatly exaggerated. In fact, once I got rid of the horribly sore throat, I quite enjoyed my few weeks in that Calcutta hospital. The doctor decided that I needed building up after ten days without food, so with each meal I got either sparkling wine or Guinness!

Each morning, you stuck your chin out from the bedclothes, and the Barber-Wallah came round to shave you. Then it was back to sleep for a couple of hours. The nurses were pretty, and the park-like surroundings were picturesque and peaceful, but eventually it was decided that I needed to escape the heat of Calcutta and go up to a hill-station in the Himalayan foothills to recuperate. This in itself wasn't so bad, but I was worried that I would miss going back home with the Band, who after Delhi were scheduled to go to Bombay and catch a troopship home. I was young and newly married, and the idea of being left alone in India until other arrangements could be made did not appeal. This has been the source of some regret ever since, as visiting that great mountain range has always been one of my ambitions, and I have never managed it – I fear that now it is too late.

I threw myself on the mercy of the doctor, who said he would do what he could. In the end I was put on a train, in a private compartment with a supply of food and drink, and spent a week chugging slowly across the entire sub-continent, to join up with my friends in what is now known as Mumbai.

We were soon on a troop-ship and on our way back to Britain, where we disembarked at Liverpool, thus bringing to an end an action-packed and never to be forgotten chapter in our lives.

Chapter 8 - The Boyd Neel Orchestra

The next 18 months or so were relatively uneventful, and very frustrating. There were a few tours with the Band, but by and large it felt as if I was just marking time, playing a couple of violin solos once a week at Mess Nights, and hearing about the blossoming careers of all my contemporaries who were now back in "civvy street". I was signed on with the Marines until far-off 1955, with no prospect of release.

This frustration was almost certainly the cause of a recurrent attacks of a most virulent form of eczema, which meant I was in and out of the sick-bay, and again receiving regular penicillin injections, by then seen as pretty much a cure-all. However, I was able to get fairly regular leave, and as mentioned in an earlier chapter, some of this time was spent having lessons with Frederick Grinke, leader of the Boyd Neel Orchestra. Grinke gave me the chance to play with the orchestra whenever I was free, and it was this generous arrangement that led to my being heard at a concert by the Labour MP for Plymouth, H.M.Medland, who then took up my cause and managed to obtain permission for me to buy my discharge. In December 1947, nearly 2½ years after the cessation of hostilities, I finally found myself a civilian again. I still have a copy of the letter informing me of the news.

I was now able to play regularly with the Boyd Neel Orchestra, and this marked the first real stage in my professional career. The BN had already carved out a unique niche for itself in the musical world, and I felt very fortunate to be given this opportunity to make up for lost time. There is a detailed and fascinating account of the Orchestra's history in " My Orchestras and Other Adventures - The Memoirs of Boyd Neel". To summarise, Boyd, from an artistic family background, was a naval cadet in Dartmouth before going up to Cambridge in 1923 to read medicine and subsequently graduate as a qualified surgeon. In 1933, with no formal musical training, he founded the Boyd Neel String Orchestra, which consisted of talented music students and performed with considerable success until the outbreak of hostilities in 1939. During the war, Boyd reverted to medicine, but kept his music and conducting on a back burner. The orchestra was revived towards the end of the war, and stayed together until Boyd returned to his native Canada in the 1950s to become Dean of Toronto University. It was during the latter part of that period that I became a regular member, one of the nucleus of 17 players who developed the characteristic string sound that became our hallmark.

It's difficult to define what made the BN unique, but the orchestra did have a distinct personality that came through very clearly however much the individual members changed. Although we tried to give Boyd's concerts and tours priority, we were all freelance London players, with a living to earn in the cut and thrust of the music profession. Inevitably conflicts arose, and Boyd maintained a pool of standby players to be drawn on when one of the regulars wasn't available.

But somehow, even with quite substantial changes in personnel, the same old BN sound shone through. We had a number of different leaders, such as Manny Hurwitz and the rising young star Manoug Parikian, an Armenian violinist who was brought up in Cyprus and arrived in England after the war. Manoug also led the Liverpool Philharmonic before moving to London in 1950 to lead the Philharmonia Orchestra.

Boyd was not by any standard a truly outstanding conductor, but he had several admirable qualities. His rhythm was impeccable, although for the most part he was able to cut individual players a bit of slack when it was called for. He had an unerring ear for tone quality. We all knew his favourite rebuke if the sound became a little edgy - "Aagh! Sounds like *knives dipped in vinegar!!*" Or worst still *"The sharpest knives dipped in the sourest vinegar!!!"* We would all go a long way in an effort to stop him saying that. It was always the bowing - the place of the bow on the string, the weight of the bow arm, the speed, the string contact. We had to sort this out amongst ourselves. Boyd wasn't a string player and couldn't tell you exactly what to do, which was in many ways an advantage. He had an ear, and knew what he wanted to hear, and he trusted us to find the right answer.

He had a charisma about him, and his thinking was clear and direct, with nothing of the poseur. He knew instinctively how to draw the best out of the talented players he attracted around him. He could be naïve, maybe occasionally lacking in subtlety, but he was completely straightforward and dependable. We loved playing for him, and our loyalty to him was absolute. I cannot remember him ever making a mistake, even in the most difficult modern works. I recall the inspirational Georges Enesco conducting a performance of the Bartók Music for Strings, Percussion and Celeste which was decidedly unsafe, but with Boyd, it was always rock-solid and clear as a bell. He always used to say "My beat never varies!" and he was right, it didn't! Sometimes we wished it would, just a bit!

Not only did we do an impressive repertoire, but the performances had a special vitality. In many ways, Boyd was the perfect musical chairman. We would play through a new work non-stop, and go back to sort out the obvious difficulties. Then came the real work. Anyone could chip in with an opinion - Boyd would just keep things in order, stop people from wandering from the point, and finally say "OK, Right. This is what we do."

He had the greatest respect for Fred Grinke, who took over from the original leader Louis Willoughby, at the start of the war. Fred was sometimes compared to the famous Hungarian player Szigeti - he was maybe not the most natural of players, but he did have tremendous vitality, musicality and audience appeal. David Martin was the principal second violin, who later gained a reputation as a teacher that rivalled Fred's. The Martin String Quartet was for a time prominent on the BBC Third Programme. David told me he often received fan mail for his performances addressed to "Dear Mr. String…."

Other violinists included Ernest Scott, my co-student at the RAM, who was for several years principal second after David left, and later played with me in the Philharmonia. There was also Kathleen Sturdy, who led the seconds when I first joined and was given me as her desk partner. She frightened me to death, but it probably did me good! Breta Graham was also a well-established member of the violin section when I joined, and has always remained a dear friend. She went on to join the BBC Symphony Orchestra, and the same career move was made by Vivien Dixon, who served as the BBC's co-leader. Felix Kok, a familiar face from my RAM days, moved on to lead the City of Birmingham Symphony Orchestra under Simon Rattle, and Derek Collier, another ex-Academy student, became leader of the Bournemouth Symphony Orchestra under Charles Groves.

The violas were led throughout my time with the BN by Max Gilbert, a larger than life character who was one of only three players surviving from the orchestra's foundation in 1933. Sam Rosenheim, who married Kathleen Sturdy, and Rosemary Green were other regular viola players.

The cellos were led originally by Jimmy Whitehead, whose style was quite abrasive but displayed considerable flair. At that time, he and Charlie Pini were the two foremost cellists in Britain, and I remember the BBC (probably inadvertently) juxtaposing performances of the Dvořák Concerto by the two of them, prompting inevitable comparisons. They were both first-rate, but my vote went to Jimmy. Charlie sounded suave and controlled, but a bit too much so for my taste - a session boy's performance. I preferred Jimmy's warmer and more temperamental approach (someone once said he had too much temper and not enough mental!)

Our second cellist was Peter Beavan, a fine chamber music player, one of the few people I have known who could play all the parts in a string quartet with equal facility. This is rare, because of the entirely different vibrato techniques required by the violin and the cello. I am totally unable to do vibrato on the cello, and I suspect that most violinists are the same, and the reverse applies to most cellists.

Other regular cellists were Hilary Robinson and another original BN member, Eileen McCarthy, who has had a long and illustrious history as a continuo player with many British chamber ensembles. Of the more occasional players, I should also mention Paul Ward, who later became principal cello with the Hallé, and made an important contribution to the Manchester musical scene. His son, Nicholas Ward, leads and directs the Northern Chamber Orchestra, of which my daughter Jeanette is now principal cello. The musical world can be a small one!

Our most notable double bass was Francis Baines, whose brother Anthony was a bassoonist, and author of a scholarly book about Baroque instruments and Baroque performance. Francis had an eccentric lifestyle - he lived on a barge in the Thames, and his frequent excuse for late appearance at rehearsals was that he'd had to stop at home to bale out! Once, on a Scandinavian tour with the BN, we arrived at the railway station in Helsinki with Francis lugging his great instrument over his shoulder. The ticket collector looked at him, chuckled and said something to his colleague in Finnish, completely incomprehensible to us but obviously the equivalent of "I bet he can't get that under his chin!" Francis turned to me and said "That's six languages I've had that in now!"

Fred Grinke left the orchestra shortly after I joined as a regular player. He had been offered the leadership of the newly formed Royal Philharmonic Orchestra by Sir Thomas Beecham, but symphonic work was never Fred's main interest, and instead he took on more solo work, along with his professorship at the RAM. He was succeeded as leader by Maurice Clare, who was proposed by Violet (Paddy) Palmer, long time sub-principal violin and manager of the Orchestra. Born in Dundee, Maurice had been a pupil of Enesco, and had lived for some time in New Zealand. Despite his obvious ability and flair, there must have been something about him that rubbed Boyd up the wrong way. Although he led the BN for at least four years, in the Boyd Neel autobiography he does not get a single mention.

Personally, I was deeply appreciative of the creative freedom I enjoyed during my time with the BN. For several years, with Boyd's permission, I led the Boyd Neel Chamber Ensemble, comprising myself, Ernest Scott and Pat Halling (violins) Rosemary Green (viola), Hilary Robinson (cello) and Francis Baines (bass). We had a wide-ranging repertoire, including on one occasion the Mozart Oboe Quartet with Leon Goossens, and a memorable performance in Bristol of the Beethoven Septet and the Schubert Octet, when the clarinettist was Colin Davis, who would later rise to fame as a conductor and receive a knighthood in 1980.

Another of Boyd's great gifts was his ability to look after the feelings of his players, and allow them to enjoy the music making. All the truly outstanding conductors I have played with have shared this gift. Somehow they manage to make you think "Yes, this is exactly how I would like to play this piece!" - not only during a performance, but also in rehearsal. You were never bored or overloaded during Boyd's rehearsals. Under a lesser baton, you can go through a session feeling that with the best will in the world you are never going to be able to remember all the detailed, no doubt admirable instructions you are receiving. It is easy to for a conductor to forfeit the respect of a band of 80 or 90 seasoned professional musicians who have heard it all before. If they feel you are lecturing them, you've lost the battle! John Pritchard got it right the day he raised his baton and said "Come on chaps, surprise me!" It worked like magic.

Another master of rehearsal technique was Rafael Kubelik (son of the famous Czech violinist Jan Kubelik), who recorded Dvořák's New World Symphony with the Philharmonia at Abbey Road around 1953. I cannot remember a more inspiring performance. Some years later I took the BBC Training Orchestra to Brighton for a week's conducting seminar directed by Kubelik. One of the aspiring young conductors was talented and full of ideas, but constantly stopped the orchestra as each new thought occurred to him. Eventually Kubelik strode onto the platform to intervene: "Mr ----, please have the common courtesy to give your players the satisfaction of playing a cohesive section of the music before stopping to make your observations. And try never to stop them in the middle of a musical phrase. It is the utmost discourtesy to a player, as it would be to an actor, if he or she is not allowed to complete the sentence being delivered."

Chamber orchestras in the UK today owe a considerable debt to the BN. Our exploration of Baroque repertoire pioneered a mushrooming revival of early music in authentic performance. Bach's Brandenburg Concerti were obvious staples, but to a large extent our programmes were built around the 12 Handel Concerti Grossi Op 6, which to my mind are fully equal in stature to the Brandenburgs. We played the big string works of the Romantics - Dvorák, Suk, Tchaikovsky, Arensky, Grieg - and a treasure chest of masterpieces by 20th century giants like Schoenberg, Bartók, Stravinsky, Honegger, Tippett, Milhaud, Bloch, and Strauss, including many works specially written for us.

Of these, pride of place must go to Benjamin Britten's Variations on a Theme of Frank Bridge. This dates back to 1937, before my time at the BN, when the Orchestra was invited to play at the prestigious Salzburg Festival, with the condition that they should play an evening of English music including a first performance of a specially commissioned English work. This offer was made in early June, and the performance was to be on August 27th, which left very little time to have a new work commissioned, copied out and rehearsed.

Boyd had already worked with Britten, conducting his Simple Symphony. There is a delightful letter from the composer in Boyd's memoirs, which throws light on the origins of that work. Boyd knew that Britten was already doing a lot of film work, and was familiar with his technical fluency. He wasted no time in telephoning him, and he accepted the commission on the spot. Ten days later he appeared on Boyd's doorstep with the complete work sketched out, and played it through to him on the piano.

So there it was - a contemporary master work for the most important engagement the Orchestra had ever had. It is no exaggeration to say that it was the performance in Salzburg that made the reputation of the Boyd Neel Orchestra unassailable. Later we regularly played Britten's Serenade for Tenor, Horn and Strings, Les Illuminations, and Prelude and Fugue for Strings, but none was more frequently programmed than the Variations. We all knew the work more or less from memory. It has never lost its technical challenge, but is still unfailingly satisfying to perform, and is always well received by every kind of audience. In his memoirs Boyd recalls the nerve-racking moment in Salzburg when an entire section of the Vienna Philharmonic appeared in the audience - one variation is a gentle but unmistakeable parody of a Viennese Waltz. The Viennese players apparently took it in very good part!

After the war, the Orchestra gradually built up a fuller calendar of engagements, helped greatly by the establishment of the BBC Third Programme, now Radio Three. We did regular programmes with Boyd, and were also engaged for many choral productions, Handel operas and all kinds of works by baroque composers lesser-known at the time. We also played for a number of visiting conductors who had been unavailable during the war years, including an extended collaboration with Paul Sacher from Zurich. He was a meticulous conductor, founder of the Basle Chamber Orchestra, and thanks to his considerable personal wealth he had been able to commission or give first performances of over eighty works by the likes of Bartók, Stravinsky, Strauss, Hindemith, Tippett, Britten, Henze and Malapiero. Some of these pieces were already in our repertoire. Sacher introduced to us a set of six Symphonies by Bach's oldest son Carl Philip Emmanuel, which were striking in their imagination and daring. He told us that the composer, frustrated by the complaints of contemporary players that his music was too difficult, had for once thrown caution to the winds and written this set of works without any regard for technical limitations. The result is certainly sometimes disconcerting, with an unprecedented freedom in modulations to extreme tonalities, but also exhilarating in its originality.

Many soloists who later became household names appeared with the Orchestra early in their careers. There was a memorable broadcast from Maida Vale No.2 Studio (a regular venue for us – ideal for our size) of Victoria de Los Angeles singing Spanish songs. We were bowled over not only by her voice, but also by her looks! She was married to a Spanish gentleman who was understandably jealous of any aspirations to his wife's favours. According to legend, one day the phone rang in their household and he answered it. A voice said " Hello, may I have Victoria de Los Angeles?" and he replied in impassioned tones "No, you may not have her! She is *mine, mine!*"

Alfredo Campoli was another example. He had been a Palm Court violinist before the war, but during the later stages of hostilities was interned on the Isle of Man; a typical piece of bureaucratic simple-mindedness based on his foreign-sounding name. Although of Italian descent, he was brought up in Soho, and had a cockney accent you could cut with a knife! Campoli - Camp to his friends - never got the recognition he deserved in the UK because a snobbish element of the musical establishment, more influential than I find comfortable, couldn't forgive his light music activities. I have no time for this blinkered attitude. All the good musicians I know enjoy playing light music, as long as it's well written.

While Campoli was locked up he revived his classical concerto repertoire, and emerged into peacetime resolved to conquer the world. He hired the Boyd Neel and the Wigmore Hall to give a fabulous evening of Mozart concertos, including the Sinfonia Concertante for violin and viola. The young Norbert Brainin, leader of the Amadeus Quartet and also a wartime internee, played the viola part, and the conductor was Walter Goehr, father of the composer Alexander Goehr.

Campoli was soon in great demand, and I remember we did a broadcast with him of what back then was a novelty – Vivaldi's Four Seasons! During rehearsals Camp was in his element, playing with the utmost virtuosity, so much so that Boyd brought proceedings to a halt to have a word in his ear.

"Camp, don't you think that movement's a bit too fast?"

"Aw no, no, no - I carn take it any slower than that - they'll think I'm practisin'!"

Some of his performances were truly mesmeric. I remember listening on the radio to a routine lunchtime broadcast with the BBC Northern Orchestra, in which he played the Bruch G minor Concerto At the end of the piece the orchestra was supposed to keep quiet while the announcer read out the final credits, but they completely forgot themselves and broke out into spontaneous cheers and clapping. I had never heard anything like it.

We had a visit from Ernest Ansermet, veteran conductor of the Suisse Romande. He was a man of the most exquisite sensibilities, as can be gauged from the numerous recordings he left behind him. One piece he did with us sticks particularly in the mind, the Petite Symphonie Concertante for Harp, Harpsichord, Piano and two string orchestras by the Swiss composer Frank Martin, a work that deserves to be heard more often for its subtle exploitation of the changes of tone colour between the three not dissimilar solo instruments. Boyd was never afraid of novel orchestration, and had an unerring instinct for what was worthwhile in contemporary music. At around that same time, we gave a performance of the 1937 Double Concerto for Two String Orchestras, Piano and Timpani by Martinu, an all-time favourite composer of mine. When I took up my next post with the Philharmonia, Walter Legge had just discovered this piece - he probably stole the idea from Boyd! He decided to make a recording of it, and the new recruit picked up some kudos as the only person in the orchestra who knew anything about it!

Another notable guest was Edwin Fischer, who did a series of Bach and Mozart keyboard concertos, both directing and playing. He was a lovable man, with a keen sense of humour. We did a week's tour of Scotland with him, and I remember three of us sharing a taxi with him out of Waverley Station when we arrived. He gestured broadly as we progressed down Princes Street past the Castle - "Aha! This is my city - Edwinburgh!" At every concert he included the little Mozart Rondo in A, K386, ending always with a cadenza just before the final phrases, which he improvised completely differently each evening while we all sat around, waiting for our time to come in. Invariably we heard the approach of the cadential sequence and raised our instruments in readiness, and invariably he would look around with a twinkling mischievous smile, shake his head and continue for another couple of minutes, to the great amusement of the audience.

For all that, Edwin was a meticulous worker during rehearsals, never satisfied with less than maximum effort from all concerned. He was accompanied on his travels by an elderly housekeeper who looked after him devotedly. She attended all the rehearsals, and evidently concluded that Edwin was being unduly hard on us.

"Tell me, Maestro - the Orchestra - they are very good, no?"

"Ja, ja, they are very very good!"

"You are sure?"

"Ja, ja, I am sure."

"Then, vy do you *hun*t them so?

But I think the members of the BN would agree that of all our guest directors, two were quite outstanding - Nadia Boulanger and Georges Enesco. Although not at all alike in their methods and personalities, they had one thing in common, an extraordinary ability to educate and inspire.

Nadia Boulanger (1887-1979) was a superb musician. Musical vitality flowed out of her in a never-ending stream. Although she worked with conductors and eminent instrumentalists, she was primarily a teacher of composers, and the list of those who had sat at her feet included Stravinsky, Poulenc, Françaix, Lennox Berkeley, Walter Piston, Aaron Copland and many others. In her youth she knew and was greatly influenced by Gabriel Fauré. As a conductor and performer she was largely responsible between the wars for the rediscovery of Monteverdi, and in 1937 at a Royal Philharmonic concert she became the first woman to conduct a symphony orchestra in London.

Her principal gift and the essence of her teaching was the ability to grasp and to make others think about the structure and form of music, its shape and its purpose. The performances she elicited were vital and full of buoyancy. She insisted on the importance of the off-beat, especially in Bach. It was never *1 and 2 and 3 and 4* but *1 and 2 and 3 and 4 and*. If she had a fault, it was that she talked with such volubility about the ideas that cascaded from her restless mind, that you sometimes felt she was not really listening to what you were doing.

Sir Clifford Curzon, the eminent British pianist, had studied with her, and her concerts generally included a Mozart concerto played by him. Sir Clifford lived with his wife, the American harpsichordist Lucille Wallace, in a most attractive house in Highgate overlooking Hampstead Heath. The Orchestra often rehearsed in their music room, which boasted a splendid collection of paintings, including a particularly fine Canaletto. At one rehearsal we were due to work on the Mozart A major concerto K488. For some reason Curzon was unable to be there, so we rehearsed without piano. Madame Boulanger (it was impossible to think of her as Nadia) sang the missing part throughout using *solfège* - naming each note as you sing it. Given the breakneck speed of the last movement, it was an amazing feat.

There are countless other stories that testify to the unique talents of a remarkable woman, but I cannot do justice to them here. For anyone who wishes to explore the topic further, I would recommend Bruno Monsaingeon's excellent "Mademoiselle - Conversations with Nadia Boulanger".

Georges Enesco (1881-1955) was the most complete musician I have ever met. He was known principally as a violinist, ranking with such greats of his time as Kreisler and Thibaud. He gained additional fame as the teacher of Yehudi Menuhin, but was also a phenomenal pianist. His reputation as a composer is less secure but equally deserved. His works were for a considerable time neglected, but are now being revived and better appreciated. It is worth remembering that in the first two decades of the 20th century there were three equally respected composers living in Paris - Debussy, Ravel and Enesco.

He had an astounding musical memory - he needed only to play or read a piece of music once, and it was clearly embedded in his brain cells, to be recalled at any time. The story goes that in 1927 he was giving a lesson to Menuhin in Paris, when Ravel came in with his newly completed violin sonata, requesting that Enesco should read it through with him. Excusing himself to his pupil, Enesco took up his violin and played the entire work straight through with the composer, who, incidentally, was not a particularly competent pianist." This is a very fine work," said Enesco when they were finished. "Would you be kind enough to let me play it once more?"

So they played it again, but this time Enesco played from memory! In view of the fact that the last movement of this sonata is a *moto perpetuo* of extreme difficulty played at lightning speed, this stretches credulity to the limit,. However I can vouch personally for another of Enesco's feats of memory, at his very first rehearsal with the Boyd Neel. We were doing a BBC broadcast, and all the sessions were in the old Criterion Studio high above Piccadilly Circus. He was ushered into the room, politely greeted us, seated himself at a piano and addressed us along the following lines (I paraphrase):

"My dear colleagues, we are here to play the arrangement of my String Octet in C Opus 7 for string orchestra. As I do not expect that many of you will be familiar with this composition, before we start work I would like you to have an idea of the music. Mr Clare will kindly play the first violin part and I will play the rest on the piano. You will excuse any uncertainty as I have not set eyes on this music for many years."

He then proceeded to play all seven other parts, flawlessly as far as we could tell, right through, without a note of music before him! It was quite awesome, particularly when you consider that the Octet is extremely complicated and rhapsodic, with lashings of late 19th century chromaticism, and lasts about 40 minutes!

Enesco could not tolerate any forcing of the string tone, I remember a phrase he often used: "Please, please, not too loud. The violin is not a trombone!" We did the Brandenburg cycle with him as we had done with Boulanger, and the differences were instructive. While she was interested in the springiness and rhythmic shape of the contrapuntal lines, he often favoured more prominence for the firm arpeggio structural passages that Bach often gives to the trumpets in the Orchestral Suites and in much of his choral music.

At the Brandenburg sessions, there was an incident that illustrated the curse of the dilettante that sometimes afflicted the Third Programme. Four of these six works have prominent solo violin parts. Maurice Clare, being our leader and a past pupil of Enesco, expected not unreasonably to be invited by the BBC to play all of these, but this was not to be. The producers in their wisdom decided to engage a different violinist for each one, based on criteria of stylistic suitability. Maurice was asked to do Number 4, which was fair enough as it suited his facility and speed, and Number 5 was allotted to Manoug Parikian. Again, a good choice, as Manoug had led the orchestra on occasions, and his classical style was ideal for this piece. Manny Hurwitz, as co-leader, was given the solo part in Number 2.

The problem came with the choice of soloist for Concerto Number 1. This is written for *Violino Piccolo*, a small violin tuned a third higher than a normal instrument, and includes various chords and double stops which are quite feasible on the intended tuning, but are incredibly difficult if attempted on a normal violin. The producers had selected to play it Antonio Brosa, the original dedicatee of the Britten Violin Concerto – a surprising choice, as his undoubted abilities evidently did not include much knowledge of the Baroque repertoire. He turned up at the first rehearsal to find that a hapless BBC secretary had sent him by mistake an orchestral 1st violin part instead of the solo part - and he didn't realise the error! To Brosa's great credit he eventually performed with aplomb, but we all sympathised with Maurice's exasperation.

One of the most memorable performances we did with Enesco was the Bach B minor Mass, which was recorded in the Concert Hall, Broadcasting House. Enesco was much impressed by the singing of Kathleen Ferrier, then at the height of her powers, and the sublime horn playing in the Quoniam of Dennis Brain. Other authoritative performances I remember include Bartók's Divertimento for Strings, and despite misgivings I have already mentioned, the Music for Strings, Percussion and Celeste.

Enesco's personality on the rostrum was quiet, modest and always most respectful of the players in his charge. He got immediate attention without ever having to ask for it. We felt free to play without fear or inhibition – there was never any question of being overawed by his celebrity. It was as if we had a kind and sympathetic spirit guiding us. Enesco had spent the war years in his native Roumania, mostly under German occupation, and had suffered both mental and physical trauma. By the time of his association with the BN, he was bent almost double, and found it difficult to keep his head upright. The fortunate few who had private lessons with him during his visits reported that he was barely able to play the violin any more. It was thanks to Menuhin that he had been rescued from his plight in Roumania and had settled back in Paris, but his financial status remained precarious. His friends could not help directly, as he was fiercely proud and would not accept charity. It is a source of some satisfaction that his engagements with the BN went some way towards addressing his difficulties, and that I can claim some part in the revival of his music. His 3rd Violin Sonata Op 25 *dans le caractère populaire roumain* had been recorded by Menuhin and Dino Lipatti, but Muriel and I later recorded it for the BBC, together with the earlier sonatas 1 and 2 and the evocative *Impressions d'enfance*, and included all these pieces in our recital programmes. I have also organised several performances of his Octet with a number of different ensembles.

Underneath Enesco's unassuming public persona lay a soul of deep passions. His wife, who travelled everywhere with him, was an amazing looking woman - thin and fragile with large black eyes, like a painting by Modigliani come to life. Apparently she was a Roumanian princess - Enesco as a young man had been invited by the Prince to play at his castle. When she heard him play, she said "This is my man!" and left with him after the performance. The invitation presumably was not repeated.

Very occasionally, Enesco's passionate nature and unswerving sense of commitment led him up the wrong path. As a conductor, his sense of tempo was uncompromising. He knew how fast the music should go, and nothing could deflect him from his instinct. We did a concert at Central Hall Westminster with Walter Geiseking as the piano soloist in Mozart's A major concerto K488. I have nothing but admiration for Geiseking as a musician, but on this occasion there was no real rapport between conductor and pianist partly because Geiseking's playing was very French, inasmuch as he favoured fast and brilliant tempi, and partly because it was generally known that he had been accused of collaborating with the Nazis during the French occupation.

In the course of final rehearsals we reached the last movement of the concerto, which begins with solo piano for four bars. The same motif is then played by the orchestra, which we duly did, but at a considerably reduced speed, following Enesco's beat, as our duty demanded.

Geiseking immediately jumped to his feet: "No, no! Is too slow! Please - faster, faster!"

"But I cannot, I cannot! You would not want I should alter the tempo? The gentleman on the bassoon - he should not be asked to play at such a speed." This referred to a notorious bassoon section towards the end of the piece. They were both absolutely convinced they were right, and neither would budge, so to cut a long story short, we played the movement that evening in two different tempi! It was a complete disaster, and strictly speaking, Enesco was in the wrong - the soloist should always have the final say in matters of tempo. In the great man's mind, however, his sole responsibility was to Mozart.

This story is a perfect illustration of the complexity of the issue of tempo. As orchestral players, we are obliged to accept the conductor's or the soloist's preference, however much we may disagree. We need to cultivate an ability to compromise, and in doing so we learn that there is no definitive speed at which music should be played. The size of the auditorium and its acoustic quality come into the equation. As with the actor or public speaker who must first and foremost deliver the meaning of his words, it is pointless to play so fast that the ear cannot distinguish the notes.

The same analogy can be applied to dynamics – just as an actor, when directed to whisper, must still be audible at the back of the gallery, there is no such thing as an exact measurement in decibels of *piano* and *forte*. Dynamics and tempo should be used as expressions of mood or emotion. Although Jascha Heifetz is notorious for his fast tempi, it is the accuracy of his technical control that often makes his playing of brilliant passages sound faster than it actually is, and consequently more breathtaking.

The difference between the ensemble player, in either orchestral or chamber music, and the individual musician, soloist or conductor, is nowhere better expressed than in Leopold Mozart's "Treatise on the Fundamental Principles of Violin Playing" translated by Editha Knocker. As a mainly orchestral player myself, I find the following passage particularly encouraging:

Decide for yourself whether a good orchestral violinist be not of far higher value than one who is purely a solo player? The latter can play everything according to his whim and arrange the style of performance as he wishes, or even for the convenience of his hand; while the former must possess the dexterity to understand and at once interpret rightly the taste of various composers, their thoughts and expressions. The latter need only practise at home in order to get everything well in tune, and others must accommodate themselves to him. But the former has to play everything at sight and, added to that, often such passages as go against the natural order of the time-divisions, and he has, mostly, to accommodate himself to others. A solo player can, without great understanding of music, usually play his concertos tolerably - yea, even with distinction - but a good orchestral violinist must have great insight into the whole art of musical composition and into the difference of the characteristics; yea, he must have a special lively adroitness to be prominent in his calling with honour, in particular if he wishes in time to become the leader of an orchestra. Perhaps there are, however, some who believe that more good orchestral violinists are to be found than solo players. They are mistaken. Of bad accompanists there are certainly enough; of good, on the other hand, but few; for nowadays all wish to play solo. But what an orchestra is like which is composed entirely of solo players, I leave to be answered by the composers whose music has been performed by them. Few solo players read well, because they are accustomed to insert something of their own fantasy at all times, and to look after themselves only, and but rarely after others.

(Footnote - I speak here nowise of those great virtuosi who, besides their extraordinary art in the playing of concertos, are also good orchestral violinists. These are the people who truly deserve the greatest esteem.)

Chapter 9 – Boyd Neel Tours

Although I began playing with the BN on an occasional basis about the beginning of 1947, I was still only able to do so during leave from the Marines, and so to my great regret was unable to accept the offer of their tour of Australia and New Zealand, leaving on 30th March that year and returning in September. This was a great success, and put the Boyd Neel name firmly on the international music map. By this time, other chamber orchestras were emerging, such as the Jacques Orchestra (conducted by Dr Reginald Jacques), the London Chamber Players (Anthony Bernard), the Kathleen Riddick Orchestra, and the Goldsborough Orchestra under the musicologist and Baroque specialist Arnold Goldsborough, which was led by Manny Hurwitz, and eventually evolved into the English Chamber Orchestra. All these ensembles provided valuable experience and income for London freelance players, and I played in them all from time to time, but during the late 40s and early 50s the BN was certainly the most prestigious, and the most ambitious in its undertaking of important European tours.

My first tour was to Portugal in the Spring of 1948. We flew to Lisbon for two concerts, and then travelled to Oporto for another two. Looking back, it is remarkable how different air travel was in those days. Flying from London, we had to stop in France to refuel, and as we had the whole plane to ourselves, we decided to take the opportunity to refuel the orchestra too! There were no catering facilities on board, so we were disembarked and led into a marquee where a delicious lunch was served. We sat round a large table and were served with red wine, one bottle between two of us.

I happened to be sharing a bottle with Boyd. I took one sip, and it was disgustingly corked!

"Augh, it's horrible. Taste it, Boyd."

He took a sip. "Hmm. Tastes all right to me! Change it if you like."

The waiter arrived, took one sniff, and promptly brought us another bottle. I had discovered the only flaw in our esteemed conductor's make-up - he was taste-blind, as others might be colour-blind! The only other musician I have known who was similarly afflicted was Dennis Brain. He was perfectly well aware of it, and said that food was a non-experience for him. Eating was just a means of stoking up the engine, there was no pleasurable sense of taste. I suppose the only consolation was that he never really knew what he was missing.

After an increasingly convivial lunch, we returned to the plane, and, already a keen photographer in those days, I reached for my camera and got the whole band to pose on the steps up to the plane. As I was doing this, I realised there was no film in the camera, but carried on anyway – I even got someone to take one with me in it! Fortunately we were all in such a complete after-lunch blur that nobody remembered to ask me for a print. It wouldn't happen today – the camera I use now is digital!

Most of our touring was supported by the British Council, so we always had to feature British music. That often meant the Frank Bridge Variations, but on this trip we did Arthur Bliss's Music for Strings. This is a rewarding work, but is not often played these days – it is very demanding and cannot be put together in just one 3 hour rehearsal. Bliss told Boyd that he composed it immediately after finishing the music for the H G Wells film The Shape of Things To Come. He was frustrated by having to work to other people's ideas, and needed a chance to be more self-expressive. I'm not sure how much the piece resonated with Portuguese audiences, but it seemed to go down well on the strength of the sheer virtuosity of the playing.

In Oporto, the Royal Box at the venue was occupied by the legendary cellist Guilhermina Suggia, who has been immortalised in her glorious portrait by Augustus John. She was born in Oporto in 1888, and lived there until her death in 1950. An impressive and still beautiful presence, she was known as the Queen of Oporto. We all met her, but she was particularly taken by Hilary Robinson, my cellist in the Boyd Neel Chamber Ensemble - so much so that he was invited to take tea at her villa the next day!

On a free day in Oporto we were invited to take a lunchtime tour of the Port Wine lodges. We took full advantage of this opportunity to sample a variety of local vintages, and as we left were each presented with a bottle of port. This led to a lively party lasting late into the night, and next day there was no port left, but we did have some premier league hangovers!

Our next important engagement, not really a tour, was ten days of concerts at the second Edinburgh Festival. The venue was the Freemasons' Hall in George Street, and we programmed an exciting range of pieces, including Britten's Serenade for Tenor, Horn and Strings, with Peter Pears and Dennis Brain. The rehearsals for this were enlivened by two incidents. First, Peter Pears was prevented from entering the hall:

"Hey, you can't go in there; the orchestra's playing."

"But I must. I am in the concert. I am Peter Pears."

"I don't care if you're Donald Peers, you can't go in." Donald Peers was a Welsh popular entertainer of the "crooner" variety, who went on to reach Number 5 in the UK Singles Charts in March 1969 with Please Don't Go, a not unpleasant update of the Barcarolle from Offenbach's The Tales of Hoffmann.

The other episode took place during the rehearsal itself. The Serenade opens with an exquisite solo horn passage, which after the final song is heard again off stage. Boyd, in an effort to achieve the right sense of distance, kept urging Dennis to move a little further away. Finally he was satisfied, and as the sound of the horn melted into silence, Boyd shouted out "Perfect, Dennis!" The only reply was the sound of the W C being flushed – Dennis was as far away as he could get!

Looking back, I don't know how we managed to cram so much work into those ten days. According to Boyd's memoirs, in addition to the Serenade and a number of shorter baroque works we played the following

Music for Strings, Percussion and Celeste	Bartók
Verklärte Nacht	Schoenberg
Second Symphony for Strings and Trumpet	Honegger
Variations on a Theme of Frank Bridge	Britten
Concerto for Double String Orchestra	Tippett
Concertino de printemps	Milhaud
Poème de l'amour et de la mer	Chausson
(with Maggie Teyte, the superb English soprano who had sung for Debussy)	
Metamorphosen	Strauss
First Piano Concerto	Rawsthorne
Apollon Musagete	Stravinsky
Serenade for Strings	Dvorák

One of our most unusual engagements was a tour of the British Occupation Zone of Germany, based in Düsseldorf and covering the Ruhr. We saw at first hand the destruction wreaked by the RAF bombing and fighting in the final stages of the war. As we drove into Cologne, the whole city seemed to be in ruins, with the great Cathedral, relatively undamaged, a dark gloomy presence brooding over the scene. Yet, remarkably, there were little shops and businesses emerging from the devastation - the economic miracle of West Germany was beginning under our very eyes.

And it wasn't just in the world of commerce. In a badly damaged but patched up theatre in Düsseldorf we attended a lively and well-produced performance of Bizet's Carmen, with a mixed cast of amateurs and professionals ensuring that as many people as possible were involved. In Hamburg we saw a performance of Mozart's Figaro in German, in a temporary auditorium that had been improvised after the opera house was almost completely gutted. We had no need of money during our stay – everything was free for British Occupation Personnel. There were Volkswagen Beetle cars were everywhere, and you could just hail one and go wherever you wanted.

Our concerts were well attended and enthusiastically received. Boyd was amused by the comments he got from local people:

"The playing is excellent – excellent! The orchestra – they are not British people?"

Boyd would assure them that we were indeed guilty as charged.

"Oh no, that cannot be so. We know that Britain is *Das Land ohne Musik* – the land without music!"

I think we managed to persuade a lot of people otherwise. We also assured them that we had met quite a number of Germans with a sense of humour!

Our Scandinavian tour in the winter of 1949 was another success, despite an early glitch courtesy of the weather. We had an overnight train journey from Oslo to Bergen, and woke in the morning to find that snow had disrupted the timetable and we were stranded amid the most breath-taking mountain scenery. We arrived late at our destination, and with little more than a cup of tea went straight to the hall to give two concerts to packed audiences of schoolchildren. Then we were free until the main concert in the evening.

Breta Graham had a Danish friend in Bergen who invited her to bring another couple of us to lunch. The eventual guest list comprised Breta, Olive Zorian and myself, so I had the privilege of escorting two of the best-looking girls in the orchestra! We were met by a very pleasant man, speaking little English, who told us that before lunch he would like to show us the famous *Holmenkollen* ski jump and the surrounding park. We boarded a train, arrived at the park, walked a considerable way, admired the terrifying height of the Olympic Ski Run, and then walked some more. The time was now nearly 3 pm. We had not eaten all day, had worked hard on the children's concerts, and were absolutely famished. Olive and I begged Breta to inform her friend of our predicament, and it transpired that lunch to the Norwegians was a substantial meal at about 4 o'clock! When we did eventually get fed it was worth the wait, but after a glass or three of wine we weren't in the best of shape for the evening concert!

Later, in Stockholm, there was a similar situation, arising from the conflicting duties of maintaining musical excellence and acting as British ambassadors of goodwill. We had a concert at 7.30, and the

British Council had unwisely scheduled a Sherry Reception at 6 o'clock, which we were expected to attend. Alcohol before playing, as before driving, is generally not advisable, but we reckoned that a couple of small British Council glasses wouldn't do much harm.

After the reception we breezed onto the concert platform, and started proceedings with a rousing Handel Concerto Grosso. The concert was broadcast and recorded, and next day we heard the play-back. Rousing it may have been, but it was also about twice as fast as we had intended!

Our final destination was Finland, with concerts in Helsinki and Turku. We travelled from Stockholm to Helsinki by boat, and were kept awake all night in our cheaper berths in the bows by the constant crash of the vessel against the ice floes. Next morning we woke in brilliant sunshine, to find the ship pushing its way through a narrow passage in the frozen Baltic. There were people walking within yards of us, and even cars and lorries driving over the ice.

We had been warned to expect extreme cold in Helsinki, and to take lots of warm clothes and underwear, but this proved largely unnecessary - it is a dry cold, not the penetrating damp you often get in Britain. Our instruments, however, didn't take too kindly to the conditions. A quick change from freezing to central heating doesn't suite old Italian wood, and Eileen McCarthy's superb Guarnerius cello developed a gaping crack in the back. But we managed to get it patched up and the concerts went well.

As usual, Boyd's duties included a lot of socialising. At one party he was talking to a distinguished looking lady, and mentioned that he would love to meet Sibelius.

"I think that could be arranged," she replied. "It so happens I am his daughter!"

Boyd spent two fascinating hours talking to the great composer. He was warned not to mention Sibelius's own music – if he did, the composer would leave the room, and that would be that. All went well, and Sibelius presented Boyd with an autographed copy of the 7th Symphony. This is now in the library of the University of Toronto.

Another composer we encountered in Helsinki was the "one hit wonder" Dag Wiren. It is true that only one piece by him is known and played, his Serenade for Strings. An appealing and tuneful work, it was a regular item in our programmes. The last movement is instantly recognisable to older television viewers as the introductory music to the popular arts programme Monitor. The TV series Dr Finlay's Casebook also has a signature tune which is very similar. It's as near to breach of copyright as you can get!

The tours were great fun, and the repertoire of the Boyd Neel provided a varied diet for any young violinist to absorb, but it did exclude the great mass of symphonic music, which I began to miss, particularly as many of my friends were in the big orchestras and getting experience that I lacked. So when in 1951 I had the chance to move to the Philharmonia, I felt obliged to take it. I remain forever grateful to the incomparable BN, for helping me not just to play music, but also to listen to myself and to others. The Orchestra was a model for what all ensemble playing, even the largest orchestra, should be. Even the smallest part is important, not only in itself but in relation to the whole.

Chapter 10 – Sascha Lasserson

A major influence on me during my time at the BN, and on many of my contemporaries working in London, was the Russian violinist Sascha Lasserson. Sascha's career is explored in the recently published book "Sascha Lasserson - Portrait of a Teacher", edited by Michael Lasserson. It is subtitled "Reminiscences of Sascha by his Pupils". Muriel and I have both contributed to this book.

Sascha was a key figure amongst the host of violinists who were taught by Leopold Auer in St Petersburg before the First World War. He was equal to any of them in technical and musical ability, lacking only the showmanship that enhances so many reputations, not always deservedly. Where he surpassed them all was in his ability to pass on his knowledge and to inspire people to realize their potential. He often used to say to me "what I tell you is not mine – it is just what I got from Auer."

In that, he was wrong. What we got from Sascha was entirely his. The bare facts that we got from him could no doubt have been gleaned from a textbook, but the genius of his teaching was that it was always given with love. I have talked to people who had lessons with Jascha Heifetz. Jascha was a magician as a player, but he was a tortured soul who didn't easily relate to others. He had a sarcastic manner that he often used in scathing put-downs, particularly when he thought someone was being presumptuous. An eminent violinist told me that he had managed by devious means to get the promise of an actual lesson from Heifetz during his visit to England in the early Fifties. He arrived at the hotel suite, knocked and entered.

"Good morning, Mr Heifetz, I would like to play to you the Sibelius violin concerto."

"Yes? Well before you do, please play to me the scale of C sharp melodic minor in thirds."

My unfortunate friend attempted this with less than perfect results.

"Thank you very much," said Heifetz. "Come and see me in a couple of years." End of lesson.

Sascha would never have done anything like that. Though never less than honest, he was always kind. You were made aware of your weaknesses, but you left a lesson with the feeling that there was hope, some way forward. - you had been shown your good points, and could build on them. It is easy to lay bare people's failings, but it takes a born teacher to point students in the right direction without destroying their self-respect. If Sascha heard a concert given by a pupil, a typical response would be, with a twinkle in his eye – "Very good. Could do better!" His philosophy was simple. Everybody has ability of some kind. The only way to progress is to develop that ability, and it is up to the teacher to find the best way of achieving this.

Unfortunately, some so-called teachers seem to think their role is quite the opposite: to point out the attributes their pupils do not have, and destroy their self-confidence. Other teachers try to turn their pupils into clones of themselves, and insist on adherence to inflexible standards. Sascha knew that everyone is different. While he had firm ideas and principles, he adapted them sympathetically to each individual. It was an approach that no doubt owed something to Auer, who is similarly remembered by his pupils.

Heifetz, although an entirely different character, had a great respect for Sascha, and whenever he visited Britain would arrange to meet him. He was younger than Sascha, and in some ways seemed to regard him as an elder statesman. When Sascha went to the Green Room on one occasion after Heifetz had played, he apparently said "What are you doing here Sascha? One conjuror should not come to watch another conjuror's tricks!" And another time, when Sascha was invited to a Heifetz recording session, Heifetz put his violin down after a couple of takes and said "It's no good Sascha – you'll have to go. You're making me nervous!"

Sascha deserves to be remembered as an important contributor to the musical legacy of this country during the 20th century. He has been unjustly neglected, perhaps partly because of his characteristic modesty, which undoubtedly prevented him from achieving the success as a soloist that his violinistic talents deserved. As she explains in Michael Lasserson's book, it was Muriel who first brought Sascha to my attention when she was doing troop concerts during the latter years of the war. I was on leave from the Marines, and she came home one day enthusing about the amazing Russian violinist she had been accompanying. She told Sascha about me, and he suggested that I should play to him. This led to several years of regular lessons while I was in the BN and the Philharmonia, which ended only when we moved to Liverpool in 1955.

Sascha made an immediate impression on us both, with his beguiling sound, impeccable technique and charming character, but he was rather absent-minded, and quite often ended a performance with his back to the audience! He was always forgetting his hat, and generally needed mothering, both from Muriel and his wife, a warm-hearted English lady who went out of her way to make his pupils welcome.

Sascha was a wonderful man, and those of us who had the privilege of studying with him will always treasure the experience. I am determined to do all I can to make sure that his memory endures.

Muriel was fortunate enough to be put in touch with an equally inspiring teacher at the same stage in her career, the Viennese pianist Franz Osborn. In addition to his solo work, Osborn did regular sonata recitals with Max Rostal at that time. Rostal was a pupil of Carl Flesch, and many of my contemporaries studied with him, but I always resisted his influence because I felt he tended to turn all but the strongest students into mere clones, who echoed his way of playing. Osborn was to my mind a more independent and original musician, and Muriel and I had several constructive sessions with him, working on the Beethoven sonatas. Sadly, he died at a relatively young age.

Osborn told an amusing story about being asked how he and Max achieved such a remarkably consistent ensemble. The two were not dissimilar in appearance, and both had a cast in one eye, Max in the left and Franz in the right.

"So you see," said Franz ,"when I appear to be looking at the music, I am actually looking at Max. And when Max appears to be looking at the music, he is actually looking at me!"

Chapter 11 – The Philharmonia

My time as a regular member of the Philharmonia began in 1951, coinciding with the Festival of Britain and the opening of the Royal Festival Hall, centrepiece of the sprawling South Bank Festival Site. This was an exciting period for London musicians. Wartime austerity was slowly lifting, and we were beginning to renew links with the European musical scene, a trend to which the Boyd Neel made a major contribution, and which the Philharmonia was to continue later. The dynamic musical entrepreneur Walter Legge had founded this, virtually his own orchestra, principally as a house recording ensemble for EMI, with the aim of attracting top soloists and conductors, and setting a new standard for British music makers.

The orchestra had been led by Leonard Hirsch, principal 2nd with the Hallé before the War, but Legge favoured the continental practice of having several concertmasters. For these positions he selected the Hungarian Jack Kessler (a pupil of Jeno Hubay), Jessie Hinchliffe (co-pupil with my father of A W Kaye in Huddersfield and at that time married to the composer Alan Rawsthorne), and Max Salpeter, former leader of the New London Orchestra, for which I had done regular work as a freelance player. When Manoug Parikian appeared on the London scene, Legge immediately saw him as a charismatic player who would make a distinctive leader, and set about his goal with characteristic ruthlessness. Leonard was also active with his excellent String Quartet, and he was persuaded to concentrate on that. Manoug became co-leader with Max Salpeter, and before long was the main man, invariably in the leader's chair for the most prestigious concerts and the visits of the most famous conductors.

The first violins also included Marie Wilson (possibly the most outstanding female orchestral violinist of her time), Hans Geiger, Granville Jones, myself and Ernest Scott, who was usually my desk partner. Leading the seconds was David Wise, former leader of the Liverpool Philharmonic. The principal viola was Herbert Downes, a down-to-earth Brummy, and the cellos were led by Yorkshireman Raymond Clarke, who played like an angel. Jim Merrett was first double- bass. A star-studded woodwind section included Gareth Morris, flute, Sydney (Jock) Sutcliffe, oboe, Frederick (Jack) Thurston, clarinet, and Cecil James, bassoon. The horns were led by Dennis Brain, with Norman Del Mar for a time playing second. First trumpet was Harold Jackson, another Yorkshireman, and the count of principals from God's own county was completed by James Bradshaw, timpani – always known as Mr Bradshaw, never Jim, at least not to his face.

In retrospect, it is clear that Legge picked all his principals not purely for their technical excellence, but for the finest possible tone quality, a sense of musical phrasing, and their strength of character. I remember them all as interesting people, and it was always a pleasure to make music together. Jock Sutcliffe's oboe sound in particular is instantly recognisable in recordings for its superb vocal quality. Remarkably enough, Jock was also an accomplished cellist, producing a similarly *cantabile* sound, and on his retirement from the orchestra spent some years teaching the cello at the Menuhin School for gifted young players.

Given such a richly diverse crew, amusing anecdotes abound. One of my favourites, because it illustrates so well the appreciation of orchestral players of anything that deflates pretentiousness, concerns Jack Thurston, who before coming to the Philharmonia had been first clarinet in the BBC Symphony Orchestra. His best friend was the first trumpet, Ernest Hall. They made an unlikely pair - Jack was very much a man of the world, conscious of his status and achievements and well able to hold his own in any company, while Ernie was a big, bluff Yorkshireman who wore his heart on his sleeve and had the affection and esteem of almost everyone who knew him. Ernie did sterling work with the National Youth Orchestra, and all the kids loved him – he was always Uncle Ernie to them.

He and Jack were both keen golfers, and one day while they were on holiday they drove to a nearby club, and Ernie approached the secretary to make a booking. A short while later he returned, and the following conversation ensued:

Jack – "Hello, what's the matter? What's happening? Why the delay?"

Ernie – "Well, 'e says we can't have a round."

Jack – "Why not? Are they full up?"

Ernie – "No, they're not full up."

Jack – "Well then, why can't we play?"

Ernie – "Well, 'e says 'e can only let in members or their friends, or people 'e knows."

Jack – "Well, that's all right. Just tell him who we are!"

Ernie – "Well, oo the bluddy 'ell are we"?

The next few years were to be the orchestra's glory days. Legge's ruthless hiring and firing policy was not universally admired –not for nothing was the Philharmonia known as the "cloak and dagger orchestra". Although the regular players were always asked first when there was an engagement, and were expected to give orchestral dates priority in return, we were all hired on a freelance basis, with only a verbal assurance of continuing work. As Sam Goldwyn so pithily put it, a verbal contract isn't worth the paper it's written on, and another anecdote illustrates this perfectly. Jim Merrett, the principal double-bass, took a few days holiday, and while he was away heard through the grapevine that his position was being offered to the principal of the LSO. He rushed back in great consternation to the orchestral office and buttonholed Jane Withers, Legge's chief assistant and orchestral manager:

"Hey Jane, Jane, what's this I hear? X--- has been offered my job!"

"It's perfectly all right Jim, nothing to worry about."

"How d'you mean, nothing to worry about? This is outrageous!"

"It's perfectly all right. Don't worry."

"Well I am worried. My job being offered around like this, behind my back."

"It's perfectly all right Jim, don't you worry. X--- doesn't want it!"

Conditions like this should have been insufferable, but morale in the orchestra was actually very good. We all felt a sense of *cameradie*, united against the evil Walter, and this gave us a channel to work through our grievances. The fact was that London players were brought up in a freelance environment, where it is perfectly natural for players to move fluidly between employers. And we were all aware that Walter, whatever his faults, was getting us the best work, the most lucrative recording contracts and the chance to play with world class musicians. We moved constantly between Abbey Road Studios and Kingsway Hall, which despite some drawbacks turned out to have an ideal recording acoustic, and was where nearly all the great Philharmonia recordings were made. We often did three 3 hour sessions a day, from 10 till 1, 2 till 5 and 6.30 till 9.30, and if all three stints were at Kingsway it was quite literally back-breaking work, because the orchestra was seated on the sloping floor of the auditorium, which meant sitting the whole day with a twisted spine. The money however was good!

At that time, Kingsway Hall was rented out more or less continuously to record companies. Beecham described it as the only Methodist Hall in the world that was making a profit! We turned up, day after day, often with no idea what we would be playing – all we had was a list of dates and times over the phone. I remember coming in one morning and seeing a stranger clutching a violin as he sat unobtrusively behind the orchestral layout, smiling benignly at anyone who caught his eye. We all thought he was a new "extra" player, and expected him to be directed to a seat at the back of the second fiddles. Instead, as we started the session, he shook the conductor's hand and climbed up onto the stage to play the Tschaikovsky concerto. It was David Oistrakh, on his first visit to Britain. What a revelation - of all the great fiddlers of that period, surely he was the greatest, for his musicality, warmth and fullness of sound, technique, assurance, and above all irresistible sense of humanity.

A number of well-known singers recorded with us in Kingsway including Kirsten Flagstad, then almost at the end of her career, and Elizabeth Schwartzkopf, in glorious voice, who had just married Walter Legge. Walter seemed almost to regard her as a Trilby to his Svengali, grooming her performances and criticizing her work in a manner that bordered on arrogance.

We orchestral players took a jaundiced view of the way that Walter set himself up as the ultimate arbiter in all matters musical, and we felt vindicated by one particular incident. Otto Ackermann was engaged to conduct a number of Viennese operettas – he was a specialist in this field, and Legge had also engaged all the top Viennese singers. At one session we were recording a champagne aria that required the sound of champagne corks popping, simulated by putting a finger in the mouth and withdrawing it with a pop. Great excitement and amusement – Walter would do the pops! He duly took his place in front of the microphone, all Jack the lad, and we began to play. It immediately became apparent that Walter could not follow the conductor – he popped all over the place, and had no coordination or sense of rhythm. Like Brendan Behan's critic, he was the eunuch in the harem. He saw the trick done every night, he knew exactly how it was done, but he couldn't do it himself. He hastily retired and one of the singers did the popping perfectly.

One final Kingsway memory. The management was always keen to attract good young players, however inexperienced. One young Academy student who got his first chance with us rather blotted his copy- book. He was told over the phone to attend a 10 to 1 session at Kingsway Hall, and arrived at half past twelve to be on the safe side!

We did several concerts during the first week that the Royal Festival Hall opened. The hall management team, made up entirely of London County Council staff, had no prior experience to guide them. The first concert included Beethoven's Choral Symphony, and it was discovered the day before the performance that the box-office had sold all the choir seats! On the day of our first rehearsal, the orchestra arrived to find that the lift up to the performing space was to be used only for concerts, and at rehearsals we would have to climb three flights of stairs. This was obviously not acceptable, and we all camped out on the lowest level until the order was hastily rescinded. Hiccups like this apart, we were excited to be in at the beginning of a new era for the London concert scene.

Unfortunately, the acoustics of the Hall proved problematic from the start. The sound was clinically clear, but there was no orchestral blending. It was terrifying to play in a section feeling that you were totally isolated, and from the audience, you got the impression that if you looked at one particular player, he or she would be the only one you could hear. Over the years there have been various attempts to improve matters, and as players we felt that the comfort factor did gradually improve. Or maybe it was just that we were getting used to it. The most comfortable acoustic for players is undoubtedly one that to some extent smoothes over the small details, and hides imperfections. Playing regularly in an absolutely clean and detailed sound environment really made us smarten up our act. You couldn't get away with any sloppy ensemble or intonation. What was all right in the Albert Hall was patently sub-standard in the Festival Hall.

The truth is that absolute acoustic clarity is not really desirable. Listen to a violin with your ear an inch from the strings and you get a horrible amount of hiss, crackle and zizz, which fortunately disappears when you stand back a little. It's like looking at a painting so closely that you can see individual brush marks - you aren't meant to be that near. A good hall not only gets rid of roughness in the sound, it is also in itself a musical instrument. Just as a great old Italian violin enhances the tone produced by the player, so do the quality of construction and proportions of the hall enhance the entire orchestra. The Musikverein in Vienna, which has a lot of wood in its construction, is a delight to play in, and an even better example is the Drottningholm Theatre on the island of Lovon outside Stockholm, which was built about 1766, and is almost entirely constructed from beautiful old pine.When I played there for a week with the LPO and Glyndebourne in 1967, doing Don Giovanni with John Pritchard, I found the sound of singing voices and strings absolutely exquisite – a perfect balance between resonance and clarity.

The faults of the Festival Hall were highlighted at one concert that first week, when we were conducted by Ralph Vaughan Williams in a performance of his Fantasia on a Theme of Thomas Tallis – a most estimable work, but better suited to the resonance of a great cathedral. Our best attempts couldn't prevent it from sounding particularly dry, and matters weren't helped by the fact that by that time Vaughan Williams was very deaf. We had the small echo orchestra, led by Max Salpeter, placed somewhat behind the main body of strings, about where the choir would be. They were quite inaudible to the composer:

"Play up! Play up a bit! Can't hear you!"

"We are playing – quite loudly!"

"Huh – can't hear you." Then to Manoug: "Are they playing?"

"Oh yes, quite loudly!"

"Oh well, if you say so!"

Even so, it was quite an experience to perform under such a venerable icon among British composers.

For a detailed account of the Philharmonia phenomenon, I recommend the excellent book by Stephen J Pettit. I do not pretend to have first hand knowledge of everything that went on, and can give only a personal account from the point of view of a rank-and-file orchestral member. My time with the orchestra, from 1951 to 1955, covered the period when Herbert von Karajan was in fact if not in name the chief conductor.

He and Walter Legge were very close. Karajan was possibly nearer to Legge in terms of aims and ideals than any other conductor. He had a clear grasp of recording techniques – it was said that he knew more about balance and placing of the players than any of the recording engineers. The other two great conductors associated with us at that time; Furtwängler and Klemperer, would rehearse to obtain the performance they wanted, then leave it to the "mechanics" (as Klemperer scornfully called them) to work on the final product.

Karajan was quite different. We would arrive for a session at Kingsway Hall, and he would start by recording the music straight through. Then he would go into the box (the room behind the stage used by the sound engineers), hear the tape through, and begin to work out what needed to be altered. He came with the aim not of reproducing his own performance, but of producing the finest gramophone record possible. The result was as near as possible flawless, but to some tastes rather too glossy.

It is worth taking a brief look at the history of recording techniques and how they have affected our concept of making and listening to recorded sound. In the earliest days of acoustic recordings, musicians had to huddle around a giant horn in the corner of the studio, which collected the vibrations and channeled them directly onto a wax cylinder. No editing was possible, and even the advent of electric recording in the 1930s changed the situation very little. When I first took part in recordings with the Boyd Neel in the immediate post-war years, we were still producing 78 rpm records, each side lasting about 4 minutes. The "takes" were made directly onto wax discs cut by a metal needle, which transferred the vibrations produced by the microphone by purely physical means. To achieve permanence, these discs had to be taken away and used to create a metal matrix, which was in turn used to stamp out the actual discs sold in the shops. It was possible to play back the original wax to hear how it sounded, but one single playing ruined its quality, and the only worthwhile reason for doing this was to provide feedback for the next attempt if there had been an obvious fault in the performance that would render it unusable anyway. The "take" to be used for the final result was always decided upon as an act of faith. You just listened very carefully to the performance, and hoped that nothing had escaped your notice! As may be imagined, those 4 minute sections made recording a nerve-racking business.

In the early 1950s, two developments changed things completely - the long-playing 33rpm record that accommodated up to 30 minutes on a disc, and even more importantly, the use of magnetic tape for the initial recording. By skilful cutting and splicing it was possible to record in short sections, cut out mistakes and do all sorts of adjustments to the original. Nothing could quite match up to a clean, uncut performance, but it was a great blessing to be able to make joins at convenient places, rather than every 4 minutes, and even more so to have access to instant replays.

Musicians are divided between those who prefer recordings featuring a clean uninterrupted performance of, say, a movement of a symphony, and those who go for the elimination of the slightest blemish by detailed editing. There are arguments on both sides. In a concert performance, some mistakes can be perfectly acceptable because the listener is carried along by the broad sweep of the music, and a performer who is too worried about perfection will sound stilted and cautious. A "warts and all" recording of such a performance may suit some agendas, but others may find it intolerable - every time you play it back, you know the mistakes are coming!

Nowadays, digital editing can be used to alter single notes and change sounds in every imaginable way, and no one can be certain how much of what you hear actually happened. It does mean that players can take more risks, safe in the knowledge that most mistakes can be rectified. One thinks of the story about the solo pianist and the conductor listening to a playback:

"It really does sound jolly good, doesn't it?" says the pianist.

"Yes," replies the conductor "don't you wish you could play like that?"

Furtwängler disdained anything that came between the actual performance and the listener. He belonged firmly in the warts and all camp. In our Kingsway Hall recording with him of Wagner's Tristan and Isolde, still regarded by many as one of the greatest of all opera recordings, there was virtually no editing or re-recording. We started work by rehearsing the 20 or 25 minute section we were due to put down in that session. After about an hour, we recorded it straight through, then the orchestra took a half-hour break to allow for a complete play-back. On returning, we recorded it through again, and that was that - one side of a 33 rpm long-play record done!

We now know that initially there was bitter disagreement between Walter Legge and Furtwängler about how the recording should be done. At one stage, the conductor refused to go ahead if Legge was in charge. In the event, Walter at least partially won Furtwängler over. He was present throughout, and masterminded the entire operation. On its successful conclusion, Furtwängler heard through the completed recording with Walter, and delivered the only publicly known compliment he ever paid him:

"My name will be on this record, but your name deserves to be on it too."

The complete opposite was the case when we recorded Beethoven's Choral Symphony with Karajan. We heard that Legge had approached the Huddersfield Choir to ask if they would take part, only to be politely informed that they recorded only with Sir Malcolm Sargent! So, at about a fortnight's notice, Legge transported the whole orchestra to Vienna, where we had a week in the Musikverein to complete the project. It was done entirely on a piecemeal basis. The first session began with about 10 minutes of the slow movement, then we jumped to another section, and so on. Admittedly it would not be practical to record that work in its proper order, as the sections with choir and soloists need balancing separately, but the way it was done gave us no sense of continuity at all. And to cap it all, when we thought we had finished and were packing up to leave, there was a sudden panic - the engineers had found a whole section of the slow movement that we hadn't done at all! We had to stay on for an unscheduled extra session to get the whole thing "in the can".

As a postscript to this, some years later, when I was leading the Royal Liverpool Philharmonic Orchestra, we hosted two important events. One was the first International Piano Competition, won by Joaquin Achúcarro, the great Spanish pianist who narrowly beat John Ogdon into second place. Joe became a close friend of our family. The next year there was the International Conductors' Competition, and the winner of the first prize, which was six months as apprentice conductor of the orchestra under John Pritchard, was Zubin Mehta. I discovered that in 1954 both these musicians had been studying in

Vienna – they were great friends, and had both sung in the choir for that Beethoven recording!

One other illustration of Karajan's approach to recording stays in the mind. When we did the Bach B minor Mass, there was a sturdy difference of opinion between Karajan and Gareth Morris, principal flute. In the *Domine Deus*, for soprano with an important flute obbligato, there is a continuous flute passage without any obvious opportunity to breathe. Gareth, of course, knew the music well, and had worked out how to take time and bend the line of notes so that it was possible to snatch a breath at certain points. He was convinced that this was what Bach intended, but Karajan would have none of it. He insisted on booking a second flute to share the part and make sure there weren't any gaps. Gareth was outraged, but had no choice but to give in.

Several years later, I unexpectedly came upon another instance of jiggery-pokery in a Bach recording. When in Liverpool I bought the Heifetz set of the unaccompanied six Sonatas and Partitas for violin on three LPs dated 1958, and found a surprising discrepancy in the Fugue of the Sonata in A minor. In bar no. 239, in the manuscript score the two semi-quavers are open G and A. But this is in the middle of a long sequential passage, and it could be argued that logically, to carry on the sequence, the notes should be G and F, which would go below the compass of the violin. And yet, somehow, this is exactly what Heifetz plays! There must have been some faking going on, because I cannot see how he could have tuned the string down so quickly in the middle of such a complex passage. Nowadays, it would be easy for the engineers to alter one note, but back in those days it was almost impossible. I always meant to write and ask Heifetz how it was done, but I was aware of his somewhat forbidding reputation, and didn't have the nerve.

As well as our recordings, we did many memorable concerts with Karajan. I particularly remember Bartók's Concerto for Orchestra at the Edinburgh Festival in 1953, and some outstanding Strauss performances, most notably Don Juan. Karajan often conducted with minimal gestures and eyes closed. In a rare moment of humour, he once said to us –"People say that I conduct the Berlin

Philharmonic, I conduct the Vienna Philharmonic, and I listen to the Philharmonia!"

In May 1952 the Philharmonia left on an extended European tour with Karajan, expressly aimed at establishing the Orchestra in the top flight of continental ensembles. It was an exhausting schedule, with concerts in Paris, Berne, Turin, Geneva, Basle, Zurich, Milan, Vienna, Linz, Munich, Hamburg and Berlin.

One item we played a number of times on the tour was Berlioz's Symphonie Fantastique. In the slow movement, the second oboe has to play offstage, and must then return for the rest of the work. Correction - that is the way it would have been under any other conductor. Karajan would not tolerate the idea of someone walking off and on during his concert, and insisted that an extra player be engaged. And so Peter Graeme, an oboist who played mainly with the English Chamber Orchestra, landed the touring player's dream job. He was needed in only one item, played just a few offstage bars each evening, and didn't even have to pack his evening dress!

Because the tour was partly financed by the British Council, we were obliged to include some British music, of which Karajan was not an aficionado. The only thing he could be persuaded to conduct was Handel's Water Music, arranged by Hamilton Harty, which we had recently recorded. Handel admittedly spent a great part of his life in London, but the fact remained that it was German music, arranged by an Irishman! Karajan was reportedly in the Abbey Road Studio one day with Walter Legge, walking past the smaller studio at the back where a chamber orchestra was playing.

"Who are they?" asked the Maestro.

"That is Harry Blech, conducting the London Mozart Players."

"Huh - London Mozart Players! I will start the Salzburg Shakespeare Society!" Karajan, like Mozart, was born in Salzburg.

On a personal level, the tour was soured towards the end when my violin was stolen from the Musikverein Hall in Vienna. This was the Ruggerius belonging to my father, which he let me use after I was released from the Marines in 1947. We arrived in Vienna after an overnight journey from Italy, and after breakfast were taken to the hall for a rehearsal. There was some confusion because the Vienna Symphony Orchestra was already rehearsing there, so we were told to leave our luggage and instruments, go out for a coffee and come back at 11 o'clock. When we returned, my violin had gone. There was great consternation, with police, newspaper reporters and a stream of sincere apologies, and in the midst of all this fuss the thief quite possibly panicked and threw it into the Danube. In any case, it was never recovered. Maybe it went to Russia. The Allies were still in Vienna as an occupying force at the time, and there were heavily armed Russian sentries at each of the four corners of the Hall. No-one walked on the pavements near them. It is not an image I recall with much affection, and for the rest of the tour I had to play on a borrowed instrument.

Chapter 12 – Toscanini

After the European tour, the reputation of the Philharmonia was sky high. The Hungarian violinist Joseph Szigeti summed it up by saying "The Philharmonia showed the Continent for the first time all the qualities of perfect chamber-music playing raised to the power of a great symphonic orchestra."

Legge knew however that Karajan had other ambitions. He had his eye firmly fixed on the ultimate goal, chief conductorship of the Berlin Philharmonic, although he was unlikely to achieve this during Furtwängler's lifetime. Understandably Legge wanted to keep his own options open, and during 1952 we worked with several other conductors, including Klemperer and Furtwängler himself. Legge also opened negotiations with Guido Cantelli, the up-and-coming protégé of Toscanini, with a view to securing concert appearances in London with the celebrated Italian maestro, who was by then 85 years old. Toscanini initially resisted the idea, feeling his age was too much of a handicap, but he was persuaded by Cantelli to hear the orchestra when we played in Milan and Turin, and on the strength of our performances there, agreed to Legge's suggestion.

Unknown to Legge, the London County Council Management of the Festival Hall had tried to engage Toscanini for the inaugural concerts the year before, but previous commitments had made this impossible. Now, however, he had the opportunity to appear in the new hall with an internationally acclaimed orchestra he had seen in action for himself. After lengthy negotiations, two programmes were agreed, consisting entirely of the music of Brahms: the four Symphonies plus the Tragic Overture and the St Anthony Variations. On the face of it a surprising choice, as Toscanini is not immediately associated with this composer. Although there were no associated recording sessions at the time, the concerts were broadcast, and in recent years they have been issued on CD. I was not hugely taken with the performances at the time, but I find distance has lent enchantment. The Philharmonia soloists are in superb form, particularly Dennis Brain on horn, Jock Sutcliffe on oboe and Jim Bradshaw on timpani. Mention should also be made of Manoug Parikian's captivating violin solo at the end of the slow movement of the 1st Symphony.

We were all aware of Toscanini's reputation for temperamental outbursts, but rehearsals went very smoothly, so much so that the Maestro actually cancelled one session entirely. If anything was not quite to his liking, he would stop, shake his head, briefly indicate what he wanted, then say "Da capo, Da capo!" He would never go back just a few bars, always right back to the beginning of the movement, to make sure he captured the full shape of the music.

The first concert had an inauspicious beginning. It was to open with the Tragic Overture - taking me back to my very first days at the Academy - followed by the 1st Symphony. The Hall was packed – tickets had been allocated by ballot, and could have been sold three times over. As Toscanini came onto the platform the atmosphere was electric. When the orchestra and audience had settled down after the National Anthem, he raised his baton, and, to our disbelief, began to conduct the Symphony instead of the Overture! We, of course, could only play what was in front of us. Toscanini always conducted from memory, partly because his eyesight was weak, so he recovered in a flash, but he was visibly shaken, and during the interval had the humility to call Manoug into his room and apologize for the error! Luckily, the incident is hardly audible in the recording.

One of my most prized possessions is a photograph of Toscanini with Guido Cantelli and some of the principal Philharmonia players, Manoug Parikian, Max Salpeter, Fredrick Thurston, Dennis Brain, Jim Merret, Herbert Downes and Jim Bradshaw.

Chapter 13 – Other Philharmonia Memories

In October 1954 there was another European tour with Karajan, this time extending as far as Palermo in Sicily. The management tried to insist that all the travelling should be by either coach or train, but some of us were equally insistent that we wanted to go by car. In the end, three of the first violins took a car full of passengers, Manoug Parikian, Hans Geiger and myself. My passengers were Marie Wilson, Ernest Scott and Derek Collier. Jane Withers was deeply disapproving of this - it would mean that if the worst happened, the orchestra would be without practically the entire first violin section! In the event, she had no cause to worry. We were in time for every rehearsal and concert, whereas the rest of the players were several times delayed by late trains and buses. It has struck me more than once that violinists often seem to be enthusiastic and skilful drivers. Maybe the levels of coordination needed are similar. Manoug was certainly a great car enthusiast, and Hugo Rignold, a fiddler turned conductor, was an outstanding driver who, it was said, would not have been out of place on the Grand Prix circuit. Karajan, incidentally, was a keen driver himself. I think he rather admired us for sticking to our guns.

There were so many outstanding recordings and concerts with the Philharmonia that I cannot possibly mention them all. David Oistrakh played the Khachaturian violin concerto, with the composer conducting, at the Albert Hall in front of a glittering audience of London's finest. We had recorded the work a few days earlier in Kingsway Hall, and the sessions had proved quite entertaining. The presence of two such prominent Soviet artists meant a host of security men, openly suspicious of the tangle of electric leads. A Russian lady was provided as an interpreter, but as she had no knowledge of music her effectiveness was limited. So we had a confusion of tongues to contend with. Manoug, being Armenian by birth, translated freely for Khachaturian, Hans Geiger translated for Oistrakh, who had a good command of German but hardly any English, and we poor folk in the orchestra struggled along as best we could! I remember Jim Bradshaw complaining that he didn't know where to come in during the last movement after several hundred bars' rest. Manoug had a brief word with Khachaturian:

"It's all right Mr. Bradshaw – he'll bring you in."

"Ah well," came back the retort, "I 'ope 'e's right!"

Our distinguished timpanist, with his North Country brogue, long skinny build and the general air of an outraged parrot, was no respecter of reputations, and as it turned out, his fears were well-founded – Khachaturian failed to give him his cue!

I have already mentioned Guido Cantelli briefly, but he deserves more detailed notice. The Philharmonia did many recordings at this time under his brilliant directorship, most notably Schumann Symphonies, Debussy "Le Martyre de Saint Sebastien" and Bartok Concerto for Orchestra As I said earlier, he was a protégé of Toscanini and was being groomed to take over the New York Philharmonic from the older maestro. It is said that Toscanini heard a concert with Cantelli conducting the American orchestra, and whispered "that is me directing this concert!" His potential as a superstar was limitless – he had every attribute of the greatest conductors, plus a charismatic presence and an appearance like Frank Sinatra. Tragically, in 1956 he died in a plane crash at Orly airport outside Paris, aged only 36. Toscanini died two months later without being told of Cantelli's death.

His conducting could best be described as incandescent. He invariably required a complete change of clothes at every interval in rehearsal or concert. Some thought his performances too theatrical and self-indulgent, but he strongly asserted that he was completely unaware of his outward appearance when performing. As could be expected he was not easy to work with, though he greatly respected our orchestra and had a particular affinity to Manoug Parikian.

One episode I specially remember. The orchestra did a trial recording session in the Festival Hall, which proved to be a complete failure as the acoustics were far too dry and unsympathetic. However, on that particular morning we were rehearsing and trying to record Ravel's "Pavane pour une infante défunte". Cantelli could not get a perfect join between the upward harp glissando and the flute entry. He tried again and again, even insisting that the harpist should sit directly before him, but nothing was right. Suddenly, he threw the baton on the floor, buried his head in his hands, sobbed "I suffer too much!" and ran off the stage. We all sat in rather shocked silence for a few seconds, then the phone from the balance box rang. Manoug answered it, and in his impeccably correct tones uttered the immortal lines – "He's lost interest!"

The summer of 1954 marked another notable recording, with a rare collaboration between Menuhin and Furtwängler in the Bartók 2nd Violin Concerto. This took place in Abbey Road Studio, and the result is an outstanding disc, with the conductor's sense of unity and line complementing the undoubted affinity of the violinist with Bartók's music. In 1943 Menuhin had commissioned from Bartók the Sonata for Solo Violin, which proved to be the composer's penultimate work. On hearing Menuhin play the finished music, Bartók paid him the ultimate compliment – a composer could not normally expect such complete realization of his aims until he had been dead at least 50 years!

The actual sessions were not entirely trouble-free. While Menuhin's playing was inspirational, it was not always technically reliable. He himself was aware of this, and in the firm strident opening to the last movement kept asking for repeat takes.

Furtwängler eventually lost patience.

"Why are you repeating so much? The more you play it, the worse it gets!"

However, none of this shows in the final result. The disc predates stereophonic recording, and the sound is not up to present day standards, but even so it is a historic recording, my favourite of this work.

Sadly, Furtwängler was to die a few short months later, on 30th November 1954. We had worked with him that Summer at the

Lucerne Festival, including performances of the Bruckner 7th and Beethoven 9th. He was never the easiest person to play for - one felt he did not entirely trust the players to follow his ideals - but it was still a privilege to be associated with such a giant of 20th century music. He could shed new light on the most familiar war-horses. I remember rehearsing Mendelssohn's Hebrides Overture with him in Euston Town Hall. There is a point just before the final coda section where the music suddenly reverts to the original key, and you feel the end is in sight. Most conductors mark this with a brief hiatus, then suddenly pick up speed. Furtwängler somehow avoided this slight but obvious gear change, and the music merged magically into its final section. His beat was so unclear that often you didn't really know what was intended! This enabled him to mould the sound; to shape it and create intricate linear designs. Many young conductors are far too literal. The role of the conductor is not to keep time. Any competent orchestra, given reasonable rehearsal, can keep together in the standard repertoire. Klemperer used to roar at us:

"You might at least play together!"

Meaning – That's your job. Mine is to shape the music.

The day Furtwängler's death was announced we were scheduled to do a Festival Hall concert with Klemperer. At short notice, the overture was cancelled, and instead we played the Funeral March from Beethoven's 3rd Symphony, the Eroica. I was sharing a desk in the first violins that day with Granville Jones, and we stopped off together for a drink after the performance. Granville was overwhelmed by the impact of the conducting we had experienced that evening. We both felt this was the dawn of a new era, and so in due course it proved. Klemperer was to become increasingly associated with the Philharmonia Orchestra, and more or less exclusively so after its reincarnation as the New Philharmonia following Walter Legge's departure in 1964.

I was to stay with the Orchestra only until May 1955, but I recall with great pleasure many notable sessions with Klemperer, including recordings of Mozart's Jupiter Symphony and the complete Four Overtures to Beethoven's opera Fidelio.

Another conductor we worked with was the Polish musician Paul Kletzki. His irascible outbursts were notorious, but never resented, as we felt there was no personal animosity, only a passionate desire to get it right. He was completely intolerant of Walter Legge's interferences during sessions, and we often thought – well, that's the last we'll see of him. Conductors who stood up to our Great Supremo didn't as a rule last very long. However, Kletzki's recordings always sold so well that Legge was obliged to put up with him. One outstanding issue was the Serenade for Strings by Tschaikovsky. My predecessor as leader in Liverpool was another Pole, Henry Datyner, who used all his influence to try to get Kletzki appointed as Chief Conductor there. This was frustrated by difficulty in obtaining a labour permit, and ironically, just when it seemed this problem was about to be solved, Kletzki died of a heart attack while fulfilling a guest appearance in Liverpool.

Walter Susskind was a regular conductor of the Philharmonia from the earliest days. He was a talented all-round musician, an able accompanist for concerto soloists, and also a fine pianist and chamber musician. I was privileged to have him as a friend and colleague later in Liverpool, and also with the BBC Training Orchestra in Bristol. While in Liverpool I persuaded him to perform the Dvořák Piano Quintet with my Quartet, and as a Czech he gave us a unique insight into this exquisite work. He was an amusing character, and very conscious of his image. Always immaculately dressed, he wore high heels to compensate for a less than average stature, was corseted against middle-aged spread, and appeared on every visit with a different, but always glamorous, lady friend.

While in Canada and America, he had worked with a number of big musical names. He told me about an occasion when Heifetz entered the green room just before the start of the concert, put his instrument case down, sat in a chair and nonchalantly lit a cigarette. When Susskind was called to conduct the overture he returned to the green room and found Heifetz just as he had left him.

"Time for the concerto, Mr. Heifetz".

"Good".

Heifetz got up, opened the violin case, took out the instrument, quickly checked the strings and walked straight onto the stage. No warming up for him - his philosophy was that if you hadn't done your practising by then, it was too late!

Heifetz , as I have already noted, didn't suffer fools gladly. He was legendary for his intolerance of pretentiousness, inefficiency and above all unpunctuality. Appointments had to be precisely kept – visitors to his house were not admitted early, and not admitted at all if they were late. He was completely uncompromising in his approach to every conceivable situation. On one occasion we were rehearsing the Brahms Concerto with a conductor who clearly did not command the violinist's respect. Heifetz took over the rehearsal, stopping whenever it took his fancy to point out faults in ensemble and balance. Belatedly the conductor tried to assert himself:

"Um, I think at bar 45 we need a little more oboe sound. Mr. Heifetz, I think you will agree?"

"Where?"

"Here, at bar 45. A little more oboe sound?"

"Huh! Sounded all right to me."

"Ah! Well – maybe – yes- OK - yes- perhaps - just leave it as it was."

"Didn't take you long to change your mind, did it?"

A great artist, but not exactly flowing with the milk of human kindness.

Chapter 14 – The London Harpsichord Ensemble

I was involved with the LHE for most of the period between 1947 and my departure for Liverpool in 1955. The founder of the ensemble was John Francis, an eminent flautist married to the harpsichordist Millicent Silver. They lived in Marlborough Place, St John's Wood, the same road where Muriel and I had lodged as students. The LHE was led by Manoug Parikian, and Hans Geiger, another Philharmonia violinist, was also a member when I joined. When Manoug left after a year or two, Olive Zorian became leader, and I was second violin. I already knew Olive from our association in the Boyd Neel. She had her own Quartet, which was active in the immediate post-war years and was highly regarded by Benjamin Britten. They recorded a number of String Fantasias by Henry Purcell, one of which was the famous Fantasia on One Note for five strings. The one note part is given to an extra viola played in this recording by Britten himself.

Sadly, Olive died in 1965, aged 49, after being forced by illness to give up playing in the early 1950s. At that time I took over leadership of the group. We were giving recitals throughout the UK, broadcasting regularly, and doing series of Baroque concerts in London. This included both broadcasts and public performances of the complete Art of Fugue by J S Bach, in the concert arrangement by Leonard Isaacs, a challenge for performer and listener alike. Conceived with the LHE in mind, it went down well with both critics and audiences, who turned out in good numbers for our performance on 24th March 1954 in the Festival Hall. We also regularly performed Bach's Musical Offering, which similarly filled an evening's concert programme.

John and Millicent became good friends of ours. By then Muriel and I were living in King Henry's Road, near Swiss Cottage, and we spent a lot of time together both professionally and socially. Their two daughters, Sarah and Hannah, were schoolchildren at that time, but went on to become successful musicians. Hannah was originally a harpist, but later concentrated on a career as a singer. We were closer to Sarah, who is well known as an oboist. We performed together often, and Sarah asked Muriel to be godmother to her daughter.

Many distinguished musicians were associated with the LHE, but Ambrose Gauntlett, who had been the first principal cello of the BBC Symphony Orchestra, deserves particular mention. I did a series of broadcasts with him of Trios by Boccherini for two violins and cello. As Boccherini was himself a renowned cellist, Ambrose's part was ferociously virtuosic, and he spent most of the time at the very top of the fingerboard. He was also an accomplished viola da gamba player, and can be heard to advantage in the recording by Menuhin and George Malcolm of the six sonatas for violin and harpsichord by Bach, where he plays the continuo cello part.

I remember one rehearsal with Ambrose when we were tackling the rhythm and shape of a particular passage, and he suddenly said "Peter, its really awful, isn't it? I've been playing all these years, and it's still the same old mistakes that keep coming up!"

Ambrose was a dear friend, and I treasure his memory.

Chapter 15 – The Violin

The violin is a musical instrument that we all take very much for granted. While there are many books about its history and its players through the years, I have found there is a widespread lack of awareness of its true significance in the context of European musical tradition. I think this would be an opportune moment to sketch a brief outline of the origins of the violin and the string family, in the hope that readers may be encouraged to delve more deeply into a fascinating piece of musical history

It is a striking fact that since its appearance in the early part of the 16th century the violin has barely altered in either form or design. It is almost as if the process of evolution suddenly stopped, recognizing that it had arrived at something essentially incapable of improvement. A visitor to the Tullie House Museum in Carlisle can see one of the very earliest violins to survive to the present day. This is from a set of six by Andrea Amati. They are highly decorated, and were constructed not long before Amati's death in 1574 for King Charles IX of France. Another of the same set can be seen in the Ashmolean Museum in Oxford.

Andrea Amati was born around 1540, and made the small northern Italian town of Cremona where he worked a byword for excellence in the field of violin-making. He founded a dynasty of luthiers which spanned three generations, ending with Nicola Amati, the teacher of Antonius Stradivarius. In due course the pupil oustripped his master to create the finest violins of all, which have been the standard model for most makers ever since.

The Tullie House instrument, although a little smaller than its modern equivalent, is immediately recognizable as a violin. The scroll is the same, and so are the curves of the outline, the inward two curves of the bouts which allow the bow to cross freely from the lower to the higher strings, the swelling curves of the belly (in straight-grained spruce), and the shape of the back, in beautifully figured maple.

Above all, the tone is unmistakably what we would expect from a violin. In about 1960, when I was leading the Royal Liverpool Philharmonic Orchestra, Manoug Parikian came to play the Beethoven Concerto with us in the Philharmonic Hall. We were scheduled to repeat the performance the next day in Carlisle, so I drove up with Manoug during the morning and went to the museum to see the Amati. To my amazement, we were given permission to borrow it for the day. We put new strings on it, made a few little adjustments, and in the evening, after the concerto, Manoug used it in his encore, Bach's Prelude in E for unaccompanied violin. The tone was not as big as his own Stradivari, but it had a unique silvery quality, and it was a sensational event for the music lovers of Carlisle. The instrument has since been played by Bradley Creswick, leader of the Northern Chamber Orchestra, during another concert in the town, when he used it for the *violino piccolo* part in the Bach Brandenburg Concerto No. 1.

Bowed instruments like the rebec existed long before Amati's time, but they often had only three strings, and were mainly oriented towards folk music. More refined string music was provided by the family of viols; bowed instruments that were used chiefly for domestic music making. A chest of viols was part of the household accoutrements of any upper-class family, and was the instrumental equivalent to the singing of madrigals. Compositions were often described as "apt for voices or viols". The viol had a gentle tone, suitable for chamber music in a small room.

Apart from its brighter, more assertive tone, the violin's most radical difference from its predecessor was the absence of frets. The viols, like the modern guitar, had these ridges on the fingerboard, showing where the fingers should be placed in order to play the various notes in tune. The fingerboard of the violin is quite smooth, and the player must learn by experience where the fingers should go. This is obviously difficult for the beginner, but it allows much more subtlety in intonation, and shape in the musical line. In his great "Harmonie Universelle" (1636-37), Marin Mersenne hailed the new violin as the king of instruments, and was one of the first serious writers to recognize the absence of frets as an advantage. It was, he claimed, actually easier to play in tune, as the fingers could be moved anywhere the player wanted! This is not a view the average violin student would share, at least not to start with, but any accomplished player knows that there is no such thing as absolute intonation, and that tuning has to be sensitively varied according to the key of the music, and to match with other instruments in an ensemble.

The violin family sound has often been compared in beauty and flexibility to the human voice. Like the voice, the violin can either move cleanly between notes, or glide smoothly up or down. It can also use vibrato to reflect the emotional content of the music, a technique greatly facilitated by the smooth fingerboard and highly effective if not overused..

Perhaps most importantly of all, violin and voice can both sing out their music in a choir. Few will disagree that the sound of a great chorus of voices is as thrilling as a great solo singer. Equally, the violin section of a large orchestra has the power to move the spirit just as much as a solo violin. Both have their place, but the new sound of strings in unison was quickly seized upon by composers as an important musical tool, and the string body became the backbone of the emerging orchestra. Wind players are mainly used as soloists, giving flavour and piquancy to the sound palette, and seldom combine in unison. A choir of 16 oboes or flutes is not easily imagined, but that number of violins is both usual and essential for a symphony orchestra, and creates the tone quality that is the basis of much of our greatest music.

It is probably no coincidence that the birthplace of modern opera in the 16th and early 17th centuries was also Northern Italy. This form of vocal and instrumental entertainment started in the courts of the aristocracy and spread to the public opera houses, fostered by a traditional Italian love of singing and a rising school of talented composers. Prominent among these, and arguably the greatest, was Claudio Monteverdi (1567-1643), born in Cremona and active as a violinist in his early years. Monteverdi was quick to appreciate the vocal qualities of the violin and its suitability as a "backing" for singers. He not only established the violin section's dominant role in the orchestra, but also originated many orchestral string effects, notably cross-string figurations, and in 1638 claimed to have invented the tremolando as a means of expressing warlike emotions.

To my mind, a close look at the history of the violin lends support to Leopold Mozart's view that its orchestral role is at least as important as its role as a solo instrument. The musical public is encouraged by many musical historians to take an almost exclusive interest in the great soloists, at the expense of those of us on the lower steps of the ladder. The Oistrakhs and Heifetzes of this world may be of inestimable value as an example and inspiration, but an army cannot function if it consists entirely of generals, and the lesser ranks, right down to the humble foot-soldier all must play their parts. Sir Thomas Beecham is reputed to have referred to his violin section in the London Philharmonic as a collection of "disappointed soloists". I prefer to look towards the public esteem which has always been accorded to the players of the Vienna Philharmonic, where every orchestral member is addressed as "Herr Professor".

The concerto grosso, a form which was developed by composers of the Baroque era such as Corelli and Vivaldi and spread throughout Europe, depended on the contrast between the solo violin sound and the sound of a body of strings in unison – the so-called *ripieno*. The Classical period saw the rise of the "symphony" and sonata form, and a gradual increase in the size of a typical body of strings to match the larger auditoriums and expanding visions of composers like Haydn, Mozart and Beethoven. This led to an explosion of sheer power in the so-called Romantic music of the 19th and early 20th centuries, with Hector Berlioz paving the way for the vast symphonies of Mahler and Bruckner.

Over the last few hundred years European music has evolved from a specialized and exotic entertainment for the aristocracy into a mainstay of recreational activity at every social level. In the UK we have monumental Festivals like the Henry Wood Proms in London, and youth orchestras all over the country that stimulate the creative juices of thousands of young people.

As someone who has devoted his life to the violin, I find it heartwarming to think that my chosen instrument has played such a vital part in this process.

Chapter 16 – Conductors

The orchestral conductor has assumed over the years a unique fascination in the eyes of the public, and time and time again, whenever people hear that I have been an orchestral leader, they want to know what I think of this or that conductor. It is true that one of the leader's duties is to act as a mediator, when called upon, between the orchestra and the conductor. Most conductors are a sensitive and intelligent enough to ensure that problems are the exception rather than the rule, but when they do arise it is up to the leader, whose ultimate loyalty is always to the orchestra, to prevent matters from spiralling out of control.

Anecdotes about conductors are legion, and it would be easy to fill an entire volume with them. I have already ventured into this territory in earlier chapters, and will return to it again in chapters about the later years of my career, but this is an opportune moment to share a few stories which to my knowledge have not previously been published.

I have only once played in an orchestra conducted by Sir Thomas Beecham, although I have often attended his concerts, particularly as a boy in Bradford. However, on one occasion in 1953 I was booked as an extra with the Royal Philharmonic Orchestra for a day's recording at Abbey Road Studios of Goldmark's tone poem Rustic Wedding, a particular favorite of Beecham's.

Jack Brymer was the orchestra's eminent clarinettist, and his wife had just given birth to a son. The players had clubbed together to present him with a silver christening cup, and at the morning interval Gerald Jackson, the principal flute and orchestral chairman, stood up and asked Sir Thomas if he would kindly make the presentation.

To get the best out of what followed, the reader must understand that Vladimir Pachmann was a pianist who was famous in the earlier part of the 20th century for his colourful and flamboyant performances, particularly of the music of Chopin. His behaviour was eccentric in the extreme, and a number of old 78rpm records exist where he can be heard volubly commenting on his own performance. Apparently they sold like hot cakes!

My father heard him in Bradford's St. George's Hall before the First World War. He reported that Pachmann came on stage, sat down, and found that the stool was a little too far away from the piano. Instead of simply moving it closer, he insisted that three strong men came on and moved the piano towards him! He then settled himself, and looked around the hall until his eye fell on a particular lady to whom he promptly took a completely irrational dislike! The concert manager was called on stage, and was informed that there would be no performance until the poor unfortunate woman was removed from the hall!

Pachmann had a starring role in Beecham's presentation speech, which I can promise was delivered completely impromptu, and was so funny that I can remember it practically word for word.:

"Gentlemen," (no women in Beecham's orchestras - he said pretty ones would distract the players, and ugly ones would distract him!) "thank you for asking me to make this presentation to our distinguished colleague, which I do with pleasure.

This puts me in mind of previous occasions when I have been asked to make presentations to musicians, most particularly the time I had to present the Royal Philharmonic Gold Medal for services to music, to the great pianist Vladimir Pachmann. This was preceded by his performance of the Chopin Concerto No.2 in F minor, which he interspersed with remarks such as 'Isn't it voonderful?' – to which I replied 'Yes it is, but for God's sake get on with it, man'.

The performance ended, and the time came for me to make the presentation, which I duly did.

Mr Pachmann, in addition to his undoubted skill as a pianist, had also a lifelong interest in the collection of precious stones and metals. This had bred in him a certain scepticism as to the validity of such objects when encountered for the first time. He took the Philharmonic Gold Medal, eyed it dubiously, and proceeded to test it by the only means available to him.

He bit it!

Slowly the realization dawned on him that it was indeed pure gold! He advanced to embrace me.

Mr Pachmann was not a pretty sight. His manager who loved him dearly had informed me previously that he bathed but once a fortnight. I retreated smartly. We encircled the grand piano three times in front of a cheering audience, and I made off down the artists' entrance!"

Many of the other stories about Beecham's *bons mots* are either apocryphal or refer to remarks actually made by others. One example concerns his wife, Lady Betty Humby Beecham, a pianist, who to put it politely owed a great part of her reputation as a player to her association with Sir. Thomas. She used to persuade him to let her play with his orchestra, and the results generally left something to be desired.

On one occasion she played the Delius Piano Concerto with the RPO at Swiss Cottage Odeon Cinema, a performance which was rescued only by Sir Thomas's magical way with the composer's music. At the interval, the orchestral manager asked some of the players to take their instruments off the platform as the piano had to be removed for the second half of the concert. Beecham is reported to have said "Oh, leave it alone – it will probably slink off by itself!"

The remark was actually made by Vince Howard, the sub-principal viola and a noted orchestral wit. Musicians love such sardonic, quick responses to orchestral situations, and one reason Beecham was so popular with players was that his sense of humour was very like theirs. No doubt that is what led to the misattribution.

A conductor with whom I had much more extensive direct contact was Otto Klemperer. One of the best Klemperer stories, however, dates from before my time. It was told to me by Lionel Bentley, a violinist whom I got to know very well in the immediate post war years. He played for Klemperer when he visited London as a young man, and remembered him as an absolute martinet who was feared by orchestral players for his vitriolic remarks and glowering presence.

He was notorious for not adhering to rehearsal timetables, and on one occasion carried on working after the orchestra should have stopped at one o'clock. In such a situation, it is up to the leader to earn his corn, and quietly inform the conductor that he must stop. But this particular leader in these particular circumstances didn't have the nerve.

Five past one came, then ten past, and still Klemperer went on. Eventually, one of the second violins stood up, put his fiddle away and picked up his overcoat. Klemperer slammed his baton down, stamped his feet and roared:

"What are you doing? Where are you going?"

"I'm sorry Doctor Klemperer, but I must go. This rehearsal is supposed to finish at one, and I have another engagement at two."

"What are you?" snarled Klemperer, "an artist or a workman?"

"Well," came the cool reply, "you want us to be workmen at 10 o'clock and artists at 1 o'clock."

I have great admiration for that violinist of long ago. I have no patience with people who demand unlimited time to complete a task. To fail to do a job in the allotted time shows incompetence and lack of consideration, and all conductors should be fearlessly reminded of this. To be fair, it is rare for such liberties to be taken, but there is always the odd megalomaniac who needs to be taken down a peg or two.

Klemperer did mellow considerably in later years, but he always retained an autocratic attitude, and often seemed possessed by an imp of the perverse that gave you the impression he was trying to see just how much unreasonableness he could get away with. Sir Adrian Boult in his entertaining book "Thoughts on Conducting" recounts the following episode and dismisses it as probably apocryphal and not really believable. It is actually completely true. I was in the Philharmonia when it happened.

We had a morning rehearsal in the Festival Hall, one of our first ever with Klemperer. At ten o'clock everyone was seated awaiting the entry of the great man. On he came, a fearsome sight, well over six feet tall with the kind of glowering, craggy visage that would give children nightmares. He shook hands with the leader, clambered on to the rostrum, sat on his stool and began a roll call of the orchestra.

"First violins, second violins, violas, celli....." – through the woodwind to the brass - ".....trumpets. Second Trumpet! Where is the Second Trumpet?"

Consternation as Jane Withers came rushing on. "I am so sorry Dr Klemperer, the second trumpet has rung to say he is delayed – he will be 15 minutes late."

"Impossible! Impossible! I cannot start without the second trumpet."

He stomped off the podium and sat like a great ogre in the front row of the stalls, smoking a dirty pipe of smelly tobacco and glaring at us all. Nobody moved or said anything. We sat there like naughty school-kids for an interminable quarter of an hour.

Eventually the second trumpet, Denis Clift, arrived and hurriedly took his seat.

"Dr Klemperer, the second trumpet has arrived."

"Good – good." He hauled himself back onto the rostrum and went back to the beginning of his roll-call. "First violins, second violins, violas, celli....first trumpet, SECOND TRUMPET. GOOD MORNING Second Trumpet....." until at last he was finished. Then "Very good; we will start. Please, Mozart Eine Kleine Nachtmusik"!!

He had the almighty gall to make us wait for the arrival of a second trumpet, and then begin the rehearsal with a piece written only for strings! No one, I'm glad to say, could get away with that nowadays.

Klemperer always got the last word in any encounter. One day we were recording the Bach B minor Suite for flute and strings with our principal flute Gareth Morris as soloist. The first run-through began, and after a short time Klemperer stopped and launched into a lengthy dissertation about our shortcomings.

"No, no. Please play with FULL tone. It is too WEAK! More strength. When I take a small orchestra, you must play STRONGLY. With BODY! More SOUND!" Und so weiter, und weiter, und weiter.

We proceeded to make a test recording, and Klemperer went into the recording room with Gareth and the ensemble leader Manoug Parikian to listen to the result.

After a time Manoug came back. "Look, chaps, Klemperer is quite right. We do need a bit more strength for the recording. It sounds all right in here, but you've just got to give it a bit more."

Then Gareth returned. "Yes, we do need more string strength. I'm surprised, because it sounded all right in here."

Next it was Walter Legge's turn. "Gentlemen, we must ask you to play with a little more body. It sounded all right in here, but for the microphone we need more."

Finally, the conductor stomped grimly back onto the podium and began the by now familiar litany. "Please play with FULL tone. It is too WEAK! When I take a small orchestra, you must play STRONGLY. With BODY! More SOUND!"

"Yes, yes Doctor Klemperer," Manoug chipped in. "We understand."

"But you must DO it!"

"Yes, we will, rest assured."

"When I take a small orchestra, I need more FIRMNESS. Strength! Better attack! With BODY! More SOUND!"

"Yes, Doctor Klemperer. We will certainly play stronger. We understand clearly now that it needs more strength in this instance for the microphone. But it sounds all right in here, doesn't it?"

"NO!!!" roared Klemperer.

Whatever the idiosyncracies of this extraordinary man, his positive qualities were fully appreciated by the Philharmonia, and his bond with the Orchestra became closer still when after I left, Walter Legge attempted to disband it. The players themselves thwarted the move by re-establishing themselves as the New Philharmonia, with the full support of Klemperer, who became conductor-in-chief. It was common knowledge that he was not the first eminent conductor to enjoy a prickly relationship with Legge, and the story went the rounds that in later years Klemperer had the following conversation with a friend:

"Today, I am sad. I am ill and I am old."

"No, no, Doctor, you are well. Everybody is happy for you."

"No, no, no! I am ill; I am old! I must soon die!"

"But, Doctor Klemperer, not just yet. And, to be sure, everyone must die sometime."

"Yes, yes, you are right! I must die. Everyone must die." Then brightening suddenly, with a malicious twinkle in his eye: "Walter Legge must die!"

Two conductors who made brief visits to Liverpool; both very different, but both high on my list of all time greats, were Pierre Monteux and Rudolf Kempe. Kempe was to my mind a paragon of conducting technique and psychology. His physical movements were never exaggerated, but always perfectly clear. His eyes were always focused directly where they were needed, with a faint trace of a smile. I always remember my great friend Marie Wilson saying "I don't look at their beat, I look at their eyes!" and she was absolutely right. You see in the conductor's eyes what he wants the music to mean, and our job is to make this happen. Conductors who use beats and gestures to produce a complicated mime are really just trying to demonstrate to the audience how well they know the score. If they stopped, it wouldn't make a jot of difference to the way the music is played!

The great conductors know how to trust their players, while reminding them of the overall shape of the music. Kempe was particularly adept at this. My strongest memory of his conducting is of the last movement of the Schumann Piano Concerto. The combination of a 6/8 and a 3/4 rhythm is sometimes seen as a test for the conductor, although in truth it demands no more than reasonable competence, but Kempe invested it with a lilt which truly brought out the reason for Schumann's use of this unusual time signature.

We had a visit from Monteux in the last decade of his life when he was over ninety, doing concerts in the Philharmonic Hall, and also in London's Festival Hall. He was a living link to a bygone age - a man who had conducted the first performance of Stravinsky's Rite of Spring, and as a viola player had taken part in string quartets with the legendary Spanish violinist Pablo de Sarasate. His mind was still needle sharp, and as with Kempe, the eyes were windows to the soul. His generous moustache gave him a benevolent air, but from my seat on the platform, directly below him, you could see underneath it a thin Gallic mouth which mirrored his quick restless intelligence.

He played Debussy with us, "L'Après Midi d'une Faune", and insisted on the utmost attention to detail and clarity. No vagaries of rhythm or balance were permitted. The impressionistic atmosphere, he said, is all written into the score - "you must play Debussy like Mozart!" The only obvious down side of his increasing age was a loss of sensitivity to higher sound frequencies. The small antique cymbals that Debussy employs in this piece were almost inaudible to him – however hard our percussionist Johnny Ward hit them, he still asked for more!

We began rehearsals the first day with Richard Strauss's Till Eulenspiegel, and at the interval he said to me "Mr Mountain, will you kindly ask the first violins not to play sharp in their introductory phrase, as the gentleman on the clarinet in his answering passage will sound flat?" I told him I agreed, we did tend to play sharp, and thanked him for reminding us.

"I will tell you a little story," he went on. "When I was in America, I had an excellent concert-master, Naoum Blinder (the teacher of Isaac Stern). He came to me one day, saying 'Maestro, we are lucky here, we have all the great violinists of our time coming as soloists. Heifetz, Menuhin, Milstein, Francescatti and many more. They are all wonderful. But, in my opinion they all play sharp. Do you not agree?'

I replied 'Yes, you are right. They do play sharp.'

'But why do they play sharp?'

'I don't know.'

'So, you agree, they all do play a bit sharp?'

'Yes, they do......and you do too.'"

It is true that any talented player will if anything err on the high side in pitch, because this adds brilliance to the sound. Anyone playing consistently flat must, in my opinion, be lacking in aural awareness. Flatness sounds horribly dull, whereas you can get away with being a bit sharp, especially in the upper register. There is an apocryphal story about an argument between a violinist and an oboist. The oboe player is accused of giving a flat A when the ensemble in tuning up.

"No, I don't – it's the strings who play sharp!"

"Well it's better to be a bit sharp than be out of tune!"

Sir Adrian Boult was a familiar figure to every player of my generation. There are mixed feelings about his conducting, as it is sometimes argued that he didn't pay sufficient attention to detail, or offer his players the clear indications that give them a sense of security. But like Kempe, his over-riding concern was the shape and broad flow of the music, and for that many of us were prepared to forgive him a great deal.

While we were rehearsing the Elgar 2nd Symphony, a work with which the orchestra was unfamiliar, I asked him "Sir Adrian, would you please let us go through this last passage slowly, to get the notes under our fingers?"

"Oh, no, I don't think that's at all necessary. Let's go back a few bars and have a RUN at it." We rocketed through the section once more, and with an imperious sweep of his moustache he delivered his verdict: "Yes, that's more the SHAPE of it!"

I can remember quite a few concerts that to us felt dangerously insecure, but were acclaimed by their audiences as memorable musical experiences. Sometimes, when playing under that long, commanding baton, you had the sensation of being carried irresistibly along, or even, if he was on the top of his form, being pulled through a hedge backwards!

Whenever a musical celebrity like Sir Adrian approaches his later years, the record producers circle like ghouls, hoping to capture as much as possible for posterity. Boult's unusual professional longevity allowed him to exploit this more than most, and as principal 2nd violin in the LPO during the 60s I was among those who reaped the benefits, from the considerable amount of studio work he secured for us.

Not that he didn't have his tetchy moments. We did a week in Kingsway Hall recording the two Elgar symphonies for a particularly fussy producer. Boult normally had the first and second violins opposite on his left and right – an uncommon arrangement at that time, but now preferred by many conductors, as it show ups the counterpoint between the two sections. The producer refused to agree to this, on the grounds that stereo records would only sell if the violins came out of the left speaker and cellos out of the right. He got his way, and Boult was furious.

Things went from bad to worse when messages kept coming from the box asking for replays of whole sections, because of technical faults which the conductor considered insignificant. At one point he roared "I think you'll have to lower your sights a bit, young man!" Finally, towards the end of the week, the producer asked for a complete repeat of one movement.

"There's no time, no time!" trumpeted Adrian.

"Oh, it will be all right – we can afford to pay half an hour's overtime."

"Well I'm going home at 5 o'clock!"

When Boult was Chief Conductor of the BBC, the Corporation had a rule that compelled orchestral members to retire at 65. When Sir Adrian himself reached that age, he was implored to stay on, but insisted on leaving the orchestra - what was good enough for the players was good enough for him. It was typical of a man of great principle, who always took the part of his players whatever the circumstances.

This could not always be said of another equally prominent figure of that time, Sir Malcolm Sargent. When it came to the great choral masterpieces, from Handel's Messiah to Walton's resounding Belshazzar's Feast, there was none to surpass him for audience appeal and sheer grandeur of effect, especially in performances with the great Northern Choral Societies such as the Huddersfield. The choirs loved him, and so did an adoring public.

Orchestras by contrast were less enthusiastic. This dated back to a specific pre-war incident. Sargent had a fairly cavalier attitude towards money, and because he loved to perform, often accepted fees lower than the going rate. At the same time, he had a lavish life-style, and was always generous to charitable appeals. As a result, when he was diagnosed as suffering from tuberculosis, there was no money in the kitty to pay for his treatment – no National Health Service in those days. The London orchestras organised a fund to help him, and a considerable sum was raised to enable him to be successfully treated at a Swiss sanatorium.

Shortly after this, it was proposed that a fund be set up to provide pensions for professional orchestral musicians. Sargent wrote a letter to the Times expressing his opposition to this, claiming that players would not give of their best if they had the luxury of such a financial safety net! Understandably, this breathtaking display of double standards didn't go down too well, but Sargent was unrepentant, and arrogantly stuck to his point of view. It was an error of judgment that blighted the rest of his career.

When he was conductor of the BBC Symphony Orchestra, Sargent tried to insist that the players should always stand up when he made his entrance at concerts. He ran into immediate opposition – it was felt that this courtesy should be reserved for particularly distinguished visiting conductors, or for special occasions. At any other time, it should be at the orchestra's discretion. It became such an issue that orchestral meetings were held about it. Some were totally opposed to standing up, while others took the view that it didn't really matter – anything for a quiet life. Things seemed to have reached an *impasse* when someone came up with an ingenious solution:

"OK, let's compromise."

"How do you mean, compromise? Either we stand or we sit, there isn't any compromise!"

"Yes there is. Let's kneel down!"

Sir Malcolm undoubtedly had his good points. His conducting technique was immaculate – if you couldn't follow his beat it was definitely your fault. His musical facility and ability to command a score were unrivalled, but unfortunately this was sometimes not matched by true musical instinct. A friend of mine who joined the BBC Symphony Orchestra during Sargent's tenure as Conductor in Chief had been sceptical of rumours that the BBC players did not like Beethoven. It was only when she eventually performed the Eroica Symphony with Sargent that she fully understood the reason. His performances of the Viennese classics were characterized by stiffness, rigidity and an imposed grandeur, lacking the subtlety and finesse that they would be accorded by an interpreter more in tune with the composer's vision.

I suppose it could be said that Sargent was a man of many contradictions. Behind the public glamour, the impeccable turnout with the ubiquitous white carnation, was a man of sensitivity who was no stranger to suffering. He sometimes came across as a bully, especially to weaker players, but was loyal to those he trusted. He genuinely loved children, and the pensions *faux pas* notwithstanding, was always most generous when confronted with cases of individual hardship. Above all, although many musicians disliked his musical sensibility, his ability to get "bums on seats" has had an impact on the profile of British musical life that cannot be overstated.

The world would have been a poorer place without him.

Chapter 17 - Freelance

When I was a student at the RAM, the acceptance of freelance orchestral engagements was definitely frowned upon. You were expected to spend any spare time in diligent practice, and in any case, orchestral playing for money was considered *infra dig*. We were there to be trained as soloists, not mere artisans! So, if we wanted to do what are now known as 'gigs', we just did them and didn't let on! I had already done one or two dates when on holiday back home, with the then Northern Philharmonic Orchestra, led by Edward Maude, and had my first experience, aged 16, of playing the Messiah, in Huddersfield Town Hall with Sir Malcolm Sargent. I remember him then as appearing exactly the same as he did years later, with the same glossy hair that miraculously retained its raven hue, although he did eventually allow a few flecks of grey to appear at the temples!

An abiding memory from that concert is the playing of the inimitable John Paley in the famous *obbligato* The Trumpet Shall Sound. He was an imposing figure of a man, reputed to be the inspiration for the painting entitled I Dreamt that I Dwelt in Marble Halls, after the aria from The Bohemian Girl by Michael Balfe, which often appeared on biscuit tin lids. It depicts a large North Country trumpeter, sitting in shirt sleeves at a kitchen table with a pint of bitter and a packet of Woodbine cigarettes fumbled open with clumsy fingers, and playing his heart out!

I had met John previously as a little boy, at one of the various local functions I was taken to by Mum and Dad to play violin solos, in the Church House in Bradford. The Bishop of Bradford was present, and John was there to play some trumpet solos and tell a few jokes. Before the show we saw him taking the Bishop into the corner and giving him a preview, to make sure everything met with his approval!

My favourite story about John was about the time he came in late to an orchestral rehearsal, and almost launched into the first movement of a symphony that the orchestra had just played, instead of the quiet second movement they were about to begin. The second trumpet, just in time, stopped him by frantic hand-waving. He lowered his instrument, and in a resonant whisper said – "By gum lad, it's a good job tha stopped me theer, or A would 'a' shifted some muck!"

In London, we young students often managed to get ourselves bookings for Sunday afternoon concerts with organisations like the Guildford Orchestral Society. One of these was led by W H Reed, leader of the LSO and an intimate friend of Elgar. The soloist was Albert Sammons, thought by many to be the most gifted violinist this country has ever produced. His recording of the Elgar Concerto with Sir Henry Wood is still unsurpassed, and his other recordings are slowly being re-issued. At this concert he played the Brahms concerto superbly, rising above the limitations of a semi-amateur orchestra and showing consummate technical command and musical poise. In C P E Bach's book on 18th Century musical performance, he describes his father, J S Bach, as playing the violin "in a strong and manly fashion", and that is exactly how I remember the playing of Sammons.

While still a student, I had an early introduction to playing in a small chamber orchestra, (which I was to do later on a regular basis as a member of the Boyd Neel Orchestra). Arthur Catterall was a distinguished British violinist, on a par with Albert Sammons, but sadly he has not left a similar body of recordings, and has consequently faded from the public memory. He was a pupil of Joachim, and early in his career led the Hallé Orchestra. There are several recordings of his in the Hallé archives, revealing an incisive technique and a clear singing tone. He was the first leader of the BBC Symphony Orchestra before leaving to pursue a successful career as a soloist. During the war years he taught a small number of students at the Academy. I never had lessons from him, but we had a friendly relationship, and when he formed the Arthur Catterall Players, a small group of young strings, I was invited to join. The group's main activity was Sunday afternoon concerts in south coast resorts and places like Stratford on Avon.

I met Catterall quite by chance one day in Marylebone High Street. He invited me to join him for lunch, where it transpired that he was en route to the Albert Hall to play E J Moeran's Violin Concerto at the Proms. Needless to say, that was my evening's entertainment organised! I believe Moeran's music is much under-rated. The Violin Concerto is a fine work, with distinctly Irish influences, and another piece well worth a listen is his Sinfonietta, which I have played and conducted many times.

During my time as a student I was also initiated into the London theatre music scene, and became a regular extra player in the orchestra for Ivor Novello's The Dancing Years. The leader, having done the gig since before the war, played from memory, and the conductor took this a stage further by busying himself during the pauses between numbers writing out the orchestrations for the next show. Novello himself, although nominally both author and composer, was actually musically illiterate, and simply picked out the tunes on the piano, leaving the harmonies and orchestral arrangements in other hands. The band was a rich *pot pourri* of musicians from a variety of backgrounds – one of the first fiddles turned out to be the brother of Albert Sammons!

After the war, I was able to renew my contacts with the West End theatres, and often played for Leslie Bridgewater, an accomplished composer and arranger who supplied incidental music to the Haymarket Theatre, a string quintet with himself on piano. The plays at the Haymarket were of the highest quality, and it meant you could see the likes of John Gielgud, Ralph Richardson and Sybil Thorndyke for free!

My biggest money-spinner was landing the job of playing the interval music at the Apollo Theatre in Shaftesbury Avenue, as a member of a trio which comprised Teddy Krish, piano, Jack Alexander, cello, and myself. All we had to do was play arrangements of soundtracks from shows like Oklahoma, Guys and Dolls and My Fair Lady, and the National Anthem at the end of the show. It was great fun. Teddy was a rather dry, sardonic character, whose main amusement was to invent complicated syncopations and rhythmic figures designed to confuse the other players. If you got through unscathed you scored a Brownie point! His hobby was writing piano arrangements of Bach Choral Preludes, and he was immensely proud of the fact that the eminent British pianist Myra Hess regularly played one of his arrangements. Jack was a typical mad cellist. He played everywhere as an extra and did a lot of light music gigs, but the Apollo was where he could let his hair down and have a bit of fun. Sometimes he let rip like a wild jazz bassist, and we had to play up to him. We often got members of the audience peering down into the pit, wondering what on earth was going on.

It was an ideal job for all of us, because we had a long list of "deps" who could stand in for us any evening we managed to get a better engagement. This meant we were in the agreeable position of knowing we would have some money coming in on any given day.

The show was called Seagulls over Sorrento and it ran for years. The star was Ronald Shiner, a brash cockney comedian. It had an all-male cast, and was a slick comedy thriller about life on a secret naval establishment in the Mediterranean. There were full houses at every performance. I was deeply impressed by the way that Shiner flung himself into the part night after night with the same undimmed enthusiasm, never giving less than 100 per cent. Real professionalism.

I must also mention here the violinist Oscar Lampe who played chamber music with Jack Alexander. For a time he led the RPO for Beecham, and recorded a fabulous performance of the great solo from Strauss "Ein Heldenleben" My only association with him was in various free-lance gigs. He was a most incredible character – a real cockney "wide-boy" and possessing a technique on the violin only to be described as fabulous. It was said that Heifetz admired him greatly, and sent some of his arrangements for Oscar to assess. I never heard him do it, but people swore that he could play Paganini "Moto Perpetuo" in fingered octaves. He had the typical "cheekie chappie" humour. Apparently in the interval of a recording session, he offered a cigarette to Beecham, proffering a case containing several dog-ends, with the immortal words "'Ere y'are. 'Ave a whole one Sir Thomas!" His general behaviour became a bit hard to take for the orchestra's dignity, and he was finally given the sack for leaving a bottle of beer on the steps of the altar in Canterbury Cathedral!

Other freelance work included BBC Light Music sessions, which could be anything from Harry Davison Old Time Dancing to backing for comedy shows. I remember doing one of the latter in a studio near Charing Cross Station, and realising only some time later that one of the comics was Tony Hancock, long before anybody had ever heard of him.

The most sought after work was of course film sessions. It was the time of the Ealing Comedies, and it was a delight to be part of a big orchestra with all the best players in London. The pay was good, and the company was always entertaining. We worked on a number of American films at Elstree, including Moby Dick, starring Gregory Peck. The conductor was Louis Levy, who many years before had written the signature tune for the Gaumont British News. Or so he claimed – some said it had actually been produced by a ghost-writer. Be that as it may, he had retained the copyright, which meant he received twopence each time it was heard. As it was played about four times a day in every cinema in the English-speaking world, he was a very rich man.

Louis didn't wear the mantle of success with much grace. He had an arrogant manner, and an alarming lack of basic musical knowledge. At one point, he urged us to play louder and louder:

"But," said the leader, "it's marked *morendo*" (meaning dying away)

"Right!" said Louis. "*Morendo, morendo,* let's have more of it!"

At another point he got himself in a muddle between *vibrato* (expressive vibration of the tone) and *portato* (the linking of notes smoothly together).

"Come on," he shouted, "more *portato,* more *portato!*"

We had no idea what he really wanted, and settled for improvising a series of haphazard slides between the notes. Louis slammed his baton down in despair.

"Not *glissando* ye buggers – *portato!*"

Life in those days was lived on different levels. Earnings from my session work went on lessons with Sascha Lasserson and buying the time I needed to practise and build up a solo repertoire. Muriel and I did an audition for the BBC, which meant that in addition to the Wigmore Hall recitals which launched us on a series of Music Club concerts throughout the country, we were offered quite a bit of radio work.

This generally consisted of 45 minute live programmes starting at 9 am. You had to get up at the crack of dawn, drive to Maida Vale BBC Studios for a balance test at 7 am, grab a rather miserable breakfast in the canteen, and hope that your metabolism would be fooled into thinking it was a reasonable time of day to give of your artistic best. Neville Marriner, who was at that time a freelance player like me, but already a master of the cutting put-down, greeted me on one occasion with this witty sally:

"Oh, hullo Peter. I heard you practising on the radio the other day!"

Muriel for her part was branching out as an accompanist, and building up a reputation with the Judy Hill Trio (Judy Hill, Olga Hegedus and Angela Dale). So those early post-war years in London were very busy for both of us.

Muriel and I had begun married life in 1945, while I was still in the Marine Band, by renting a two roomed first-floor flat at 92 King Henry's Road. This served us well enough at first, but the birth of our son Paul in August 1949 soon put impossible demands on a space already stretched by the arrival of Muriel's mother, who had left Coventry and come to live with us. As a temporary solution we found her a good room in nearby Eton Avenue, but the need for more room was still pressing, and suitable accommodation was hard to come by. By sheer good luck we became friendly with the Irish proprietor of an estate agent in Chalk Farm, and by telling him the story of my supposed Irish ancestry, I was able to play on his heart strings and persuade him to let us have a house at 130 King Henry's Road. We moved in during November 1949.

Although our earnings were starting to pick up, we were still far from well off, so as the move was no more than a quarter if a mile, we did without the services of a removal firm, and shifted our meagre belongings with a wheelbarrow and a cart at dead of night. In this we were assisted by a friend of the Brenners called Marcel, who had been stationed in London during the war and was a full Colonel in the Free Belgian Army. I was not long out of the Marines, so I felt a measure of discomfort when I found myself furtively pushing our worldly goods along a dark Hampstead road assisted by such an impressively uniformed high-ranking officer!

Our new home had ample accommodation and an attractive garden. We set up a spacious music room which was ideal for chamber music rehearsals, and many of our friends and colleagues became regular visitors. A number of musicians lived in the area - it was convenient for our work. Muriel was by then a full Professor at the Academy, and could take the two mile walk to work through the pleasant greenery of Primrose Hill and Regent's Park.

As we now had space to spare, we let rooms to musical friends. Niven Miller was a singer we got to know in this way. He eventually emigrated to Australia and enjoyed a successful career there. He had our large front room, and every week held rehearsals for a student madrigal group, which was regularly directed by Imogen Holst, daughter of the composer Gustav Holst. She was a dedicated, enthusiastic musician, who in many ways reminded me of Nadia Boulanger. In later years I took part in several recordings of her father's music ,which she directed with the English Chamber Orchestra. I also did a BBC recording of Holst's Concerto for Two Violins with Manny Hurwitz during my time with the BBC Training Orchestra in Bristol.

Our second child, Alison, was born in 1954. Muriel was friendly with a vivacious singer, Sybil Ghilchik, who performed Gilbert and Sullivan with the D'Oyly Carte Company. They often gave recitals together. Sybil's father, David Ghilchik, was a well-known cartoonist and member of the Savage Club. David enjoyed using his contacts to help out his friends, and insisted on trying to get Muriel into Queen's Hospital, as he knew a prominent obstetrician who could "pull a few strings". What he hadn't realised was that the consultant could refer only abnormal pregnancies to Queen's, and as Muriel and baby both proved to be in rude health, that was the end of that!

We settled for a more than adequately comfortable hospital on the Mile End Road. This wasn't ideal for visiting, although several orchestras I worked with at the time did hold rehearsals and recording sessions at the People's Palace, a theatre in the area. But I didn't really mind this minor incovenience - it meant that our first two offspring were born deep in the East End of London within the sound of Bow Bells, and can claim to be true Cockneys!

I was by now beginning to get a fair amount of concerto engagements, notably the Mendelssohn with the Bournemouth Orchestra and Charles Groves. The Midland Light Orchestra, somewhat surprisingly, asked me to play the Bach E major Concerto, and I did a whole series of concerto dates with the BBC Welsh Orchestra in Cardiff, conducted first by Arwel Hughes, and later by Rae Jenkins. These included the Pibroch Suite by Sir Alexander Mackenzie, a former Principal of the RAM. Based on Scottish themes, this rarely played piece for violin and orchestra was dedicated to Sarasate.

Despite these successes, however, part of me was still hankering to fulfil a prophesy that Ernest Read had made back in the Academy days, when he told me I would make a good orchestral leader. I had done some leading of chamber groups, and some occasional guest orchestral leading, but the ultimate goal had so far proved elusive.

The chance eventually did come. Olga Hegedus, cellist in Muriel's trio and later to lead the ECO cellos, had worked with a bright new star in the conducting firmament, John Pritchard, who wanted to bring his Nottingham String Orchestra to London. Olga suggested me as a leader, and I played with the orchestra in a concert at the Wigmore Hall. One thing led to another, and in 1955 John was appointed joint Musical Director with Efrem Kurtz of the Liverpool Philharmonic Orchestra. He asked me to become his leader, and in May 1955 I played my first date in Liverpool's Philharmonic Hall. It happened to be a televised concert, so I was in at the deep end!

During that summer Muriel and I moved from London with Paul and Alison to the pleasant Liverpool suburb of Blundellsands, Crosby, where we had bought a house from my predecessor as leader, Henry Datyner.

BOOK 2

Chapter 18 - Liverpool

The Royal Liverpool Philharmonic Society can claim to be the fifth oldest surviving concert-giving organisation in Europe, being antedated only by the Leipzig Gewandhaus (founded at the end of the 18th century), Vienna Gesellschaft der Muskfreunde (1813), London's Royal Philharmonic Society (also 1813) and the Paris Conservatoire Concerts, which began in 1828. (The Vienna Philharmoniker of which the Gesellschaft was proprietor did not begin its regular concerts until 1842, being thus two years junior to our own.

Two Centuries of Music in Liverpool Stainton de B Taylor

Liverpool's Philharmonic Concert Society gave its first concerts in 1840, considerably earlier than its Manchester rival the Hallé Concert Society, which first performed under Sir Charles Hallé in 1858. For a long time thereafter the same pool of players was drawn upon for orchestral concerts in both cities, and indeed in most of the North of England.

It was only in 1940 that both the Hallé and the Liverpool Philharmonic began to employ full-time salaried musicians. The Phil's original principal conductor was Malcolm Sargent, and the principal players were drawn from the disbanded BBC Salon Orchestra that had been evacuated from London. The leader was Jean Pougnet, followed towards the end of the war by Henry Holst, a distinguished Danish violinist who for much of his working life made his home in England. Holst had given the first British performance of the Walton Violin Concerto, written for Jascha Heifetz and premiered by him in America in 1941. The score was ferried across the Atlantic at the height of the German U Boat blockade, and Holst, remarkably, learned it in a fortnight. I heard his performance on BBC radio, and was deeply impressed.

When Holst left, principal second violin David Wise took over as leader. He was followed in 1946 by a very young Manoug Parikian, and in 1947 by the Polish violinist Henry Datyner. Datyner was appointed by Hugo Rignold, who in the same year succeeded Sargent as principal conductor.

A period of unrest and strife ensued. Rignold, himself a talented violinist, was known mainly as a light music player, and had appeared regularly with the dance-band leader Jack Hylton. Although he was a very capable conductor, equally at home with the classics and with giants of the early 20th century romantic and impressionist repertoire such as Debussy, Ravel and Sibelius, some elements of the Liverpool concert-going public could not forget his antecedents.

It was also a period of transition for the membership of the orchestra. The principals in strings and wind from the BBC Salon Orchestra had returned to London, and many of the remaining players were elderly. Rignold took upon himself the role of new broom, initiating a drastic cull of the old guard and replacing them with a virtually new orchestra of bright young players fresh out of college. Changes were undoubtedly needed, but the process was handled badly by Rignold and Wilfred Stiff, the manager. They aroused the ire of the Musicians' Union, and were forced to reinstate all the original players. The repercussions of this were still being felt when I arrived, shortly after the appointment of John Pritchard. Wilfred Stiff was still manager, and it wasn't until he was replaced by Gerald MacDonald eighteen months later that the latter's diplomatic skills finally healed the rift.

For his first year at the Phil John Pritchard was not solely in charge, as on Rignold's departure the Committee had decided to have two music directors. The other was Efrem Kurtz, who had conducted all over the world, from Houston Texas to La Scala Milan. His recordings with the Philharmonia often became best-sellers, and he had charisma and audience appeal in abundance, but his technical shortcomings soon became apparent to the players. He often tried to conduct from memory to impress the public, even when his detailed knowledge of the score was less than perfect.

At the first Tuesday Subscription Concert in the autumn after I arrived, Kurtz insisted on doing the Second Suite from Ravel's Daphnis and Chloë without a score. During the piece he made an error, from which we quickly recovered, but at the point where the same phrase is repeated in the final pages, he gave the same wrong beat. Although I have no clear recollection of this, members of the front row of audience later reported hearing me hiss in anguished tones "The silly bugger's done it again!" After this *débâcle*, Kurtz did at least have the grace to apologise to me!

Whether or not to perform from memory is a vexed question. It's said that Béla Bartók, who was a brilliant pianist, refused to play without a score, insisting that the safe expression of the composer's intentions was much more important than indulging his own vanity. On the other hand, many musicians find the memorising of music relatively easy, and feel that this allows closer contact with their fellow musicians and the audience - "have the score in your head, not your head in the score".

Although nowadays more and more people are not ashamed to perform with the music in front of them, not long ago this was unthinkable for any concerto soloist, except in the case of a modern piece that is particularly difficult or obscure. Muriel, whose work playing chamber music, accompanying singers or sight-reading orchestral parts always involved the use of a score, nevertheless had an excellent memory - she always said that you didn't really know a piece unless you could play it without the music. Musicians who often play solo are as accustomed to performing without notes as are actors who routinely learn their lines. Some people find this easier than others, and as in all things, practice breeds confidence. On the other hand, musicians who play only in orchestras do not habitually memorise music, and some make a practice of never doing so in any circumstances.

The best course of action, in my opinion, is to make a firm decision and stick to it. In 1958 I was given the important assignment of playing the Britten Violin Concerto with the Liverpool Philharmonic. I worked at it consistently over a six month period, and eventually felt confident enough to do without the score. We did a short tour of venues that included Preston and Sheffield, with Stanford Robinson as conductor, and I felt this had gone very well. At the end of the week we finished with a live broadcast from the Philharmonic Hall. In view of the occasion, I opted to play safe and have the music on a stand, to refer to in emergency. It was a decision I regretted. Having the notes there, I found I couldn't take my eyes off them. The performance went well, enough, but it lacked the spirit and spontaneity of my earlier efforts. To me it sounded distinctly stodgy, and I wished I had taken the risk of playing from memory.

In the end, it's a question of horses for courses. As a teacher, I generally encourage pupils to play from memory if possible, but there are exceptions. Some children can absorb music so quickly that they never look at the printed page, and consequently become poor sight-readers. Memory and sight-reading are equally important, and the American violinist Joseph Silverstein passed on an excellent exercise that his father made him do to improve both skills. Take a piece of unfamiliar music, look at just one bar of it, then turn round with your back to the music and play it. Do this until it becomes quite easy, then do the same thing with two bars, then three, and so on. This means you always transfer the music into your mind before playing it, and never actually play while you're looking at it.

After twelve months of job sharing, John Pritchard emerged as principal conductor, and we entered into several years of very happy cooperation. I had the greatest admiration for John, for his musical talent and for his wit, which was fully equal to Beecham's and gained him the esteem of the players. The biblical proverb "a soft answer turneth away wrath" might have been coined for John – he had an intuitive ability to defuse difficult situations. In one hall he found that just one desk of the violins was raised above the others, and that both occupants were well past the first flush of youth and no oil paintings. He told Johnny Murphy, the orchestral manager, to make them change places with two pretty girls, and one of the old boys, affronted, demanded to see John for an explanation. The interview ended as follows:

"Well, I'm not all that bad looking."

"Yes, but you're not my type!"

Some accused John of being frivolous and lacking the commitment to work steadily at improving standards. He certainly used his quicksilver brain to hide the fact that he sometimes came to the rostrum inadequately prepared, and it was also true that he'd had very little previous experience of the symphonic repertoire. If he was conducting music that appealed to him and the concert was an important occasion, the results could be magical. One of his most spectacular successes was a series of monthly concerts entitled *Musica Viva*, which by clever programming managed to achieve creditable audience numbers for music by contemporary composers.

On the other hand, if things were not going well he could easily become bored. I remember one time when we played Dvořák's 8th Symphony in G for three consecutive nights. John had not played the work before, and I don't think he particularly liked it. During the last concert, in front of an unusually unresponsive audience, he lost patience. As I was preparing to go on for the Symphony he said "Peter, pass the message around, no repeats in the last movement!" He had either forgotten or didn't realise that in the last movement, where a number of short eight-bar passages are repeated, in some of the instrumental parts they are written as repeats, but in others they are fully written out. The horrible confusion that resulted when we tried to follow his instructions certainly livened up the proceedings!

John, of course, was "gay", a term not generally used in a sexual context at a time when practising homosexuality was a criminal offence. Many people involved in the Arts were known to have partners of the same sex, and although jokes about this were common currency, it never implied any disrespect. Alderman Harry Livermore, a successful criminal lawyer in the city, was also an enthusiastic Chairman of the Philharmonic Committee. He was particularly adept at persuading prominent figures to support the orchestra, and regularly wined and dined them before sharing his box with them at concerts. On one occasion his guest was the celebrated judge, Mr Justice Laski. When John Pritchard flounced onto the stage in his own inimitable way, Laski reportedly leaned over to Livermore, and in a sonorous stage whisper growled "Gave a chap five years for that this morning!"

Livermore was an excellent Chairman. The fact that he was almost entirely unmusical was more an asset than a liability - we had a Vice-Chairman who fancied himself as a musical connoisseur, and he was a nuisance, always wanting to air his knowledge and interfere. Harry was a sound judge of character, and if he felt people could do a good job he would trust them, although he was quick to disagree with anything he considered unwise or impractical. I remember him saying "Peter, I love coming to the concerts at the Phil. I shut the door of my box, and for the next two hours nobody can get at me!" On another occasion he said "Very good concert tonight, Peter. The strings looked fantastic!" **Looked** fantastic - how they sounded didn't really concern him!

The success of this chapter in the history of the Liverpool Phil was founded on a body of good orchestral members who worked well together, backed by the dependable triumvirate of Livermore, MacDonald and Pritchard, who seemed to have the knack of playing to the city's strengths. Liverpool, like Glasgow where I later worked, is to my mind the ideal size for a city. It has a wonderful variety of backgrounds, cultures and amenities, drawing on the wide racial diversity typical of a long established seaport, but at the same time a unity whereby central institutions are recognized and valued throughout the community.

London is too big and sprawling to have this unity - it is more like a country made up of a number of separate counties, with no real joint allegiance or recognition of the centrality of cultural bodies. In London, if one was identified as a member of the LSO or the LPO, people would react - so what? In Liverpool, membership of the Phil has a certain *cachet* that transcends social boundaries. Note that it is invariably the "Phil". Ask a taxi driver to drive you to the Phil, and you will be unhesitatingly taken to the Hall in Hope Street. If you ask to go to the Philharmonic, you will very likely be dropped outside the rather grand pub called the Philharmonic Hotel, diagonally opposite from the concert hall. Mind you, this is well worth a visit. The beer is excellent, and the interior architecture is rich in wonderful mahogany features, many of which were rescued from old Cunard liners dismantled in the city's dockyards.

Liverpool's civic pride and awareness are well illustrated by a story I was told on my arrival in the city. My predecessor but one, Manoug Parikian, had wanted to drive a car when he arrived in Merseyside, having been used to driving in Cyprus as a youngster. He was already an expert driver, but to comply with British regulations of course had to take a test. He duly drove all around the city with the official examiner by his side, and after the examination, the following conversation took place:

"Well, Mr Parikian, you are obviously a very competent driver. You controlled the car well and safely. However, I am afraid that I must on this occasion fail you."

"Oh dear, why is that?"

"Well, unfortunately, when we were going round the dockland area, there was a bollard at one turning that said *Keep Left,* and you ignored it. I am aware that it was not absolutely obvious, but in my opinion you should have noticed it, and as you broke the law, I have no alternative but to fail you."

Manoug accepted this verdict with good grace, and walked back to the office with the examiner.

"By the way, Mr Parikian, what is your job?"

"Well, actually, I'm the new Leader of the Philharmonic Orchestra."

"The Leader of the Phil? Oh, my God! I had no idea. The Leader of the Phil? I can't fail the Leader of the Phil! Well - now - please promise me that you will never do that again! OK, a pass! Goodbye, and I look forward to seeing you at the next Tuesday Subscription Concert!"

The Philharmonic Hall is situated midway along Hope Street, which boasts at one end the new Roman Catholic Cathedral, and near the other end Gilbert Scott's magnificent Anglican Cathedral. The original Hall on the same site was completely gutted in a disastrous fire on the night of 5th July 1933. When after lengthy negotiations no agreement could be reached on a replacement, the Philharmonic Society took matters into its own hands, and at considerable financial risk commissioned the distinguished Liverpool architect Herbert J Rowse to design the present building. Opened on 19th June 1939, it survived superficial bomb damage during the war, and apart from a few minor alterations and renovations remains the same much loved edifice today. The audience is ideally seated, and the acoustics are to my mind superb; a perfect balance between clarity and warm resonance.

Upon completion of the Hall, the management negotiated its sale to Liverpool Corporation. The agreement was that the Corporation could let it out for public and private functions, on condition that the Orchestra should have first call on the facilities free of charge. In effect this was a substantial indirect subsidy, of a kind that no other orchestra in the country enjoyed. The other condition was that the Philharmonic Committee should be reconstituted. Up till then the Committee had been comprised entirely of private individuals, but half the members would now be Liverpool councillors. Later, the independent members would include a representative of the Arts Council. The Chairman would be a nominee of the Corporation, and would have a casting vote, while the Committee was to appoint a Musical Director and a General Manager who would report to it at monthly meetings.

The success of such a venture depends heavily on the temperamental compatibility of the people involved, and in this respect we were particularly fortunate. Muriel and I often socialised with members of the Committee, and formed many lasting friendships. Gerald Macdonald, an outstanding Manager who was fair and open in all his dealings, also became a lifelong friend. His wife, Joyce Pearson, had been a fellow student with us at the Academy. She was a pianist and a viola player, and for a time had been a member of the BBC Symphony Orchestra. Joyce's birth name was actually Jeanette, and our third child, born in Liverpool in November 1956 and now a distinguished cellist, was named after her.

Chapter 19 - Sir Charles Groves

In 1963 John Pritchard resigned, and his successor was Charles Groves, already one of the most highly acclaimed conductors in Britain, who would go on to be knighted in 1973. I already knew Charles quite well, having played a concerto with him when he was conductor of the Bournemouth Orchestra, and since my arrival in Liverpool he had made regular guest appearances. His appointment ushered in a long period of professional harmony and artistic success that was a tribute to both his warm personality and the single-minded pursuance of his aims.

As Malcolm Sargent once said to me, being a guest conductor is easy. You do a few good concerts, the orchestra welcome a change, you flatter the players, and everyone says what a jolly good chap you are. The principal conductor is different. After a relatively short honeymoon period, your particular foibles become clear to the players, you have to make a few unpopular decisions, and suddenly everything is not quite so rosy. Sargent himself had a pretty rough time as conductor in chief of the BBC Symphony, partly as a result of his own relatively abrasive personality. Charles was a much more lovable character, and to my mind a much better musician, but everyone has strengths and weaknesses. The weaknesses are quickly noted and complained about by players who work together every day, often in a way that flies in the face of logic and reason.

As I have already mentioned, John Pritchard had his detractors, particularly towards the end of his stay: "Oh, John's fine if it's a big occasion, and he's playing something he likes, but if it's a routine out-of-own date, he doesn't bother. What we want is someone to get down to the hard graft of bringing the orchesta up to scratch. John's more interested in popping off to Glyndebourne, or doing recordings wth the LPO. Then John left, and Charles was warmly welcomed. But within a month or so we were hearing from the same people: "Oh dear, Groves is terrible. He over-rehearses; doesn't allow any spontaneity. Whenever a guest conductor comes he's always lurking around. Why doesn't he leave us to ourselves? It's all so dull! When we had Pritchard it was so much more exciting.….!"

In the end, however, Charles's blend of sound musicianship, fair dealing and openness won over the critics. His Mahler series happened at just the right time. The great Austrian composer's reputation in Britain was at last in the ascendancy, and Charles undoubtedly caught the wave. The climax of the series was the 8th Symphony in E Flat, the Symphony of a Thousand, performed in Liverpool's Anglican Cathedral with the combined Liverpool and Manchester BBC Orchestras, every brass player north of Watford, and a vast conglomeration of northern choirs. To those of us in the middle of it all it was a bit of an acoustic jumble, but the BBC sound engineers did an immaculate job and the resulting tape sounded crystal clear.

I was very fond of Charles, and it was always a joy to work with him. It was an inspiring experience to hear him at the piano reading from the most complex orchestral scores. On the rare occasions when he played for instrumentalists or singers, it was obvious that if he'd had the time to devote to it, he could have been the finest of accompanists. Like John before him, he had a ready wit that he often used to ease inevitable tensions. I was recently reminded by Ernest Scott, my colleague from Philharmonia days, of an example of this. The orchestra had just finished a heavy schedule, were feeling tired and unruly, and were about to rehearse an obscure, turgid and boring modern symphony. "Ladies and gentlemen," said Charles solemnly. "I bring you nothing for your delight.….!"

If Charles had a fault, it was that he was over-sensitive. Ideally, a conductor should be able to work through a disagreement or misunderstanding, and turn up next day with the whole thing forgotten and the slate wiped clean. Charles couldn't do this. If he ever had occasion to use firm words, which after all is part of the job, then next day he would stand up in front of us and express his regrets about what had happened before launching into a rehash of the whole business. He had obviously been thinking it over all night. We felt obliged to listen, but secretly we were all wishing he would leave it alone and move on. Muriel used to say that Charles had all her worst faults, which may have been something of an exaggeration, but I knew what she meant. Like Charles, Muriel tended to extremes of moods, either all up or all down.

I know that when in 1966 I decided to leave Liverpool, Charles took it as a personal slight. It was not in any way intended to be so, but I regret that he felt that way. It is greatly to his credit that never once in later years did he allow this to interfere with our friendship and frequent subsequent collaborations. I shall always be gateful to him for years of wonderful music making.

Chapter 20 - The Orchestra

It will not be possible to mention all my Liverpool friends and colleagues in the detail I would like, but I have never worked with a more congenial set of musicians, and the eleven years I spent with the Liverpool Phil were among the happiest in my life. Our family was growing up, and we were comfortably settled in the house we had purchased from Henry Datyner, an arrangement which led people to describe it as the Chequers of the orchestra! Henry's wife, Cherry Isherwood, had also been a fellow student at the RAM. She was a pianist and harpist, and from her Muriel inherited the post of Orchestral Pianist.

Although I didn't know most of the orchestra when I arrived, we quickly established an excellent working relationship. My deputy leader was Tom Rowlette. Tom and I sat together on the front desk, day in and day out, for the whole of my eleven years, and there was never a cross word or disagreement. Tom came from South Wales, and as far as I could gather was almost entirely self-taught, a natural in both his actual playing and his musical instinct. Although intensely loyal, he could always be relied on for witty and caustic remarks about life in the Orchestra. Occasionally his passions would run away with him and inconsistencies would creep into his arguments, as is evident from the following exchange:

"Look, Peter, it's not good enough!"

"What's the trouble, Tom?"

"I've just found out that Alan Stringer is getting five quid a week more than I am."

Alan Stringer was our principal trumpet, the finest exponent of his art in not only the North of England, but possibly the entire country.

"I know Alan's good," Tom went on. "He's a marvellous player, but any bloody fool can play the trumpet! I play the violin – a difficult instrument, and I work at it. I'm a principal in the orchestra. I lead when you're not here - it's a responsible job. I don't see why the first trumpet, whoever he is, should get more money than me!"

I sympathised. "Well, Tom, I see your point. Go and have a word with Gerry MacDonald and put it to him. You know I'll back you up."

A fortnight later Alan Stringer suddenly announced he was leaving to take up the post of principal trumpet with the LSO, and an exasperated Tom came looking for me.

"Peter, the idiots on the Committee want their bloody heads examining!"

"What's the matter, Tom?"

"Because of them, we've just lost the best trumpet player in the country. And Alan has told me himself; he went personally to see the Committee and said he'd stay on if they'd only give him five quid a week more!"

To put this in a modern perspective, a rank-and-file player in a contracted provincial orchestra presently receives an annual salary of between £20,000 and £25,000, which is by no means excessive in view of the skill and training involved. This has more or less kept pace with the cost of living over my lifetime, which is one reason for the preponderance of women players in many orchestras. It may not be entirely politically correct, but such a figure is widely perceived as a comfortable income for a single person with no liabilities, but less than adequate for a married man with a family to support.

As it turned out, Alan found life in London uncongenial. He had strong social roots in Liverpool and after a year returned, much to everyone's joy. A well-known conductor once said to me that the two absolute necessities for a good orchestra are a strong first trumpet and a strong first horn. (A strong leader comes third!) If they are weak, that's the first thing the public notices. The Phil had no worries in either department, with Alan as first trumpet and Ifor James as first horn. Ifor later moved on to the Hallé before furthering an illustrious career first in London and then in Germany.

Shortly after I left the Phil in 1966, Tom also took up a new post, as leader of the BBC Scottish Orchestra in Glasgow. He enjoyed considerable success there, but sadly suffered a heart attack in 1974 and died relatively young in 1982.

Trevor Connah, our Principal Second Violin, went on to hold the same position in the BBC Symphony Orchestra, and also was a member of the Academy of St Martin in the Fields. He possessed a particularly fine Nicholas Amati violin, and his sense of ensemble was exceptional. He was also something of a musical detective, with an unerring eye for the slightest misprint or discrepancy, even in the most sacred of cows like the Beethoven symphonies! He had an identical twin brother, Geoffrey, who was a pianist. Geoff lived in London, but often visited us in Liverpool, which gave us the chance to play a favourite joke on guest conductors. After the interval of a morning rehearsal we would send Geoffrey on to the platform in Trevor's place, and our bemused maestro would find that his leading 2nd violin, previously a model of excellence, had suddenly become completely incompetent!

The violas were led by Robert Braga, a sensitive player with a great love of chamber music. He and his wife, the pianist Rosemary Beckett, made a delightful couple, and Bob was godfather to our daughter Jeanette. On his retirement he did great work in Liverpool organising chamber music sessions for school children with players from the Phil. Bob was brought up in Macao, now a special administrative region of the People's Republic of China but in those days a Portuguese colony, and had picked up a smattering of Chinese pidgin English. A piano, he told us, was known as "Box you fight him, him sing out!"

Oliver Vella was the leader of the cellos when I arrived, but left shortly afterwards to go to the Hallé. His replacement was Denis Vigay, who had studied at the RAM not long after my time there. Denis led for about three years before being tempted back to London, and was succeeded by Christopher Catchpole, another gifted chamber player with a beautiful singing sound. Chris and I became lifelong friends. After I left the Phil he emigrated to Canada to join the Vancouver Symphony Orchestra, and Muriel and I were able to enjoy his family's hospitality when we visited the city in 1994.

The Double Bass Principal was Roy Watson. Although Roy was a brilliant player, and an impressive presence on the platform, I have to confess he was my one *bête noir* in the orchestra. His father, Victor Watson, had been principal bass for Beecham, and a famous figure in London orchestral circles. Roy was very conscious of his august musical lineage, and put on (to my mind) insufferable airs and graces. He got himself elected Chairman of the Orchestral Committee, and often made Gerald MacDonald's life a misery by dredging up every conceivable real or imagined shortcoming in the way the orchestra was run. He and I had quite a few spats, both in private and, on the odd occasion when he took advantage of the inexperience of a visiting conductor to give him a hard time, in full view at rehearsals. Eventually we arrived at a degree of mutual tolerance and possibly even respect, but I can't say I was sorry when he too went to the Hallé and was succeeded by Ray Hutchinson, an equally fine player who was much easier to work with.

The first flute was Fritz Spiegl, a character if ever there was one. He was born in Salzburg on the same date as Mozart, 27th January, which was the source of some good-natured humour during my second year at the Phil in 1956, the bicentenary of the great composer's birth.

Fritz was a true Renaissance Man. He came to London as a Jewish refugee from the Nazis, at the age of 16, without being able to speak a word of English, and developed a remarkable parallel career to his flute playing, as a journalist and broadcaster. He became renowned for his musical witticisms, displaying an eventual command of the language and an awareness of its idiosyncrasies that put many native English speakers to shame. Not only that, he was also trained as a draftsman, and when anything amusing happened in the orchestra, there was sure to be a Fritz cartoon pinned up on the band-room notice-board.

One of the most looked forward to dates in Liverpool's musical calendar was the annual April Fools Concert that Fritz booked the orchestra for at the Philharmonic Hall. This was always a sell-out, and if he couldn't get the hall in April he delayed the booking until the next month, calling it Nuts in May! I remember Fritz being resentful of the success in London of Gerard Hoffnung, who put on similar concerts at the Festival Hall and published several books of musical cartoons. Fritz claimed that Hoffnung had stolen his ideas and received undeserved credit for them. That may have been so, but I would have to say that Fritz never did anything quite as funny as Hoffnung's concerto for Vacuum Cleaner, his quartet of tubas playing Chopin Preludes, or the Concerto for Hosepipe and Strings, played by Dennis Brain and based on an actual Horn Concerto by Leopold Mozart.

When Fritz left the Phil to concentrate on his other activities he was followed by Atarah Ben-Tovim, whose tone on the flute matched a warm and voluptuous personality on the platform! Atarah's performance of the Mozart concerto for Flute and Harp with our harpist Mair Jones was something very special. Eventually she created a group called Atarah's Band, which toured the country giving imaginative and original concerts designed for younger audiences.

First oboe Keith Wood, together with his glamorous cellist wife Betty, joined the Phil just before I did. At that time the ill-fated Yorkshire Symphony Orchestra, based in Leeds, had sadly been disbanded, so they were among a number of good players migrating to Liverpool. The first clarinet was Tom Gilbert, brother of the flautist Geoffrey Gilbert, whose career took him to London, where he acquired a towering reputation both as an orchestral player and as a soloist. I suspect that Geoffrey's success may have given Tom something of an inferiority complex, although in fact he was a fine, sensitive musician in his own right.

Manfred Arlen, who made up the woodwind team, was a bassoonist of distinction, who in contrast to Tom had no shortage of self-confidence. If he got the idea that a conductor was in error, he would never hesitate to speak out. I recall one stormy rehearsal with Kurtz on the podium. Efrem expected all his players to be completely ready when he raised his arms, which meant bows on strings and wind instruments to lips. Like many bassoonists, however, Fred preferred to keep the reed away from his mouth and pop it in at the last minute, so a clash of wills was inevitable:

Kurz raised his baton and glared round the orchestra. "Be ready!" Pause. Baton lowered. "You are not ready!" Again - "Be ready!" Another pause. He glowered across to the woodwind - "Bassoon, you are not ready!" No response, so he repeated the whole spiel and pointed the baton at Fred. "You - you are not ready!"

"Yes I am, Mr. Kurtz."

"Don't answer me back!"

In the breathless silence that followed, Kurtz took his baton, broke it in half, then in quarters, threw the fragments to the floor and stalked off the stage. As leader, it was my job to follow him off, smooth his ruffled feathers, remind him we had a concert to put on that evening, and tell him everybody loved him, it was all just an unfortunate misunderstanding and of course no one thought he was a ranting megalomaniac. From such episodes, and we had quite a few of them with dear old Efrem, orchestral legends are born.

The trombone section were another two Freds, Devlin and Cooke, both very experienced and reliable players, and on bass trombone the energetic Tom Wrigley. Ifor James, first horn, was possibly the greatest natural talent in the orchestra. Born in Carlisle, like his father he was steeped in the tradition of brass band playing, while his mother was the soprano Ena Mitchell, famous for her oratorio work, and in later life a highly respected singing teacher.

Ifor was a sparkling character, with an unstoppable flow of jokes and anecdotes, sometimes to the point where you felt you could have too much of a good thing. During his time in the Hallé he was a great favourite of Barbirolli's - his wicked impersonations of Sir John have passed into folk lore - and in his days with the ECO he was held in the highest esteem by Barenboim. When Antal Dorati recorded the complete Haydn symphonies, Ifor was specially engaged to play the notorious high horn parts in the Paris Symphonies, numbers 82 to 87. He had a high degree of natural all-round coordination, and could easily have been a professional footballer. In fact, looking back he was probably not dissimilar in personality to George Best, though thankfully without the Irishman's self-destructive tendencies.

The timpanist was Jack Casson, whose authoritative playing was always admired by visiting conductors. Jack spent his whole career with the Phil, and like many orchestral players exposed to consistently high decibel levels, suffered the occupational hazard of partial deafness. It isn't hard to imagine that the sound erupting from those great drums, when you're standing directly over them day after day, must take an inevitable toll.

Percussionist John Ward, a protégé of the legendary Jimmy Blades, was notable for his single-minded devotion to his art. I remember the first of several visits to the Phil of the Vienna Philharmonic's Willy Boskovsky, famous for his world-wide "Viennese Nights" tours. The first thing he asked me was - did the percussion player know all the funny business required in the Thunder and Lightning Polka, involving watering cans, umbrellas, raincoats, and thunder-sheets? He needn't have worried. Johnny had watched every New Year television broadcast from the Musikverein in Vienna. He knew every single antic that his Austrian counterpart got up to, and had invented several of his own. He did the whole thing with a Buster Keaton deadpan expression that was perfect, and brought the house down.

In later years, we were invited to a 70th birthday party for Johnny in Liverpool. It was a genuine complete surprise for him and his wife Jean, who had often played 2nd percussion. Almost 200 colleagues gathered for lunch, speeches and entertainment in the Philharmonic Hall. In Johnny's heyday, a number of young apprentice players had studied with him. Some of these went on to reach the heights of the musical profession, and on this illustrious occasion two of them were able to attend. They were both natives of Liverpool - the pianist Peter Donohoe and the conductor of the Berlin Philharmonic Orchestra, Sir Simon Rattle!

This is by no means a comprehensive survey of the players I worked with during my 11 years in Liverpool, but I think it gives an idea of the calibre of the people we had at that particular time. In the light of the amazingly high standard of present day performers, and the overall excellence of many modern concerts and recordings, it would be easy to fall victim to a slight feeling of inferiority about one's past achievements, but in taking this trip down Memory Lane I have realised anew that I have much to be proud of. We were at the centre of many unforgettable occasions, and the standard we produced was unfailingly high, but above all the members of the Liverpool Philharmonic were people with a sincere and committed attitude to their music making that was second to none. The friendships Muriel and I made have been an enduring treasure, and along with many of my older colleagues in the profession, I am unapologetic about looking back on that era in Liverpool as a golden age.

Chapter 21 - Programmes and Personalities

At one time the distinction between musical life in London and in the "provinces" was much more marked than it is now. Muriel and I were both brought up as students and young professionals to see this as the natural order of things. The idea of leaving London was not to be thought of, and when I was first offered the job in Liverpool, Muriel was horrified! Friends and colleagues thought we would be crazy to give up the advantages of living in the Capital. Because few recordings of orchestras outside London were made, thanks largely to the trouble and expense of transporting the bulky old-style recording equipment, people began to assume that provincial standards must be unacceptably lower. These days, recording can be done anywhere, and people buy CDs by orchestras like the Hallé, the Liverpool and the Bournemouth just as readily as recordings by the London ensembles. It is a much healthier state of things that high quality music making should be seen to exist throughout the country.

One advantage of working in a provincial orchestra was immediately clear to me. I saw that in London, mainly due to commercial pressures and recording strictures, the orchestral repertoire was often limited to what the public expected, what was "box-office", and what sold on records. For instance, the Philharmonia seemed to specialise in Brahms's 1st Symphony to the exclusion of the other three, while with Beethoven it was the Eroica and the Pastoral. Karajan often played the Berlioz Symphonie Fantastique and Bartók's Concerto for Orchestra, but there was much standard repertoire that he never approached. Of course we did play all sorts of other music, but it was not the same as presenting a balanced series of programmes aimed at keeping the broadest possible interest of a regular and loyal local public, and as a so-called experienced London musician, I sometimes felt ashamed that I had such limited knowledge of so many important parts of the musical landscape. It was a real education over the Liverpool years to perform a wide, balanced spectrum of almost the whole orchestral repertoire, and to feel that you were playing it for a discerning local public who were close to you and valued your work.

As Charles Groves didn't take over as Conductor in Chief in 1963, most of my time in Liverpool was spent working with John Pritchard, who, like Charles, later went on to be knighted. Looking back through old programmes, I am struck by the distinctly modern feel of John's selection and arrangement of repertoire, and his imaginative choice of soloists. His flair for doing or saying the right thing at the right time was an asset that wasn't always fully appreciated. I remember Gerald MacDonald being disappointed with the box office takings from one of the short Prom seasons we used to do every summer in the Liverpool Stadium (now demolished). He decided the next year to adopt a no-risk strategy and fill every programme with established popular favourites - well known piano concertos, Gilbert and Sullivan, famous operatic arias and symphonic barnstormers like the Dvorák New World. The result was an even bigger flop. People thought the prospectus looked ordinary, and stayed away in droves! Gerry was big enough to admit he had been wrong. "I should have let John make up some programmes with a bit of imagination," he said. "You can't build success on statistics."

Having said that, one of the earliest Liverpool concerts to stick in the mind was conducted by Efrem Kurz on November 15th 1955. As well as the infamous performance of Daphnis and Chloë, this featured the 13 year old Daniel Barenboim as soloist in Mozart's K271 piano concerto in E flat, known appropriately enough by its nickname "Jeunehomme", although it is now thought that this is a corruption of the surname of Victoire Jenamy, the pianist daughter of a friend of Mozart's, for whom he wrote the piece in 1777. It is the first of Mozart's truly great works in this form, and Barenboim played it with amazing maturity. He also gave us a preview in the Green Room of the equal fame he would eventually attain as a conductor, with a precocious series of impressions of British maestros like Beecham, Boult and Sargent!

A month before this there had been a remarkable performance of the oratorio King David by the contemporary Swiss composer Arthur Honegger. The conductor was Pritchard, and the important part of the narrator was taken by Emlyn Williams, then at the height of his fame as playwright, actor and film star – a big catch for the Phil. To ensure a full house, the posters had his name in immense capitals, then King David fairly small, and in miniscule type at the bottom the name of the poor composer!

In 1956 there were widespread appeals in the West to help the casualties of the Hungarian Uprising, the anti-Soviet revolt of that year which was suppressed with the utmost severity by the Soviet military. Anywhere from 25,000 to 50,000 Hungarian rebels and 7,000 Soviet troops were killed, thousands more were wounded, and nearly a quarter of a million left the country as refugees. Among these was the eminent pianist Béla Siki, who played with us often. I was able to approach him and suggest that the orchestra would like to do something to support the Lord Mayor of Liverpool's Fund for the victims, and that we would value his support. The upshot was a conductorless concert on December 9th, with Siki as soloist. It attracted huge interest and a full house, raising a considerable sum in the process. The programme included Purcell's Trumpet Voluntary, Bach's Brandenburg Concerto No.3, Mozart's Piano Concerto K.459, Schubert's Unfinished Symphony, and of course Berlioz's Hungarian March. The press gave it good coverage, and we were pleased by the comments of Neil Barkla, the music critic, who praised a well sustained long diminuendo and crescendo in the Bach which, he said, would have normally been noted as a particularly felicitous contribution by the conductor, if there had been one!

Earlier that year, John Pritchard had enticed to Liverpool a notable pair of soloists in the French composers Jean Françaix and Francis Poulenc. Françaix played his own Piano Concerto, and the two joined in Poulenc's equally witty and urbane Concerto for Two Pianos.

After the concert, both men stayed and spent some time with us in the Green Room. Françaix, although very friendly, was quite reserved and chose his words carefully. I remember Nadia Boulanger saying that his main joy was in the act of composition. After he finished a piece, he lost interest in it, and had to be nagged into collating the material, submitting it to the publisher and all the other necessary evils that didn't really concern him in the slightest. All he wanted to do was start writing the next opus. Muriel and I had played his delightful Sonatine for Violin and Piano in our debut recital at the Wigmore Hall, and it appeared regularly in our programmes therafter.

Poulenc was quite different, a natural raconteur who kept us in fits with an endless stream of anecdotes and recollections. I told him that my wife and I had often played his Première Bagatelle for Violin and Piano, which we rated very highly, and were interested in locating the other Bagatelles. He replied that there were no others - he had called it the First Bagatelle just in case he decided to write another one!

It was well after midnight before we called it a day, which must have sorely tested the patience and understanding of the janitorial staff at the Phil!

As previously mentioned, I had the unusual experience in my first year with the Phil of working with two Musical Directors. They both knew that after a year, only one of them would be chosen to carry on. John Pritchard was wise enough not to press his case too hard, but Efrem Kurz took every opportunity to try to bring influence to bear in the right circles. Perhaps he had already seen the writing on the wall, and was determined to go down fighting.

To be fair, Efrem's occasionally erratic conducting and quirky manner were underpinned by genuine musical knowledge and insight. He was always excellent company, if you indulged his need to be the centre of attention. With his cellist brother Edmund, he had fled from Russia before the Revolution, and they had both landed firmly on their feet. Edmund somehow acquired one of the most famous Stradivarius cellos ever made, and played it in all the major musical centres. Efrem conducted all over the world, and seemed to know every single person of any celebrity. He had a favourite phrase in rehearsal whenever he wanted to emphasise a point -"You know who told me that? -Rachmaninov!" Or it might be Shostakovitch, or Prokofiev, or even Elgar. Sometimes we half expected it to be Mozart! I remember Efrem joining a crowd of us in a restaurant in Preston before a concert.

"Look, I show you something!" He made a complicated pattern with some matches on the table. "Now, how do you convert this into.….?"

It was something that seemed utterly impossible, and none of us could do it. He moved three matches and hey presto, it was done, to our fulsome acclaim.

"You know who showed me this? Einstein!"

Kurtz was a great showman, and always had an eye on maximum popular appeal. He once whispered to me just after I had done a concerto with him "Look, if I am appointed here, you will be able to do lots of concertos, because I know I can bring the audiences in, so we don't need to hire half so many expensive visiting soloists!" He would never end a programme with the New World Symphony, on the grounds that the slow diminuendo to nothing after the last fortissimo chord kills the applause! His favourite trick was to play The Stars and Stripes March as an encore, and walk off through the orchestra during the piccolo obbligato, leaving us to finish on our own. It always brought the house down.

It was actually true that Efrem knew a phenomenal number of people. He was married to an American flautist, Elaine Schaeffer, who recorded with Yehudi Menuhin, and the two of them often entertained us at the Adelphi Hotel. On one occasion, when we were in the foyer there, Efrem was warmly greeted by none other than Louis Armstrong, and I had the privilege of shaking the legendary Satchmo's hand and enjoying an all too brief exchange of pleasantries!

Like any major orchestra, we had our share of visiting conductors. Sir Malcolm Sargent was a regular guest, and we did a number of concerts with the Huddersfield Choral Society under his baton. During my time we recorded Handel's Messiah, Mendelssohn's Elijah and William Walton's Belshazzar's Feast, all in the magnificent acoustics of Huddersfield Town Hall. A fine hall can undoubtedly play a major part in enhancing the reputation of the group most often associated with it. The choir in Huddersfield is banked up almost vertically, and the sound is projected straight at the audience. Sargent was in his element there, and in the big choral works there was no one to surpass him. By this time musicians were beginning to pay more attention to issues of authenticity in the performance of Baroque music, and even then some of us considered Sargent's Messiah over-inflated and stylistically sterile. All the same, I recently heard some of that old performance on a tape, and I cannot deny that it still has tremendous impact.

Other notable guests included Hugo Rignold, Walter Susskind, Norman Del Mar and someone who has always been a special friend, George Hurst. George arrived on the London scene while I was in the Philharmonia, and made an authoritative Festival Hall debut appearance with a programme that included Tschaikovsky's 2nd Symphony, the Little Russian. Ever since then he has been a lively presence in British music making. For several years he was conductor of the BBC Orchestra in Manchester, and I played a concerto by Thomas Pitfield with him.

George's most spectacular guest appearance with the Phil, a follow-up to Charles's Mahler 8th, with similar combined forces, involved a performance in Liverpool's Anglican Cathedral of the Berlioz Grande Messe Des Morts. Incredibly, George conducted this colossal work entirely from memory! Since then he has been mainly associated with the Bournemouth orchestras. He studied conducting with Pierre Monteux, and, as his many devoted students at the Canford Summer Music School can testify, is one of the very few people who can actually teach conducting.

I am firmly of the opinion that a conductor should be able to use his baton to express the music – too many of them substitute the tongue for the stick. Some of our foreign visitors were seen as a welcome relief because of their limited grasp of the English language, and, I have to confess, as a reliable source of amusement for their frequent grammatical vagaries. Hermann Scherchen, a German conductor who has written an interesting book about his art, was accustomed to the highly disciplined orchestral etiquette prevalent in his own country, and although he learned to tolerate our more relaxed standards, he occasionally felt the need for a gentle pull on the reins. This once resulted in this memorable pronouncement: "Ladies and gentlemen, please, please, sometimes a joke I like, yes, but always, my God, never!"

Perhaps the most remarkable of our visitors from overseas during my time in Liverpool was the charismatic Romanian musician Constantin Silvestri, who took over the Bournemouth Symphony Orchestra in 1962 and transformed its reputation almost overnight. As a very young man he had been marked out for future greatness by his older compatriot, Georges Enescu, and Silvestri returned the compliment by conducting many of Enescu's compositions when they were virtually unknown. Like Enescu, he was a multi-talented musician, a fine composer and virtuoso pianist as well as an outstanding conductor. Not everyone agreed about his merits or subscribed to his often controversial artistic values, and his output was sometimes uneven, but at his best he was capable of scaling the highest peaks of imaginative and poetic insight.

His performances of Dvorak's 8th Symphony in G and Tschaikovsky's Symphony No. 4 in F minor were particularly memorable. In the introduction to the Tschaikovsky, he adopted a startling approach that divided critics, audience and orchestral players alike. Up till then the opening four bar fanfare had usually been phrased across the bar lines, with the phrase breaks occurring halfway through the bars, but in private conversation. Silvestri pointed out to me that the composer had actually indicated phrase breaks on the bar lines. He was absolutely right, and the difference in impact this makes is remarkable, but the change wasn't achieved without a struggle. Silvestri, knowing that the players were used to doing things the old way, made us exaggerate the new phrasing in a way that produced what felt like a horribly obvious hiccup at the end of each bar. Some players hated it. The second horn couldn't restrain himself at one point: "Why can't we play it in time?"

I remember an occasion when Silvestri replaced another conductor who had defaulted at the last minute. The programme began with Richard Strauss's Don Juan, and there were to be six hours' rehearsal on the Monday, with three on the Tuesday and the concert in the evening. At the Monday rehearsal, Silvestri informed us that he had not conducted the Strauss before, but had stayed up all the previous night in order to learn the score. Unfortunately, he had been able to learn only the first half, so when we had played that, he closed his score, thanked us and said he would know the rest by the next morning! Our pleas to be at least allowed to play through to the end of the piece fell on deaf ears - the idea of conducting anything without proper preparation was one he just couldn't entertain. So we duly rehearsed the second half on the Tuesday, and I would have to say the eventual performance was pretty sub-standard. He also presided over a less than inspiring performance of the Sibelius Violin Concerto, with a soloist whose artistic sensibilities were clearly a long way from his own. These minor blips were however very much the exception rather than the rule.

Silvestri was not insensitive to criticism, whether positive or negative. One comment he particularly valued was from a writer who compared him to both Toscanini and Furtwängler. To my mind, this was right on the mark – Silvestri's musicianship showed a rare combination of the former's textual integrity and firm rhythm, and the latter's poetic feeling and elasticity.

Silvestri listened to music constantly, and kept recordings of thousands of broadcast performances. His knowledge of these was encyclopaedic. He could tell you exactly, for instance, what tempo Elgar took in his recordings of the Enigma Variations, which bore little relation to what is heard in many so-called "traditional" performances. In one conversation I had with him, he extolled Elgar as a great symphonist, in contrast to Sibelius, whom he surprisingly dismissed as an "atmospheric" composer:

"What do you see in Sibelius's music? Only flying in a plane over Finland. Lakes and forests and rivers and so on. Elgar is real constructed music of substance."

In another of my many valuable and constructive conversations with him, Silvestri explained how as both composer and conductor, he often had to consider *tempo,* the actual speed of music, from two very different viewpoints:

159

"When I write music I am always very meticulous to specify an exact metronome mark for each different section. When I come to perform the music I find the marks are nearly always wrong - not always too fast or always too slow, but different. You can never tell the tempo of a piece until you actually perform it."

This echoes Beethoven's experience. When he was introduced to the metronome by its inventor, J N Maelzel, he enthusiastically added metronome marks to his previous compositions, but later abandoned the practice as unreliable.

Although an orchestra may build its reputation on the skills of those who wield the baton, nothing has quite the box office appeal of one of the great piano concertos in the hands of an acknowledged master. During my time with the Phil I was privileged to take part in performances with a generation of truly outstanding pianists. Many of today's players have prodigious technical ability, and often a fine appreciation of the composer's intentions and ideas, but I remain convinced that the flowering of talent we had back then was something really special. Lev Pouishnoff was renowned for his brilliance in the romantic repertoire, but to my mind the greatest of them all was Benno Moiseivitch, viewed by many as a reincarnation of Rachmaninov himself. Indeed, some would say that Moiseivitch even surpassed his great mentor, because his ability encompassed both the classics and the later virtuoso concertos. I recall one concert when he played the opening figure of the Beethoven 3rd Concerto in C minor which such rhythmical and spatial purity that I can never hope to hear it better.

Myra Hess's magical opening statement in the Beethoven 4th Concerto – how was our following string entry supposed to live up to that? - was another memorable moment, but Solomon, a consummate classicist, was her equal if not superior in Beethoven. He was a master of dynamic gradation and subtle rhythmic control, but did suffer very occasional memory lapses, and I wonder if the tension of public performance might have led to the massive stroke that hit him in 1956, terminating his playing career at the age of 56. It happened just as he was about to finish his recordings of the complete Beethoven Sonatas. He had a favourite conductor, Herbert Menges, who directed many of his concerts and most of his recordings, and I remember many first-class sessions in the Philharmonia with them both. At the end of every work, Solomon would always thank the orchestra with the utmost sincerity, and apologise, quite unnecessarily we thought, for any retakes caused by his own mistakes!

Gina Bachauer was formidable in both Brahms concertos, both for her playing and her impressive personality on the platform, while Cyril Smith was another who shone in the Rachmaninov concertos. Cyril Smith later lost the use of his left hand after a stroke, but was able to continue a career, playing duets for three hands, many of which were written specially for them, with his wife, Phyllis Sellick.

Shura Cherkassky brought a unique and breathtaking approach to the late romantic and virtuoso repertoire. He used to say at the end of a rehearsal "Thank you very much, ladies and gentlemen. Please watch out. It will be completely different tonight!" Like Vladimir Pachmann, Shura was prone to the odd eccentricity. He had an obsession about his piano stool. Once he got it to the right height at rehearsal, he wouldn't let it out of his sight. During the afternoon between rehearsal and concert, he had it carried into the Green Room for practising, and poor John Charles, our assistant orchestral manager, had to follow him with it where ever he went!

After one rehearsal I followed Shura into the Green Room and asked if he would like a cup of coffee. He said he would, so I rang down and in a few minutes a tray with two cups duly appeared.

I was just taking the one nearest to me when Shura suddenly burst out "Oh please, please, excuse me, I think they meant *me* to have that one!"

"But they're both the same!"

"No, no, no, please. They meant that one for *me*. Please, please!"

There was no point in arguing, so we solemnly changed cups and drank our coffee in rather embarrassed silence. What he was thinking about I hadn't the slightest idea, and I didn't like to ask! Apparently, he never owned a home, and spent his entire life in hotel rooms. It is reported, possibly apocryphally, that a lady approached him in the street in Berlin:

"Oh Shura! How lovely to see you after all this time!"

"Yes, Madame, how nice to see you too. But you must excuse me. I am afraid I have forgotten your name."

"But Shura, I'm your wife!"

Clifford Curzon, though an exquisitely gifted player, suffered agonies of nerves before a performance. He used to huddle in the corner of the Green Room, with his hands clasped around a hot water bottle, not speaking to anyone, waiting for the concert to start. Once on stage, he became the embodiment of whatever work he was presenting, which when he performed with us was usually one of the Brahms or Mozart concertos. He told us that he always had the music with him when he did Mozart, because he had a nightmarish fear that if he were playing from memory, he would emerge at the end of the cadenza into a completely different concerto!

Artur Rubinstein played the Brahms D minor and the Tschaikovsky B flat minor, with Pritchard conducting, on Tuesday and Wednesday April 5th and 6th 1960. He was bitterly disappointed to be allowed to play only one concerto each night - he was fully prepared to play them both at each concert, although he was also giving a marathon Chopin recital in the same week! He played effortlessly with total command, despite complaining that the keys of our piano were too slippery, and was the life and soul of the Green Room, where he kept up a non-stop flow of anecdotes about Stravinsky, Heifetz, Bernstein and countless other giants of contemporary music.

Tamás Vásáry guested with the Phil several times, and often came to visit our family at home. He was brought up in Budapest, where he studied with Zoltán Kodály. Kodály, he told us, had an insatiable urge to widen the scope of his knowledge. He recalled visiting the composer's flat when he was in his late eighties, and on the stairs passing a Greek Orthodox priest who was just leaving. It transpired that Kodály had regretted his lack of knowledge of the Greek classics, and had decided to have lessons in Classical Greek so that he could read them in the original tongue!

Vásáry was particularly fine playing the music of Mozart and Chopin, and I have fond memories of playing Mozart violin sonatas with him both at home and at the Walker Art Gallery concerts. Later, he was made Director of the Northern Sinfonia in Newcastle, and it was he who appointed our daughter Jeanette, not long after she graduated from College, as principal cello, a post she held with great distinction for a number of years. During that time I occasionally acted as guest leader for the orchestra, and greatly enjoyed taking part in recordings of the Chopin Piano Concertos with Vásáry playing and directing.

On 30th December 1960 Eugene Istomin was due to perform the Brahms B flat, but cancelled the day before, and an emerging young local talent called John Ogdon was invited to step into the breach. When asked if he knew the work, John said he did, although what he meant was that he had never played it, but knew more or less how it went. He arrived to rehearse on the day of the concert, with the music. Muriel turned over for him, and it was quite obvious, both visually and audibly, that he was actually sight-reading the notes. In the afternoon, John Pritchard and Ogdon's teacher Gordon Green spent three hours going through the score with him. It was an early indication of the young man's ability to soak up musical knowledge like a sponge - in the evening he gave a convincing performance that sounded as if he had been playing the piece for years.

Gordon Green lived in Hope Street, and in a nearby house his wife Dorothy ran the 51 Club, a superb little restaurant much frequented by Philharmonic audiences and artists. After concerts we were often invited to parties chez Green, where talk about all things musical went on long into the night. Their son, Nicky, was about 8 or 9, and used to creep out of his bed and listen in from the top of the stairs. Apparently Nicky's teacher at school had asked the class if any of them knew anything about Mozart.

Dead silence, then Nicky put his hand up. "Please Miss, he's a friend of my father's!"

Although piano concertos may top the box-office charts, the violin concerto is not far behind, and we had frequent visits from many top players. Menuhin appeared with us several times. On one occasion he was booked to play the Beethoven, which would normally have guaranteed a complete sell-out, but on the evening of the concert a pea-soup fog, the kind we used to get before smoke abatement legislation was brought in, descended on Liverpool, and the audience numbered barely sixty. I myself was late, despite running at full speed across the town, and didn't reach the hall until after the overture had started. I can still picture the expression on Yehudi's face when I burst into the Green Room, eyes streaming and completely out of breath.

Campoli was another regular visitor. I overheard a typical exchange between him and Gerald MacDonald which went something like this:

"Ah Gerry, Gerry! How about booking me for something soon? It's a long time since I was up to do something with the orchestra."

"But Camp, that's what you're here for now – you know, the Bliss Concerto with Sir Arthur conducting it?"

"Oh, yes yes yes, that's OK. But that's not what I mean. I mean a *reel* concerto, like the old Mengleson!"

The premature death of Ralph Holmes was a great loss to British string playing. His performances had a clean and forthright quality, and we were always amused by his archetypically English personality – a bit like Harry Wharton in the Greyfriars stories of Frank Richards!

Among the many gifted violinists I have played with, one of my particular favourites is Ida Haendel. She and I are of an age, and when I was a student in London she was already playing regularly as a soloist. It was sometimes said that she achieved such prominence only because the war had isolated us from wider musical circles, but I cannot subscribe to that viewpoint. Throughout her long professional life Ida's authoritative and commanding style of playing has entitled her to be ranked with the very best, and she deserves more recognition than she is often given. Maybe the British public became too familiar with her, but for me, her performances of the Beethoven concerto are unsurpassed.

Ida has never taught - she believes that if talent is there, it will find its way, and if it isn't, there's nothing to be done about it! As a little girl, she picked up a violin and said "Mummy, I can play this!" - and she could. According to one story, by the time she had started lessons with Carl Flesch, she was able to play all the well-known concertos, but Flesch felt that she needed to broaden her musical awareness and asked her to play some Beethoven violin sonatas. It was at this point that he realised she could barely read music, and had been playing entirely by ear!

I remember working with Ida and Charles Groves on the Shostakovitch Second Concerto. She was outraged that in rehearsal Charles thought she was tending to rush the difficult virtuoso passages, making it hard to maintain ensemble with the orchestra, and she cornered me in the Green Room afterwards.

"Mr Mountain, please tell me – am I rushing?"

She played the passage in question, and I said tactfully "Well, maybe a little, but it sounds wonderful rushing! It's up to us to go with you."

Visits from the Polish violinist Henryk Szeryng were always a sensational success. A colleague of mine described him as the most honest of violinists, meaning that everything he achieved was without the slightest trace of what might be called faking. His technique was honed to the highest degree, and his interpretations were considered and shaped to the smallest imaginable detail. I was lucky enough to have some help from him, and he once invited me to his room in the Adelphi Hotel to play to him. When I arrived, I found him practising the Beethoven Concerto with the music on a stand, although he had played it with us the two previous nights from memory, and to our ears quite flawlessly.

"You should never practise without the music," he explained. "Small errors can creep in. With the music before you, you can see more and more of the composer's true intentions, the true shape of the phrases, the overall line and construction of the music. Playing without music is learning like a parrot. Real practising should always be a voyage of discovery."

Wise words. Some people found Szeryng overbearing and opinionated, and he was certainly not lacking in self-confidence, but if he was conceited, it was not without cause! I was especially privileged to play the Bach 2 Violin Concerto with him at one concert, and will never forget his help and support.

The violin of course is not the only string instrument to have concertos written for it, and our visitors to Liverpool included a number of distinguished cellists. Paul Tortelier's concerts were always lively and produced playing of the very highest calibre. Unfortunately, Paul also had conducting ambitions that were not entirely matched by his actual ability in that department, and I remember a tour of Wales we did with him, both as soloist and as conductor of a decidedly erratic Beethoven 7th! Paul's son Jan Pascal Tortelier, on the other hand, started his career as a violinist and has since become one of the outstanding conductors of his generation.

Of the many other fine cellists I worked with, none was more notable than Jacqueline Du Pré. I played with her only once at the Phil, in 1965, when she was still only 20. Her marriage to Daniel Barenboim was to follow in 1967, and it was all too soon after this that she began to suffer the symptoms that led to a diagnosis of multiple sclerosis in 1973, and eventually to her untimely death in 1987 at the age of 42.

In a chapter entitled Programmes and Personalities, it would be impossible not to come back to arguably John Pritchard's greatest contribution to the Liverpool musical scene, the *Musica Viva* concerts. These were modelled on a series started in Munich by the composer Karl Amadeus Hartmann. They were in three parts, first an introductory talk with musical extracts played by the orchestra, then the concert proper, and then a discussion group, chaired by a distinguished independent musician. The programmes typically contained three works; a major established 20th century piece such as Bartók's Concerto for Orchestra, a modern concerto item, and an up to the minute contemporary work, often a first performance with the composer present.

They were exciting occasions, skilfully conceived to attract wide audiences, and a much more honest way of introducing people to modern music than the apologetic slipping of pieces into a classical programme, as if they are something to be ashamed of! Where else would I have got the chance to play an epoch-making piece like Hartmann's *Concerto Funèbre* for violin and strings? Hartmann was profoundly anti-Nazi, and this work was written in 1939 as a lament at the outbreak of war. I also did the Violin Concerto by the American composer Roger Sessions, notable for the fact that the orchestra is without violins, thus making the soloist stand out more. It is also quite the most difficult piece I have ever tackled!

Pritchard loved opera, and was already closely involved with Glyndebourne, so it was not surprising that he soon began to negotiate a link between his two main activities. This led to a two-week visit in September 1956 by the entire Glyndebourne Opera Company to the Liverpool Royal Court Theatre, with all the top stars, including Joan Sutherland, Sir Geraint Evans and Ian Wallace. Vittorio Gui was associate conductor with Pritchard, and the full Glyndebourne productions of three operas were presented - Mozart's Figaro and Don Giovanni, and Rossini's La Cenerentola. Not the most adventurous of choices, but financially it was a high risk venture, and we had to keep our eyes fixed firmly on the box office.

Even so, initial bookings were disappointing, and there were a few bitten fingernails among the management team. After the first night, however, there were rave notices in the press, and suddenly the whole series was sold out. In the second week there was a gala banquet at the Town Hall, which began very formally, largely because the city councillors of Liverpool were uncertain how to behave with such strange bohemian creatures. But it wasn't long before the ice was broken, as the Glyndebourne crew launched into a series of arias, duos, and eventually the Sextet from Lucia di Lammermoor, which brought the house down. We ended up migrating next door into the grand Council Chamber, where Ian Wallace took over the

Lord Mayor's throne for an impromptu performance of the famous Flanders and Swann Hippopotamus Song:

Mud - Mud -Glorious Mud

Nothing quite like it for cooling the blood

The Town Hall has seen nothing quite like it indeed, either before or since!

Opera at Ingestre, Lord Shrewsbury's ancestral home, got off to a good start in 1958, and promised to become the Glyndebourne of the North. The first season included two double bills, the first of which began with Purcell's Dido and Aeneas. The title role of Aeneas was taken by a Swedish baritone of advanced years, sporting a hearing aid distinctly unTrojan in appearance. His pronunciation of his lines was rich with comic potential, which as usual we failed miserably to resist. To his heartfelt "Vot lengvidge sall I uuze to shaw my looove?" the orchestra would shout back "Try English!"

The orchestral parts we had were in an edition with all the vocal cues printed in German, another regular source of amusement. One of my favourites came at the end of the hunting scene when the storm breaks, when Belinda the Lady in Waiting (sung by Heather Harper) has the quick, virtuoso aria "Haste, haste, to town!" This emerges in German as "Schnell, Schnell zu Stadt!" - guaranteed to dislodge any false teeth!

The second half of the bill was Master Peter's Puppet Show by Manuel de Falla, a beguiling little opera for puppets, based on the story of Don Quixote. It is a great shame that the music from this is so seldom heard. We joined forces with the Hogarth Puppets, whose founder Ann Hogarth gave the world the legendary Muffin the Mule, and the singers were behind the stage.

The other double bill featured Venus and Adonis by John Blow, and the delightful comedy Dr Miracle by Bizet, in which the hero, Silvio, gets into the house of his beloved by pretending to be a cook, and is obliged to produce an omelette to feed the assembled guests. At this point he hisses to the audience "This is the moment I've been dreading!" and immediately the first violins have a presto passage of the utmost virtuosity, testing them to the limit. Bizet obviously had an orchestral player's sense of humour! When the guests eat the revolting omelette and are all violently ill, Dr Miracle - Silvio in another disguise - is hastily sent for, with the rib-tickling summons "Quick Quack, Quick!"

John had organised the Ingestre project in cooperation with Nadine Talbot, Countess of Shrewsbury, herself a well-regarded opera singer. Unfortunately it foundered after a sensational divorce case in 1959, when a judge refused Lord Shrewsbury's petition on the grounds of adultery because the Earl had committed adultery himself. The family's finances were ruined, and the whole estate had to be sold.

In 1960, John had a final throw of the operatic dice when he booked Geraint Evans for a series of performances of Cimarosa's Il Maestro di Capella, where the singer, in 18th century costume and wig, conducts the orchestra in a hilarious burlesque. This was particularly enjoyable for the orchestra because many of the jokes happened to be at the expense of my old sparring partner, principal double-bass Roy Watson!

I'm sure it was part of John's master plan to establish a permanent operatic presence in the North, and I suspect that with the failure of Ingestre, his position with the orchestra started to lose some of its allure. He didn't have the temperament or inclination to do for the Phil what Barbirolli was doing for the Hallé, and that, I think, is why in 1963 he left us to take up conductorship of the London Philharmonic.

1963, coincidentally or otherwise, was also the last year of the Annual International Competitions, alternately for conducting and piano, which had been run by the Philharmonic Society since 1958. The first Conductors' Competition, in May 1958, was judged by the formidable American maestro William Steinberg, who irresistibly put me in mind of the bald-headed and moustachioed ruffian often seen in Laurel and Hardy comedies. He had the unnerving habit of prowling around the back of the orchestra while competitors were performing, and whenever he detected a mistake in the playing he would clap his hands loudly, bring the music shudderingly to a stop, and demand whether the poor nerve-shattered wretch wielding the baton had also heard it.

Now and again, however, he unexpectedly met his match. One competitor, a young American boy, had an immensely rich American father, who had literally bought him an orchestra back home in Texas to practise on. Although not prodigiously talented, he had a winning, pleasant manner, and we all took to him immediately. He was thrashing his way with us one morning through Debussy's La Mer, and Mr Steinberg, with a thunderous scowl on his face, was lurking behind the woodwinds.

Clap clap! We all stopped.

"Well, well, did you hear it? A mistake on the second flute? Yes?" He turned to the villain of the piece. "I'm not blaming you - anyone can make a mistake. But he should have heard. Did you hear it? Yes? Answer me!"

"Gee, Mr Steinberg," came the reply, in an accent straight from the Deep South. "I didn't hear a thing. Sounded marvellous to me! Wish it was like this back home!"

Needless to say it had us all in stitches, with the possible exception of Steinberg, who wasn't best pleased when it made the first page of the Liverpool Post next day!

That first competition, as touched upon in an earlier chapter, was won by Zubin Mehta, who has of course gone on to build an international career at the highest level. During the six-month apprenticeship he received as a prize, on 15th November 1958, I played the Glazunov Violin Concerto under his direction, which, in retrospect, was quite a prestigious addition to my CV. Zubin left the Phil at the end of the six months, and went to America with his father, Mehli Mehta who had been a violinist in the Hallé. Neither of them had any definite prospects, but within a few months Zubin struck gold, landing engagements with a number of top orchestras and rapidly becoming a world-wide star.

"Why don't we have Zubin back for a concert with us?" I said to Gerry MacDonald, a little over a year after the maestro's departure from Liverpool.

Gerry's response was swift and to the point: "We can't possibly afford him!"

Reactions among the Phil to the conducting competitions were always interesting. Orchestral players are notoriously intolerant of musicians they suspect of having ideas above their station, and to anyone who hasn't been there, it's easy to resort to old clichés like "*anybody* can beat four in a bar" or "the baton is always in tune." Among the budding conductors were a number of highly respected instrumentalists, and we all assumed they would do well, but to our surprise, more often than not they turned out to be fairly clueless! It began to dawn on people that maybe conducting wasn't so easy after all, and there was more to it than just waving a stick about.

In the first Piano Competition, won as previously mentioned by Joaquin Achúcarro, the two judges were Cyril Smith and Solomon, both giants of the keyboard who had been stricken in mid-career by paralysing strokes. Gerry Macdonald used to give us inside information about their reactions in the jury box, which illustrated how artists tend to be over-critical of anyone they perceive as operating in their own special territory. When a competitor was playing a Beethoven concerto, Cyril Smith would award high marks, and Solomon would invariably disagree, whereas when Rachmaninov or Tschaikovsky was played, the reverse would be the case. This is possibly the mindset Kreisler was referring to when he said he could never bring himself to teach, because to play at the highest level it is necessary to be so completely convinced you are right, that you are unable to conceive of any other way of playing the music.

Before I draw a line under the Liverpool days, there are a couple of other highlights that deserve mention. I was asked to play Max Bruch's well-known G minor Concerto at a Saturday concert on 16th February 1957, with Efrem Kurz conducting. Bruch had been Principal Conductor at the Philharmonic from 1880 to 1883, but no one in either the audience or the orchestra, including myself, realized the full significance of the occasion until the actual evening. During the interval of the concert, our Chairman Harry Livermore came onto the stage to announce that the Orchestra and the Society had been granted Royal Patronage, and that henceforth we were to be known as the Royal Liverpool Philharmonic Society. It was a very well-kept secret - no leaks!

Finally, there is one personal achievement of which I am particularly proud. In 1956, I recruited the Phil's principal string players to form a String Quartet, which played and broadcasted regularly in the North. Realising that it needed a base for the focus of its activities, with the help of Liverpool University I started a series of Chamber Concerts in the beautiful Walker Art Gallery in the centre of the city. These took place monthly during the winter on Monday evenings, and by careful negotiation I was able to engage many of the well-known soloists who were already booked to appear in the Tuesday Subscription Series. We did piano quintets, individual solos, Mozart arias - all kinds of ensemble items. Some of these were comparatively rare, and were guaranteed a good audience by the participation of big names. John Ogdon in the Brahms Piano Quintet, Walter Susskind in Dvořák's Piano Quintet, Szeryng in a selection of sonatas played with Muriel, April Cantelo (first wife of Colin Davis) in an entrancing programme of Mozart Concert Arias - there are too many to mention them all. The concerts were invariably sold out, so they were a financial as well as an artistic success. Even if you didn't like the music, you could sit back and enjoy the paintings!

So, 1955 to 1966 was a golden period for us. Our children were growing. Paul was doing well at Merchant Taylor's School - a keen rugby and tennis player, getting good all-round grades in class, and showing considerable promise on the violin, although it wasn't until later that he committed himself to the pursuit of music as a vocation. Alison was already showing a leaning towards the visual arts, and Jeanette was fortunate in having Amos Moore, a dedicated and conscientious teacher who was a member of the Phil's cello section, to give her a firm start in her career. Amos also taught Colin Carr, who was the same age as Jeanette and went on to achieve conspicuous success as a soloist and teacher on both sides of the Atlantic.

At the same time, Liverpool was buzzing with vitality as the epicentre of the Pop revolution. Lily, our domestic help, had a son who managed a nightclub in Southport, where he used to book the Beatles, in their earliest days, for £30 a night, and later, as a teenager, our son Paul was a regular at the Cavern Club. Heady days!

However, I was beginning to get itchy feet. When we had been in Liverpool for little more than a year, I had been invited to go back to London to sit with Paul Beard as deputy leader of the BBC Symphony Orchestra. I hadn't accepted, because I wanted to concentrate on one thing at a time, which I still feel was the right decision and one I don't in any way regret.

But after ten years in the job, I started to get the feeling that I was being taken for granted. This feeling came to a head at a party attended by Committee Members and some of the orchestral players late in 1965.

"Things are going well," someone said. "The orchestra sounds exceptional. We're getting good notices in the national press, we have a great conductor."

"And we have a very good Leader," someone else chipped in.

"Oh yes," said the first speaker. "We know that!"

The realisation hit me that I was being classified as part of the furniture, and going home in the car, it suddenly became clear what we had to do.

"Right," I said to Muriel. "We're leaving!"

And so at the end of the winter season in 1966 we were on our way, not without some regrets, but determined to find fresh fields and pastures new.

Chapter 22 - Back to London.

We bought a house in Myddleton Park, out Barnet way. Times had moved on, and the area between St Johns Wood and Hampstead that had previously been our favourite part of London was now prohibitively expensive. For the sake of the family, we were looking for somewhere to put down roots, and we were not to know that this stage of our cavalcade through life was to last only a little over two years. If life has taught me one thing, it's that however much you try to plan ahead - whatever future possibilities you envisage, however diverse - what actually ends up happening will more often than not be something quite different!

We arrived in London without any kind of job prospects, but we had many friends in the city, and when word got around the phone began to ring with offers of freelance work. Muriel resumed teaching privately and at the Academy, and doing *repetiteure* work for the London Opera School, while I did a number of sessions with the English Chamber Orchestra, led by my friend Manny Hurwitz. We recorded a series of Mozart Piano Concertos with Barenboim directing and playing.

The manager of the ECO was the violist Quin Ballardie, another friend from Academy days. Quin also asked me to lead the orchestra in Britten's Noye's Fludde at the Aldeburgh Festival, conducted by Norman Del Mar and closely supervised by Britten himself. This was quite nerve-racking. The orchestra comprised a string quartet, wind players, Jimmy Blades leading a variety of percussionists, and an array of young people playing simple string parts. It was our responsibility to organise the youngsters and keep them in order, which often meant that just as the TV cameras were beginning to roll, you would have some little violinist coming up to you with the plaintive lament "Please Sir, my bridge has fallen down....!"

Norman Del Mar was in every sense a larger than life character. His conducting was vigorous, to say the least, and during energetic passages he almost took off! As mentioned earlier, he began his career as a horn player, and when I was first in the Philharmonia he was second horn to Dennis Brain. Beecham took him up as a conductor, and his career subsequently blossomed. I worked closely with him for several years with the Training Orchestra and the Academy of the BBC in Bristol, and we were always good friends. He was in Bristol during the time that the BBC downgraded us from a full symphony orchestra to a chamber orchestra, a move that he resisted strenuously, although unhappily to no avail.

Norman's knowledge and preparation of the music were always exemplary, and his writings (particularly the three books on Richard Strauss) have a unique and unmistakable style - you only have to read a page and you can hear Norman speaking. The last of them was published in 1973, and for some time prior to this, while he was chief conductor of the BBC Training Orchestra, his every spare moment was devoted to writing and correcting the final drafts. One reviewer marvelled that anyone could possibly marshal such a vast array of detailed facts in such a masterly fashion, while at the same time working a full schedule as a conductor.

Although he was admired for his detailed grasp of everything he conducted, Norman sometimes stretched the patience of his players by finding problems where they didn't really exist. Manny Hurwitz put it perfectly when he said "Norman is very good, but he's a bit like a Sherpa guide. He's marvellous on Everest, but you don't really need him on Snowdon!"

Norman also had the endearing habit of inventing adjectives and adverbs of his own to suit a particular situation. On one occasion when I was driving him to the Bristol studio for a rehearsal, traffic was heavy and I couldn't find a parking place. It looked as if we would be late, so I said "You jump out here, Norman. I'll find somewhere else to put the car."

"Are you sure?" he asked, eyebrows typically raised. "I feel a bit *rattish*!"

When Norman's wife Pauline was expecting their first son Jonathan (now a distinguished musicologist and conductor) the couple were at Dartington Summer School. At the first signs of Pauline's labour pains, Norman, instead of going to a local hospital, insisted on driving her at breakneck speed to her nursing home in London, arriving just in time. Unable to be present for the birth, he visited next day. Breezing into the ward, he ignored Pauline completely, went straight to the cot at the foot of the bed, lifted the covers to inspect his infant son and delivered his verdict.

"Hmm - that's the sort of thing!"

And then breezed straight out again! Or so legend has it. Not having been there, I can't actually vouch for this, but it is certainly the kind of story that sprang up around Norman. He was often exasperating, but was always on top of any task he undertook. I felt he was under-appreciated in some quarters, and find it hard to understand why he never joined the ranks of British conductors honoured with knighthoods.

That year, Aldeburgh's main theme was the music of Tschaikovsky, a favourite of Benjamin Britten's. Ben conducted a memorable concert with the ECO in the Snape Concert Hall, with Rostropovich as soloist in the Rococo Variations and other smaller cello pieces by Tschaikovsky. The ECO players, used to a more refined diet of Haydn Symphonies, had very little experience working in a larger orchestra, and were somewhat taken aback to be confronted by a programme opening with Tschaikovsky's Romeo and Juliet. On the back desk of the fiddles, Henry Datyner and I were the only ones in the band who knew anything about that kind of music, and felt very superior!

There are other concerts at Aldeburgh that stick in the mind. One was a performance of Haydn's oratorio The Creation, again inspirationally conducted by Britten, in the Parish Church. It was recorded by the BBC and is still regarded as a classic account of this masterpiece. Another was a couple of years later, in 1969, when the BBC Training Orchestra's conductor Meredith Davies invited me to lead the orchestra in Britten's A Midsummer Night's Dream. The Festival started disastrously when the Snape Hall was completely gutted by fire on the first night, and our production had to be transferred to the Theatre Royal in Bury St Edmunds. Even so, it proved to be a great experience, with Britten attending several of the performances, and incredibly, by the time I returned to the Festival next year, the Snape Hall had been completely restored to its former glory, as if nothing had happened.

My other engagements with the ECO during my second stint in London included a tour to Prague and Bratislava, with concerts conducted by Sir Charles Mackerras and Daniel Barenboim. At the time of our visit, Czechoslovakia's Communist rulers were struggling to cope with the widespread disaffection, led by Alexander Dubček, that was to culminate in the Soviet invasion of 1968. The signs of austerity were everywhere. There were long queues for everyday food items, and the beautiful architecture of Prague was going to rack and ruin through sheer lack of maintenance. As foreign visitors, we had been warned not to talk to chance acquaintances who might be government agents, but the local people expressed their hatred of the Communist regime quite openly. In Bratislava we were taken on a tour that passed an immense ugly Soviet war memorial on the top of a hill, and were told that the Russians had demolished several beautiful churches and buildings nearby because they slightly obscured the view of the monument.

In spite of this powder-keg atmosphere, we had excellent audiences, and were given a warm welcome everywhere we went. In later years, after the "velvet revolution" of 1989, I revisited Prague and Bratislava while on holiday with Muriel, and it was heart-warming to see how lovingly these great historic cities had been restored.

In the summer of 1968 Amaryllis Fleming and I were invited to take charge of chamber music at Canford Summer School. Amaryllis (known to all as Amo) was one of the finest cellists I have ever known. Strikingly beautiful, she was the half sister of James Bond's creator Ian Fleming, and the illegitimate daughter of the painter Augustus John. John did some stunning preliminary sketches of Amo playing the cello, and if he had lived long enough, might well have produced a painting to equal or even surpass his portrait of Guilhermina Suggia, the great cellist of an earlier era.

The family came down to Dorset with me, and Muriel, Amo and I gave a joint concert at the end of the course. We began with the Beethoven Piano Trio in B flat Op. 11, Muriel and I played 5 Madrigal Stanzas by Martinu, and as a finale Amo gave a performance of the Bach Suite No.1 in G for solo cello. I sat in the audience to listen, and with me was our daughter Jeanette, then aged 11, who was herself already beginning to tackle the Bach Suites. Jen's party piece at the time was the Minuets I and II that form the penultimate part of the first suite, and I had told her that Amo would be playing them. As the final Gigue came to its energetic conclusion, and Amo was graciously acknowledging her ovation, I heard a plaintive little voice:

"She never played my piece!"

"Jen, are you *sure*?" I said, startled.

"Yes, I am!"

Jeanette was possibly the only person in the hall who had realised that Amo, playing from memory, had accidentally gone straight from the Sarabande to the Gigue. We went round to see her in the Green Room.

"Amo, that was tremendous," I said. "But you missed out the Minuets."

"Bloody hell - are you sure?" Poor Amo was mortified, and by way of apology I seem to remember she sat down there and then, and played them especially for Jeanette!

Amo never received the public recognition her talents merited. She once told me she felt her career had been stolen from her by Jacqueline Du Pré. Among her fellow musicians she was universally respected, particularly for her chamber music and for her teaching. Raphael Wallfisch was an eminent pupil of hers from an early age, and Jeanette studied with her for several years after leaving Joan Dixon at the RCM. Amo herself had worked with Casals, Fournier and Tortelier, as well as a number of internationally renowned violinists, and it was a privilege to be associated with a musician of her pedigree and calibre.

Early in 1967, I was invited to be principal 2ⁿᵈ violin in the LPO, and accepted with pleasure, as it would mean working again with John Pritchard. The orchestra at that time was led by Rodney Friend, later to lead the New York Philharmonic and the BBC Symphony Orchestra. Rodney was from my neck of the woods, having been brought up in Huddersfield and had early lessons from the wife of Arthur Kaye, my father's teacher. We hit it off from the start, and have remained firm friends ever since.

This was the first time I had played second violin parts regularly in my career, and I found it quite an eye-opener. People assume that the second part doesn't generally go as high, so it must be easier and doesn't require such good players. In fact this is far from the case. The first violins nearly always have the tune, which is much easier to hear in your head, easier to read, and on the whole I suppose more aesthetically appealing. The seconds, on the other hand, are constantly switching between the melody line and the inner harmonies that are nowhere near as easy to grasp aurally, or to read. This imposes its own peculiar demands, particularly when the seconds are placed opposite to the firsts, to the right of the conductor, which can lead to a quite scary sense of isolation.

In the event, I found I rather liked that set-up – it engendered a real sense of independence, rather than the feeling of being a mere pale shadow of the brilliant firsts. I was also intrigued to discover that the really great composers always write more exciting second fiddle parts. In my first season at Glyndebourne we did Donizetti's L'Elisir D'Amore - a charming comedy, but with a deadly boring second violin part. By contrast, Mozart's Figaro is terrific fun. Beethoven, Tschaikovsky and Wagner also write interestingly for the seconds, but Brahms, perhaps surprisingly, is less inspiring, often simply scoring just an octave down from the firsts.

My time with the LPO encompassed two Glyndebourne seasons, which served to emphasise the drawbacks of living in the north of the city. It meant a lot of driving in heavy traffic on days when we had to do an opera performance as well as a recording session at Abbey Road. We often recorded with Sir Adrian Boult, then in his later years, and another prominent figure was the Russian Evgeny

Svetlanov, who conducted notable performances at the Festival Hall of Rachmaninov's 1st Symphony and Tschaikovsky's Manfred Symphony, in those days both rarely heard. Svetlanov to my eyes was the spitting image of the film comedian Bob Hope, although I'm not sure he'd have found the comparison amusing!

I did two foreign tours with the LPO, both conducted by Pritchard. The first, in September 1967, was of Scandinavia with Glyndebourne Opera. It was the nearest thing to a paid holiday I have ever experienced. We performed one opera, Don Giovanni, for several days each in Stockholm, Oslo, Gothenburg and Copenhagen. In each place there would be a brief seating rehearsal to settle into the theatre, and then, apart from performances in the evening, our time was more or less our own.

It was a special pleasure to perform in the Drottningholm Theatre in Stockholm, mentioned in an earlier chapter. This is the only perfectly preserved 18th century theatre in the world that survives complete with its own original scenery, which is operated backstage by a complicated system of levers and wheels. All this happens in dead silence, apart from subdued creaking of the machinery, and in full view of the audience, as there is no curtain for the stage. The only partitioning curtain is one half way up the stalls, which comes down at the interval so that the aristocracy at the front (including two large thrones for any royalty present) are not obliged to mingle with the *hoi polloi* behind!

This kind of setup is ripe for a classic operatic disaster, and sure enough, things duly went pear-shaped in the graveyard scene, where Giovanni comes across the statue of the Commendatore, Donna Anna's father, whom he murdered in the first Act, and invites him to dinner. Just before this encounter, a trapdoor was supposed to open on stage, allowing the statue to be lifted into full view, and on the second night, the process ground to a halt halfway through. After several abortive attempts to get it going again, with much creaking and groaning, it became obvious that there was a real danger of the whole thing going into reverse, so the luckless singer playing the part was left knee-deep in the stage. The two Royal Princesses in the audience then got a highly infectious dose of the giggles, especially when Leporello the manservant was told by Giovanni to read the inscription on the statue, and dutifully examined its upper legs! Sad to relate, the singer concerned failed to see the funny side - he'd never been so humiliated in his life!

We also did an extended European tour with John Ogdon as soloist. This trip finished in Paris, at a time when relations between France and Britain were not particularly cordial. During the first part of the concert the atmosphere was distinctly frigid, and the applause pointedly lukewarm. John, generally the quietest and most peaceful of characters, was fired up by this. He came onto the stage after the interval and gave the most devastating performance of the Tschaikovsky Concerto I have ever heard. To say it brought the house down would be the understatement of this or any other year. It had the audience on its feet and roaring its approval, entirely forgetting that John was one of those evil Rosbifs.

There was one performance on the tour that for some reason Ogdon could not do. I think it was in Munich. As a substitute, we played the Tschaikovsky violin concerto with the veteran Russian Mischa Elman, then aged 76. Elman died later that same year, but on that particular evening he was full of life. It was a historic experience for all the string players, especially for me. My teacher Sascha Lasserson had gone to school with Elman in St Petersburg, and they had both studied the violin there with Leopold Auer. There is a wonderful photograph of Auer's class in St Petersburg about 1900, with Mischa and Sascha sitting in the front row as little boys.I had heard Elman give a recital at Drury Lane Theatre just after the war, and it was incredible to be actually on the platform with him. The fact that the playing was not technically immaculate was of little importance. Elman was world famous for his individual sound, and that was still there, along with his forceful personality and breathtaking originality. He did things with the phrasing that no one else would have dared. From close up, I was amazed by the length of the nails on his left hand - they were so long that he played with almost flat fingers. How he managed to negotiate the technical passages was a mystery to us mere mortals.

There are many stories about Elman. Many people, including Sascha, while admiring his formidable talents, criticised his taste and showmanship. From his earliest years as a child prodigy he had done nothing but continuous world tours, eventually becoming almost a caricature of himself. Apparently it was belatedly recognised, in his early adult years, that he had missed out on most of the essential experiences of childhood and growing up. It was decided that among other things, it was about time for him to have the chance to experience sex. Money was provided for this purpose, but his guardians discovered to their consternation that he was spending it on sweets! First things first!

Overall, although there were undoubted high points, those short years in London are not a period I look back on with a great deal of pleasure. Muriel and I were both working hard, with a lot of travelling and not enough time together and with the children. Coming back to the Metropolis after an eleven year absence had made us realise how much the quality of life for musicians there had decreased in the interim.

Chapter 23 – BBC Training Orchestra

I was engaged for a short time as violin coach for the National Youth Orchestra of Great Britain, and helped with an excellent performance by them of Bartók's Concerto for Orchestra. The composer Herbert Howells was on the board of the NYO. He came to one of the concerts and was particularly impressed with the quality of the string playing. I subsequently heard that he had mentioned my name to Sir William Glock, then Head of BBC Third Programme, who was looking for a suitable violinist to direct the BBC Training Orchestra, then only one year old. The present director, Leonard Hirsch, was no longer willing to continue as a player, and would only conduct.

The orchestra was a completely new venture, which had came about as a deal between Musicians' Union and the BBC, who wanted to negotiate an agreement for more "needle time" as it was then known, i.e. the amount of air time they could earmark for playing gramophone records. In return for this they agreed to do something to help budding orchestral musicians, and the result was this brainchild of Sir William's - a kind of postgraduate orchestra, to be based in Bristol, designed as a stepping-stone into the profession for instrumentalists who had graduated from music college.

It was an inspired idea, and I worked with it for nearly eight years, which in some ways were the most rewarding and enjoyable of my career. Of the huge number of young players who passed through the orchestra, not one of the many I have met in later years, in every branch of the music profession, has recalled that time in Bristol with anything other than pleasure and appreciation. It is a great pity that the project did not lead to the establishment of a permanent institution, and was discontinued in 1976. The reasons for this are complex, but I will try to give a brief synopsis.

With the benefit of hindsight, it can be seen that several unwise decisions were made. Glock was an idealist, and wanted to make sure that the highest possible standards were achieved by the project. He didn't want it to be something that people joined as a last resort because they couldn't get a job anywhere else, but a reasoned first step in their careers, which would improve their prospects later. In line with this philosophy he decided to pay salaries equal to those offered by the other provincial BBC orchestras. Not only that; the Training Orchestra would actually produce less air time than the others. The plan was that they would do one programme a week, plus the occasional public concert, but would benefit from more rehearsal time and facilities for chamber music, with coaching from the Amadeus Quartet and the finest wind players in the country. Meanwhile the other orchestras were producing two or three programmes a week for the same money in much less ideal conditions. One can imagine the resentment of experienced older players, struggling to bring up families on less than bountiful BBC salaries, on finding that young, inexperienced kids fresh out of college were receiving such preferential treatment.

The BBC then compounded this misjudgement by failing over the years to maintain pay levels relative to the cost of living. It was a time of high inflation, and orchestral incomes in general, protected by experienced negotiations on the part of older players and the Union, rose accordingly. The Training Orchestra salary, however, stayed the same, so from being comfortably well off its members soon found they were reduced to existing on less than a student's grant. The Union, dominated by players already in the profession, did nothing to help, and when the very existence of the orchestra was threatened by the BBC, it took no action. The orchestra existed as long as it did only through the sterling work of its young members, who were immensely loyal, and appreciated its worth.

Around 1970, with the whole country facing financial problems, the BBC began an attempt to renege from its agreement and disband the orchestra. After prolonged negotiations, it was agreed to reconstitute it as a smaller chamber-type orchestra. The actual name had long been a subject of controversy (it was disparagingly referred to as the BBC Straining Orchestra!) so the new title was Academy of the BBC.

It was a move in the wrong direction. What the members needed was experience of the big orchestral repertoire, but now they had to subsist on a diet of Haydn symphonies and specialist modern chamber orchestra items, in direct competition with top-drawer outfits like the ECO and St Martin in the Fields. They gave it their best shot, but with a constantly changing membership it was not possible to maintain a consistently high standard. In 1975 I felt obliged to accept another offer, and disbandment followed shortly afterwards.

To look on the positive side, the orchestra was extremely well organised. It was controlled by Philip Moore, Head of Music BBC West; a sensitive man and an excellent musician with whom I worked very happily. I was appointed to lead the orchestra, to coach the string players and to arrange day-to-day orchestral seating, so that different players had the chance to sit with me on the front desk. I also conducted from time to time. The members were auditioned by myself, Philip Moore, and our regular wind and percussion coaches.

Members normally joined the orchestra immediately after graduation from College, and were accepted for a minimum of one year and a maximum of three. This gave them a reasonable spell of training, then two years to provide stability to the ensemble and to make inquiries about future employment. It was a good arrangement, because new entrants learned from the example of the more experienced players. The main value of the orchestra, however, was the regular public platform it provided by way of well rehearsed weekly broadcasts with first rate soloists and conductors. When the orchestra disbanded in 1976, there was an attempt by Goldsmiths College in London to start a similar body, but it did not last long. Because it was recreated as a new orchestra each year, it was unable to match the continuity we had, and it also lacked the pressure of regular broadcasts to maintain a sense of urgency in the work.

My interview for the post was with Sir William Glock himself. He said he had discussed the project with Leopold Stokowski, who had favoured the idea of having at its head a musician who would act mainly as an orchestral leader and instruct by example, sitting with the young players in rotation rather than imposing ideas on them from above. In the continental tradition, the job was to have the title of Concertmaster.

For the first year I worked with Leonard Hirsch, a gifted orchestral musician but not a real conductor. His replacement as principal conductor was Meredith Davies, who became a close friend. Meredith's wry sense of humour was often expressed in the debunking of pretentiousness in his fellow musicians, which probably militated against his rising as high as he might have done in the estimation of the musical establishment. When he left to pursue other commitments in 1972 he was followed by Norman Del Mar.

George Hurst, who has always been very supportive to young musicians, was a frequent guest conductor. His uncompromising respect for the music and his refusal to accept any false values made him a particularly good role model. Three of George's performances stand out in the memory. The first was the Berlioz Grande Messe des Morts in Liverpool, which I have already mentioned. The second was a broadcast of Mozart's Jupiter Symphony, with all repeats in the slow movement and the last. It seemed to go on forever, but emerged as a towering masterpiece. The third, which I heard in Bristol's Colston Hall, was a performance of Stravinsky's Rite of Spring with the Bournemouth Orchestra. That season, their home town audiences had been disappointing, but for some reason the Rite appealed to the Bristol public, and it was a complete sell-out. George rose to the occasion, and I don't think I have ever heard a more exciting rendering of this electrifying work.

We had Sir Adrian Boult as guest conductor a few times, notably for a broadcast of Job by Vaughan Williams. This remarkable piece was originally conceived as a masque for dancing, but can be presented with a spoken commentary of the story of Job, interspersed between the various movements. This is the way we did it, with the words eloquently delivered by Douglas Vaughan, our regular BBC announcer in Bristol. Boult established a great rapport with the young orchestra, and I still enjoy hearing the broadcast, which I taped.

One other occasion when we worked with Douglas ended less happily. Edgar Cosma, a regular guest conductor, had spent a hard week rehearsing the orchestra in Walton's 1st Symphony. It was eventually recorded in a venue that we often used, an army drill hall in Whiteladies Road, almost opposite the BBC buildings. The actual recording went very well, although we needed every minute of the allocated time to get all the details fixed. After the last take we had to vacate the hall as quickly as possible, because it was needed for something else. Everyone lent a helping hand, none more so than Douglas, who had done the announcements and was one of the orchestra's most enthusiastic supporters. The big circular can, which contained the tape of all the work we had done on the final recording, was lying on a table, and when Dougie was handed one of the microphones by the engineer dismantling the equipment, he put it down on top of it, not realising that a microphone contains a powerful magnet. This corrupted the tape, leaving a mark that could be heard twice on every revolution and ruining our entire week's work!

In the early days of the BBCTO, when we were a full symphony orchestra, most of our recordings were done in the Colston Hall, which had an excellent acoustic and provided valuable experience of performing in a major concert venue. Beecham once said the Colston was the only concert hall known to him where the conductor, sitting on the loo in his dressing room, could, by slightly opening the door, watch the public coming into the concert. This is quite true, I can vouch for it personally!

When the Orchestra was downsized and became known as the Academy of the BBC, we were often recorded in the small BBC studios in Clifton, or in various church halls such as St Adhelms, which became a regular venue. This did help accustom the players to studio techniques and playing in small environments, but it is essential that musicians also get experience of playing in larger halls, which demand an effective projection of their performances, and this is what we missed in the later years.

Players who cut their musical teeth in Bristol at that time are today the backbone of our profession all over the world. I am often amazed by encounters like the one I had on a recent visit to Perth in Western Australia, where I met Peter Moore, who was a bassoonist with the Academy of the BBC. I remember conducting the orchestra when he was soloist in several Vivaldi concertos. Peter is now on the staff of the Music Department of Perth University, and is in charge of all the Youth Orchestras in Western Australia. His wife is clarinettist

Lorna Cooke, with whom I crossed paths a little later in Scotland, when I conducted a youth orchestra for her performance of the Finzi Clarinet Concerto. Lorna is now a member of the Perth Symphony Orchestra.

My son Paul is another whose entry to the music profession owes much to the Bristol Orchestra. Although he had obvious talent, music was not Paul's first choice of career. He graduated from university with a degree in Economics and took up a teaching post in Taunton, where after two unhappy years he realised that after all his great love was music. He gave up his job, practised solidly on the violin, with lessons from me, Manny Hurwitz and Yossy Zivony, and applied to join the Training Orchestra. Obviously I had to stand down from the audition panel, but the other members were more than satisfied, and he was with us for two years, after which he secured a position with the Philharmonia Orchestra in London. Subsequently he has had a busy and influential career in music education in Leeds, notably as conductor of the Leeds Youth Orchestra.

Paul's example is a valuable reminder that the lack of a conventional music college education, if you have the talent and the desire, need not be a barrier to employment as a professional musician.

Chapter 24 - Auditions

Anyone involved in music performance will have had to endure auditions, either doing them or listening to them, both of which can be deeply unpleasant experiences. There is nothing more forbidding than having to play to a row of glowering monsters portentously scribbling notes, and occasionally whispering what you are sure are derogatory observations as you struggle through your set pieces. Even worse is to play to a screen that hides your inquisitors, or (as in BBC auditions) to a microphone in a deserted studio, with a panel of torturers, in your fevered imagination, probably laughing and joking in a nearby invisible and inaudible balance box.

Audition stories are legion. One of my favourites is about the violinist who is trying for entry to the Covent Garden Orchestra. When asked what his sight-reading is like, he replies "My sight reading is fantastic. Just show me the opera I can't read." They put up Rosenkavalier and he says "That's it! Thanks very much. Goodbye!"

I remember auditioning violinists for the Liverpool Phil with John Pritchard when one contender came on to play the Adagio from the first Sonata for Solo Violin by Bach. It was reasonably competent technically, but the rhythm was so distorted that it made the music practically unrecognisable so John asked me to go down and tell him to play it again in time.

"Excuse me, thank you very much, but would you kindly play it again, with really correct rhythm, so that we can tell if you have a good sense of timing?"

"Oh well, yes," came the reply. "But my teacher told me to muck it about a bit!"

On another occasion I was again auditioning with John when a young hopeful came in to play the Mendelssohn Concerto, without accompaniment. It was immediately obvious that his strings were tuned about three semitones too low. I went down onto the stage and said. "Excuse me, before you play any more, would you kindly tune your instrument up to pitch? Here is the piano A."

"I'd rather not," he said. "These are the only strings I've got!"

He didn't want to risk tightening them up properly until he was sure he had got the job, and could afford to pay for breakages! Sadly we were not amused, but now and again even we glowering monsters did find it hard not to laugh. One well-known London orchestral violinist, a regular applicant for various posts, was asked what he had chosen to play.

"Well," he said. "if you can't tell what it is within the next few seconds, we're all of us wasting our time!"

Auditions, by their very nature, cannot be an entirely accurate guide to an applicant's strengths and weaknesses, and a successful audition should always be followed by a trial period in the orchestra. I recall one player who gave such an impressive performance of the Brahms violin concerto that he was immediately accepted without even a sight-reading test. He subsequently proved to be completely unable to blend into the section, or to read standard orchestral repertoire, to the extent that it attracted adverse comment from members of the public. Although other members of the section were having lessons from him that they valued highly, he had to be asked to leave.

The reverse can apply. Some potentially valuable orchestral members may go to pieces when asked to do an audition. Playing demanding violin concertos or Paganini Caprices is not their *forte*, although they can be excellent at fitting into a section and playing second violin in a Mozart symphony, an exacting task in its own right.

Sight-reading is another bone of contention. The ability to play orchestral passage work competently at first sight is not an automatic plus mark. There is always the chance to rehearse and practise difficulties before performance, and it would be my preference to give players a second or third try at a difficulty, just to observe their coping strategies. Another effective procedure is to allow half an hour before the audition for preparation, or even to send the music by post a few days in advance.

One test I adopted in Bristol and later in Scotland was to ask candidates to perform violin duets with me. Anyone with a natural aptitude for chamber music will always be valuable in an orchestra and I am suspicious of players whose only interest is in virtuoso performance. A player who thrives on the give and take of chamber music is likely to have broader artistic instincts, and is also more likely to have the kind of sociable personality best suited to the stresses and strains of orchestral life.

Music is a not an easy way of making a living. Every professional musician has at some time or another suffered the pangs of disappointment and rejection, and it is important to develop the strength and resilience of character to deal with these setbacks. The opinion of one set of adjudicators can be diametrically opposed to another, and provided the ability and self-belief are there, the chances of eventual success are high.

The ups and downs are both well illustrated by one final cautionary tale from my Bristol days. I was often asked for advice about auditions, and invariably told violinists that they should at a moment's notice be ready to play one Mozart and one other standard concerto. The fact that you may never be asked to play such music in public is beside the point - by demonstrating a high level of technique you are proving that you are unlikely to struggle with the lower technical demands of orchestral music. You must also actively practise sight-reading. I was giving lessons to one boy who was a very agreeable character, but not the best of our players, although I was sure he would make a perfectly acceptable good rank-and-file violinist. He told me he had been offered an audition with the Bournemouth Sinfonietta, to be held when they visited Bristol a few weeks hence. Could I *please* help him with his sight-reading?

I gave him a very good tip - have a look at the programme the orchestra is playing at the time, because it is most likely that they will just take out something suitable from the first violin parts for use at the auditions. He went away and came back with the news that they were playing the Bizet Symphony. "Oh, my God!" I groaned. "The last movement is a real test! Get the part from the library and we'll have a go at it right away!" So he did, and we worked on it ceaselessly until the day of the audition, by which time he could play this notorious passage quite impressively.

When he was called for his ordeal, he played his audition pieces reasonably well, and then came the sight-reading. The panel, by nature kind-hearted people, decided that it would be unfair to expect someone of my pupil's standard to tackle the last movement at sight, and gave him the first movement instead. He was completely unnerved and made an absolute mess of it!

I'm glad to say that he did eventually succeed, and was for many years a valuable member of the ensemble, always giving his all - especially in the Bizet Symphony!

BOOK 3

Chapter 25 - Scotland RSAMD

By 1975, it was obvious that the battle to save the Bristol orchestra was more or less lost. The BBC wouldn't renew my contract for more than one year at a time, and although we still were attracting a good standard of applicants, they were now promised only one year's engagement. Muriel and I began to make plans for an eventual return to London, where we could count on freelance work and explore the possibilities of a permanent orchestral post for me. We did this with a heavy heart, as there had been much to enjoy about many aspects of our work during our eight years in the West Country.

I have always been a firm believer in giving 100% effort to any project I undertake, but there have been points in my life when I felt I had done all I could in one particular field, and that I was ready for a change. At such times I have often found serendipity coming to my rescue. Serendipity, according to the Oxford English Dictionary, is the faculty of making happy and unexpected discoveries by accident, and it certainly seemed to work for me as the Bristol years drew to a close.

I was contacted by Manoug Parikian, with whom we had kept in touch since I left the Philharmonia for Liverpool back in 1955. Manoug knew the violinist Louis Carus, Head of Strings at the Royal Scottish Academy of Music and Drama in Glasgow. Louis was leaving to take up the post of Principal of the Birmingham School of Music - would I be interested in applying for the vacancy?

Muriel was initially less than enthusiastic about moving to Glasgow. Although she had been born in Carlisle and brought up in Coventry, she was entirely Scottish by descent, on both sides, and her memories of Glasgow were all of family visits to aged aunts and cousins, or being persuaded to draw on her budding skills as a pianist to play at Burns Suppers. However, the prospect of returning to London was even more unappealing, so she plumped for a return to the land of her ancestors.

The autumn of 1975 duly found us settled in an imposing and gigantic (by English standards) terraced house in Kingsborough Gardens, in the West End of Glasgow. Muriel always had the main input when it came to our choice of houses, but I was happy to rely on her taste, and to be persuaded to agree with her selection! We were lucky to have congenial neighbours in Bill Rankin, a surgeon at a local hospital, and his wife Shirley. Bill, underneath a gruff exterior, was the kindest and friendliest of men when you got to know him, and Shirley was a marvellous conversationalist and writer whose long letters always kept us entertained while we were away. I often thought she could easily have made a living as the author of best-selling novels.

Unfortunately, our first nine months in Scotland proved financially disastrous when we fell between the house purchasing systems north and south of the Border. Having made an offer for the Glasgow house we were legally committed to it, and in the meantime the sale of our home in Bristol fell through, so we had a horrific bridging loan to cover for nearly a year. Be warned, anyone planning a move to the North!

After this difficult start, our fifteen years in Glasgow - the longest stay we ever had in one place – turned out to be very happy, productive and musically varied. We weren't strangers to this part of the world - Muriel's family connections meant we had been on frequent visits to see her relatives, and we had spent several holidays in Scotland. I had also made a few professional contacts, never suspecting how useful they would one day be. I had coached the Edinburgh Youth Orchestra on a number of occasions, and in 1972 I had become involved with the National Youth String Orchestra of Scotland. The NYSOS ran a large-scale Summer School for string players, consisting of a Senior Orchestra, a Junior Orchestra, and three other preparatory orchestras catering for younger children. These last, in order to avoid any implication of a pecking order, were given their own whimsical names, which I think were Troubadours, Cavaliers and Minnesingers. I remember meeting a rather tearful little girl on the first day of the course, clutching her child-sized violin and standing forlornly in the corridor.

"Please sir, I don't know where to go."

"Oh dear, I am sorry. Can you remember which orchestra you're in?"

"Please sir, I think I'm a Paratrooper."

The School was held initially in Aberdeenshire, and subsequently in various other locations. For several years it took place in Perth, where it benefited from the organisational skills of my good friend Henry Neil, a major musical figure in the area. Conductors of the Senior Orchestra included Bryden Thomson, Meredith Davies and John Currie. I was chief coach of strings for some time, and eventually took over the conductorship until we left Scotland on my retirement in 1990. Through this long association with the NYSOS I have been able to keep in touch with many eminent players, from their earliest childhood until their emergence as professional musicians.

I began work at the RSAMD in the autumn of 1975, in the old building, situated between the two parts of West George Street in what was shortly to be renamed as Nelson Mandela Place. For a brief history of the Academy I am grateful for permission to include this extract from their website:

The history of the Academy can be traced back to the creation of the Glasgow Athenaeum in 1847. The Athenaeum was established to 'provide a source of mental cultivation, moral improvement and delightful recreation to all classes' - in today's terminology, that would be described as a mission statement and it is one to which, even at this distance in time, today's Academy could happily subscribe. Notably, the Athenaeum's inaugural address was delivered by Charles Dickens - very appropriate given the great expectations of the far-sighted founding fathers (yes, they were all men) of that new and exciting institution.

From its inception, the Athenaeum offered classes in music and, in 1886, drama was introduced into its curriculum. Music proved to be so successful that, in 1890, a School of Music was formed as a discrete department of the Athenaeum, with its own Principal (Allan Macbeth, a graduate of the Leipzig Conservatorium) and its own prospectus of courses. It was from the Athenaeum's School of

Music that the Scottish National Academy of Music was formed in 1929. Building upon that very firm foundation, the new Academy of Music grew in prestige and, in 1944, its position as an Academy of international standing was recognized by King George VI, who approved that the prefix 'Royal' be added to the Academy's title, making it the 'Royal Scottish Academy of Music'. At that same time, the then Queen Elizabeth graciously assumed the role of Patron of the Academy, a role in which she continued as Queen Mother until her death in 2002.

These exciting developments were by no means confined to music. 1950 saw the creation in Glasgow of the College of Dramatic Art which had the very clear and focused aim of training actors and directors for the professional theatre. Very quickly however, the College's curriculum expanded to include technical courses and, in collaboration with the University of Glasgow, diploma courses with a strong academic element. In 1962, the College opened the first television studio to be located within a UK drama school - evidence of a pioneering spirit with which the present day Academy is still imbued.

It was in 1968 that the title of Royal Scottish Academy of Music and Drama was approved which, of course, reflected the happy union of music and drama in a single Academy, dedicated to excellence across the spectrum of the performing arts.

Throughout the 1970's and 1980's, the Academy continued to develop its course provision and enhance its international reputation. This period saw the introduction of the Academy's first degree courses which, at that time, were validated by the University of Glasgow. However, in session 1993/94, the Academy became the only UK Conservatoire to be awarded its own degree awarding powers by the Privy Council, a decision which followed an extensive review of the Academy's approach to the maintenance and promotion of the quality of its courses. The Academy is justifiably very proud of that wonderful achievement - particularly as the Academy remains to this day the only UK Conservatoire to have achieved that particular distinction. Following the achievement of degree awarding powers, all of the Academy's courses were up-graded to degree level and, over the intervening years, those courses have been refined to keep pace with the demands of the professions. New undergraduate and postgraduate courses have also been added to the Academy's portfolio so as to meet new and future needs. In session 2000/01, the Academy recruited its first research students which represents another key milestone in the Academy's development, particularly as the Academy's approach to research is, in itself, radical in that it is firmly practice-based.

The Academy's physical development has kept pace with its artistic and academic development. In session 1987/88, the Academy moved from its original Victorian home to the splendid custom built building it occupies today - the building having been opened formally by Her Majesty, Queen Elizabeth the Queen Mother in 1988. A mere ten years later, Dame Janet Baker opened the magnificent Alexander Gibson Opera School, which provides rehearsal and coaching rooms, together with a stunning performance space used by both music and drama students.

In 2003, HRH Prince Charles The Prince of Wales (or the Duke of Rothesay as he is known in Scotland) graciously accepted the Academy's invitation to succeed his grandmother as Patron of the Academy, thereby maintaining the Academy's royal patronage for over half a century.

We hope that you have enjoyed this very brief historical note. The Academy has come a long way since the 19th Century Athenaeum and is now a mature, confident and vibrant Conservatoire for the 21st Century with its doors wide open to the talented performers of the world.

I worked with three different Principals at the Academy. The first was Dr Kenneth Barritt. His immediate predecessor had been Henry Havergal, the first independent Principal. Historically the post had been held *ex officio* by the Professor of Music at Glasgow University, and the Academy had been little more than just one part of the University Music Department. Havergal, previously music master at Winchester School, virtually created the Academy as an independent institution, which would eventually exist on the same level as the three other royal British music education institutes, the RAM, the RCM in London and the RNCM in Manchester. Kenneth Barritt had been Director of Music under Havergal, and succeeded him as Principal on the latter's retirement shortly before I arrived.

As can be surmised from its name, both music and drama are taught at the Glasgow Academy. The Principal is invariably a musician, and under him are the Heads of Music and of Drama, who run more or less independent structures. Although this works quite well, as the two disciplines can interact and use each other's facilities, I often wished that there could be more cooperation between them. Performing musicians have also to be actors, and too many students are narrowly concerned with the nitty-gritty of playing their own particular instrument, forgetting that they have to project the music to the listeners - in other words to act it, to sell it.

In 1975, the Academy, while creatively vibrant and able to boast many illustrious figures among its alumni, was in terms of administration and accommodation still living in the past. The building, although characterful, was really quite unsuited to modern demands. Its main chamber, the Stevenson Hall, was a lovely, elegant room, with all the charm that goes with a great artistic tradition, but was big enough for only small ensemble recitals - a full orchestra filled the entire area of the stage and auditorium. Orchestral concerts had to take place in the Glasgow City Hall, a good mile away. Not only that, the Stevenson's large glass windows were not at all sound-proof, and in recital programmes, a beautiful pianissimo would often be completely wrecked by a police or ambulance siren passing by.

The Academy's sense of tradition was also evident in the abundance of august musical figures in its table of past teachers. When I arrived, the fabulous Horace Fellowes had just celebrated his hundredth birthday by giving a concert with his local admirers, at which he had played the Bach E major Violin Concerto with a string ensemble, and a selection of Kreisler violin solos. Horace had studied in Vienna, and had played for Brahms! On returning to England, he had been involved in founding the Buxton Music Festival, and had at one stage led an orchestra that was conducted by the father of Sir Thomas Beecham!

In my early years, I played the Mendelssohn Concerto with the Bournemouth Orchestra conducted by Charles Groves, and Horace was in the audience. We met after the concert and had a happy evening together. When I moved to Glasgow, my friend Jimmy Durrant said "Oh, you must go around to see Horace - he would love to see you and have a chat. But for goodness sake, don't tell him you have anything to do with the Academy. He's never forgiven them for making him retire twenty-five years ago when he turned seventy-five!"

Sadly, before I could make this appointment, Horace died. He wrote a marvellous account of his life in music, which regrettably is no longer available. Many people in Glasgow at that time remembered him for his enthusiasm, his remarkable playing, and his glowing personality and love of his students.

The legacy of "old school" icons like Horace is to be treasured, and I can't deny that I spent twelve happy years in the old building before it was replaced by a new "state of the art" complex in 1987/88. Indeed, many of us felt quite a pang at the time of the move. When I first arrived, the Academy was dominated by the forbidding presence of John (Jock) Scott, the Registrar, who ruled every aspect of the administration, and especially the expenditure, with a rod of iron. Every purchase was scrutinised with the greatest rigour. There was one photocopier in the main office, and any request for its use was usually refused, unless it was for something deemed absolutely essential.

There were of course no computers, and no telephones except in the office. To be a Head of Department didn't entitle you to any administrative equipment or any kind of job "perks". After his interview for the post of Head of Wind, a year or two before my arrival, my colleague, Edgar Williams, received a charming letter from Jock Scott:

"Dear Edgar, I am delighted that you are coming to join us in Scotland. I'm sure you will be very happy....with very best wishes.... yours, Jock."

Emboldened by this, Edgar wrote back in similarly friendly terms, concluding "By the way, as I shall be moving up from Bournemouth to Glasgow, I wonder if the Academy would be able to help me with the considerable expense involved?"

"Dear Mr Williams, " came back the reply. "On no account will the Academy make itself responsible for your removal expenses. Yours faithfully, J Scott."!

Obviously it was by no means all bad. We, as heads of the various departments, were relatively unencumbered with routine administration. Our concern was with the music, the students and the actual teaching. We were closer to our pupils, and were required to involve ourselves first and foremost in performance and teaching, by both precept and example. Nowadays, teaching staff, and especially departmental heads, spend far more time in meetings, writing reports and filling in forms than ever we did. I get the impression that administration is taking up more time, energy and funds than the actual teaching does, with constant rounds of upgrades to computer systems, office space and the organisation of teaching posts. 40 years ago we were managing quite well without all this paraphernalia - all you need to teach music is a room, a piano and a music stand! More and more teaching is undertaken by part-time staff, often on short term fixed contracts, while the numbers of full-time office staff and administrators seem to grow in inverse proportion. Music and drama are of course not the only fields of education affected by this malaise - my daughter Alison, who teaches art to University students, assures me that the same has happened in her discipline.

In 1977, David Lumsden was appointed as Principal. David did much to bring the Academy gradually into the modern age, while maintaining the best of the old traditions. He was closely associated with the planning and construction of the splendid new accommodation on Renfrew Street, although it was not completed until several years after he left in 1982 to be Principal of the RAM in London. Philip Ledger was Principal for the rest of my stay, and his forceful character brought the institution fully up to date. Philip presided over an impressive official opening of the new building in the presence of Queen Elizabeth the Queen Mother, our Patron for many years.

Head of Music was David Stone. Like me, David had attended the Academy in London, and studied the violin with Rowsby Woof, but he was much more of an all-round musician than I was, being an excellent pianist as well as a composer. His career had taken a very different direction from mine, into teaching, administration and producing music programmes at the BBC. He has also written some excellent elementary music for young string players, and a series of arrangements of well-known classical pieces playable by school orchestras. He obtained his post when Kenneth Barritt became Principal, and soon demonstrated that his administrative abilities were perfectly complemented by fine musicianship. I was deeply grateful for David's generous help in guiding me through the initial stages of the job.

At the time of my appointment, the other Heads of Departments were Wight Henderson, piano (always known as Jackie), Edgar Williams, woodwind, and David Kelly, singing. Other notable members of staff included Lawrence Glover, piano, and his violinist wife, Mabel. Lawrence was a pianist of sensitivity and stature. He had been a pupil of Gordon Green in Manchester at the same time as John Ogdon, and some said that Gordon valued Lawrence's talent the higher of the two. Lawrence became Head of Piano when Wight Henderson retired, but sadly developed a cancer that proved untreatable. The entire Scottish musical establishment attended his funeral, to mourn the premature death of a great pianist, musician and colleague.

Joan Dixon deserves special mention. Her sister, Hester, was also on the staff, teaching piano accompaniment, and the two were from an Edinburgh family that had been closely linked to Donald Tovey. Joan was a formidable figure, with a nation-wide reputation in string teaching. In 1975, she was teaching more or less full time at both the Scottish Academy and the RCM in London, which involved a punishing schedule of weekly train journeys.

In previous years, when based mainly in Scotland, Joan had worked very closely with Henry Havergal in establishing the RSAMD as a credible advanced conservatoire for music education. Although I was now the official Head of Strings, she still exercised a strongly proprietary role in the department, and was quick to question any decisions I might make. Although at times this could be irritating, I learned a lot from Joan. As a player, she was a founder member of the Edinburgh String Quartet, which still exists today after several transmogrifications. She was the original cellist in the Scottish Piano Quartet which I played in for several years with Jack Henderson, but by the time I got to know her she had virtually given up public performances, apart from occasional sonata recitals with Hester.

Our daughter, Jeanette, studied with Joan for three years at the RCM in London. She found that while Joan's teaching was excellent, it was closely geared to the lowest common denominator of her classes, and perhaps because Joan was not primarily a player herself, couldn't offer sufficient inspiration to the more talented students. It wasn't until later, in the course of her postgraduate studies under Amaryllis Fleming, that Jeanette was able to make the move to a higher level.

Jimmy Durrant, *doyen* of Scottish viola players, was one of my closest friends at the RSAMD. Although not Scottish by birth - like Edgar Williams he moved north from the Bournemouth Orchestra - he is a prominent bulwark of the Scottish musical scene. I had already met him as a fellow coach with the Edinburgh Youth Orchestra, so he and his wife Dawn, a terrific percussion player and an accomplished artist as well as mother of a fine family, were welcome friendly faces to guide me through a labyrinth of musical and social activities both within and outwith the Academy.

Jimmy was very straightforward and down to earth, and got on well with his students Like me, he was essentially an orchestral and chamber music player, although he was also a very capable soloist, commissioning many works for viola from Scottish composers. I could always count on his support against any teachers who denigrated orchestral playing as an inferior activity, and wanted all their students to perform concertos. Jimmy had led the violas in Bournemouth and in the Scottish National Orchestra, and knew the difference between a flashy operator able to rattle off a few showpieces, and the well schooled, all-round player who would be welcome in any ensemble.

I felt I was leaving the department in good hands when he took over my post on my retirement in 1990.

Before my arrival, the Academy's orchestra was conducted mainly by Kenneth Barritt. Kenneth, although he was a distinguished and knowledgeable musician, was not a natural conductor, and I made it a priority to bring in visiting conductors to do the main concerts. We were also often able to invite conductors who were already booked for appearances with the SNO or the BBC Scottish Symphony Orchestra to come in during the day and take the students in rehearsal.

On one occasion we managed to persuade Paavo Berglund, the Finnish maestro, to rehearse the orchestra in Sibelius's 2nd Symphony. Berglund had enjoyed a successful spell as chief conductor of the Bournemouth Orchestra. A former violinist, like all string-based musical directors he was particularly fussy about bowings, and although this was only a one-off morning session, he turned up with a complete set of his own parts, which he insisted we used. Berglund conducted left-handed, which was rather off-putting for the students, but his imposing physical presence commanded their respect, and they learned a lot that day.

He and I had never crossed paths professionally, and his manner when we met struck me as somewhat curt and unfriendly. He possibly thought I was one of those accursed administrators who might try to interfere with what he was doing! He began to warm slightly when he realised that I had been in orchestras, and when I mentioned that I had played in Helsinki with the Boyd Neel Orchestra in 1950 his eyes lit up. "Ha!" he roared – "Aha! Boyd Neel! I was at that concert. I was ten years old! It was very good! You played Handel's Concerto Grosso in D, Britten's Variations on Frank Bridge, Tschaikovsky's Serenade…." He went on to detail the whole programme, and after that, we were the best of friends!

Rudolf Barshai, the well-known Soviet violist who attained his greatest fame as conductor of the Moscow Chamber Orchestra, was another who rehearsed with the orchestra, and was a particular inspiration to the strings. Visitors who had full concert engagements with us included Meredith Davies, George Hurst and Christopher

Adey. Chris had been a violinist in my section when I was leading the second fiddles in the LPO, but was now branching out as a conductor. Very much at home working with young people, he gave some stunning performances at the Academy, and also later with the Scottish National Youth Orchestra, of which more anon.

There was one memorably stormy episode with George Hurst. George made no concessions to the age of his players. He demanded, and invariably got, absolute dedication and attention to the music. Every moment was important. I wouldn't have liked to be in the shoes of the unfortunate girl from the office who opened the door and came in with a list of names:

"Excuse me, Mr Hurst, but I've got to take these students out of your rehearsal for an hour or so - they are required for their end of term interviews."

George was incandescent. "How can I work with an incomplete orchestra? What is more important - music or an interview? Can I believe this!!!"

It took all my powers of persuasion to stop him storming out of the building and taking the first plane south!

During David Lumsden's reign, the Academy began to invite distinguished musicians as visiting teachers. This led to a happy relationship for me with the Alberni String Quartet, who became regular visitors as artists in residence. The quartet's leader Howard Davis and his wife, harpsichordist Virginia (Ginnie) Black, became close personal friends of ours, and often stayed in our house. The Alberni gave many outstanding public concerts at the Academy, and were all greatly respected by the students, both for their playing and their extensive experience in chamber music coaching. They had the enviable ability to find the right word at the right time, and bring out some point with a lightness of touch that would make it memorable.

Cellist David Smith had a particularly ready wit. At one lunchtime concert the quartet attended, the first item was a violin solo played by one of the best students I have ever had, Jane Murdoch. Jane went on to lead the Edinburgh Quartet for a time, and also led several other orchestras and chamber ensembles. The piece was the Habanera by the Spanish violinist, Pablo de Sarasate, which includes double-stopping, harmonics, left hand pizzicato - every possible flashy device in string technique. Jane played it in fine style and sent the audience into raptures. As the applause faded, Dave leaned over to me and whispered "Thank Christ he never wrote any string quartets!"

Chapter 26 - Other Activities in Scotland

As soon as my appointment in Scotland was announced, I was invited by John Currie to follow in the footsteps of Louis Carus, my predecessor at the Academy, and lead the small orchestra that accompanied his chamber choir in an annual series of concerts. It was a most enjoyable activity that lasted throughout our time in Glasgow. The members of the orchestra were all first-rate freelance instrumentalists, and all the singers in the hand-picked choir were capable of tackling solo concert roles. Especially memorable were the sopranos Pat McMahon, who has produced many fine singers as a teacher, both at the Academy and privately, and Irene Drummond, who worked often with Muriel.

The repertoire of the Singers' concerts was thoughtful and varied. We performed all the Masses and choral works of Haydn, which unlike some famous compositions of this kind contain some wonderful string writing. Indeed, I always used to contend that to play one of those great pieces was just as enjoyable as playing through three or four complete Haydn String Quartets, and nothing could be better than that! Haydn is often under-rated and taken for granted by musicians who seem to forget the sheer scale of his achievements, their variety and originality, and the unfailing wit and good humour of the music. If I were able to meet just one of the great classical composers, I would certainly choose him.

Among the standard choral items we tackled, John's Messiah, generally at Christmas but sometimes at Easter, was always lively and stimulating. Handel's masterpiece is always a pleasure to play, but the heavy-handed approach of some conductors can take the gilt off the gingerbread. The Singers also regularly commissioned modern compositions, so some of the concerts were pretty hard work!

For several years, John Currie was closely associated with the Perth Festival, and staged regular meticulously crafted productions of all the great Mozart operas. The orchestra was involved only during final rehearsals, just before the actual run of performances, but regular rehearsals started much earlier. This meant at least a couple of weeks' detailed and enjoyable work for Muriel, who played continuo for all the shows, using a fortepiano made for us by Lionel Gliori, a lavishly talented instrument maker based in Pencaitland near Edinburgh.

Lionel's astonishing output includes harpsichords, clavichords, violins, baroque violins and bows. He has an insatiable urge to know more about music and the making of music. He plays the violin, not as a professional, but as the best kind of amateur, with real passion. For a long time he had wanted to construct a fortepiano, so we offered to commission one. This was before such things became the vogue amongst early music *aficionados* - nowadays, you can buy kits of prefabricated parts, and assemble an instrument like this at home, as if buying it at IKEA. Lionel saw it differently. He wrote to the Smithsonian Institution in Washington DC and bought a blueprint of the 1784 Viennese Fortepiano by Johann Andreas Stein, complete in every detail. This was the instrument that Mozart loved, but from all accounts had not been able to afford.

Lionel's reproduction, constructed from the bare wood, was a thing of beauty, and had a responsive and beautiful tone colour. I had had a Richard Duke 18th century English violin, inherited from my father, converted back to its original baroque condition by the violin restorer Lambert Houniet, then living in Edinburgh but now returned to his native Holland. With these two instruments Muriel and I performed all the Mozart Violin Sonatas, and also many 18th century works by Scottish composers of the time.

The Stein fortepiano was a great success in the Mozart operas, both with the public and the critics. As an accompaniment to the recitatives, I am convinced that Mozart himself might have preferred it to the harpsichord, which produces a monochromatic sound with no variation of dynamics. The fortepiano is able to respond sensitively to changes of mood, and has a far greater expressive range.

1979 marked the inauguration of the National Youth Orchestra of Scotland, with a series of concerts in Falkirk, Aberdeen and Dundee. The seeds of this had been sown in 1976, when Edgar Williams and

I had both been involved in the early discussions. William Webb was in due course appointed Director, with Edgar and myself in charge of instrumental coaching.

The very first concert took place in Falkirk, where an enthusiastic orchestra of over 100 young musicians was conducted by Nicholas Braithwaite. The performance was in a gigantic marquee that had seen similar service with the Berlin Philharmonic. Unfortunately the day was blighted by a thunderstorm, followed by hours of torrential rain, and although the concert went ahead, there were several times when some of the violinists and a substantial section of the woodwind had to shift their seats to avoid a drenching. In the event, the dramatic weather conditions were actually an enhancement to the final item, Respighi's Pines of Rome. The balancing of the recorded song of the nightingale in the 3rd movement, *Pini del Gianicolo,* was problematic - if we played it at normal level it was drowned out by the sound of the rain on the roof, and if we turned it up too much it sounded like a demented starling! But the gradual crescendo and final brass outbursts of the 4th movement, *Pini della Via Appia,* were a triumph, and set the foundations of the excellent reputation the Orchestra still enjoys today.

Nowadays the organisation comprises several subdivisions, including preparatory ensembles and jazz groups, but in those days there were just two annual courses, each consisting of a concentrated rehearsal period followed by a tour of concerts. This followed the example of the National Youth Orchestra of Great Britain, except in one respect. We were limited to musicians with Scottish connections, and to compensate for our smaller catchment area we did admit Music College students.

An early member of the percussion section was Evelyn Glennie, a young schoolgirl from the Aberdeen area. I was amazed when Bill Webb said to me "You see that girl playing side drum in the percussion? She's completely deaf!" Before long, Evelyn gained an international reputation for her part in bringing percussion to front stage in the musical world. She did a tour with the Youth Orchestra, playing a percussion concerto specially written for her by John McLeod. The virtuosity of her playing is complemented by a winning personality that endears her to audiences. She lip-reads perfectly, and in her company it is easy to forget that she is indeed deaf.

Before we left Bristol, I had been approached by the North East of Scotland Music School, with the offer of doing some visiting teaching for them, based in Aberdeen. Following the discovery of oil in the North Sea, the Granite City had suddenly become a boom town with a rocketing economy. Glasgow and Edinburgh were too far for students to travel for specialist tuition, so the School was looking for higher level input to reinforce the work of local music teachers, and had already persuaded eminent teachers like Ifor James and Denis Matthews to come for one day, three times a term. The distance and expense were no problem, they said. I could drive to Heathrow, fly to Aberdeen, be teaching by 10 am, do a full day's work and be home in Bristol by late evening!

While discussions were still progressing, I had resigned from my Bristol post and joined the RSAMD. Now it was a different story. Someone only good enough to work for a home-grown institution couldn't possibly pass muster as an eminent visiting teacher. Instead the post was offered to Manny Hurwitz, who travelled up and down for a couple of terms before deciding it was too heavy a commitment in view of his busy London schedule. He wrote a letter of resignation, saying "Why don't you ask Peter Mountain; he's more or less on your doorstep?" I was approached again, and began a long and happy association with the School and its organiser and moving force, Dorothy Hately. The most warm-hearted of people, Dorothy met us off the train or plane, saw to our lunch, fixed all the last minute crises, looked after the pupils, and even put us up for the night if necessary. It was a sad loss for everyone who had been involved with the School when she developed a cancer and died in 1996.

For most of our time in Scotland I had a similar teaching commitment in Belfast at the Ulster School of Music, to which I was introduced by my colleague, the pianist Jackie Henderson. It was run by another remarkable woman, Daphne Bell, in a down at heel mansion just off the Belmont Road. Unlike Dorothy in Aberdeen, who might have been best described by that wonderful Scottish word "couthy", and in complete contrast to the shabby rooms and general air of make do and mend that we taught in, Daphne was flamboyant. Everything about her was extreme - her clothes, her hats, her general demeanour. But like Dorothy, she certainly got things going, and the whole concern would have fallen apart without her energy and drive.

Members of the Ulster Orchestra did some coaching for her, but Daphne loved her regular visitors - we were all Professors, and were always to be addressed as such. Daphne could smell out promising pupils, and there was a constant stream of talented children for us to teach. The main teaching room was named the Paul Barritt Room, in honour of one of the School's most successful former pupils. I knew Paul later as leader of the Northern Sinfonia, and he has led many other orchestras, including the Philharmonia, the ECO and the Hallé. He is unambivalent about Daphne's influence on his career. "If it wasn't for Daphne," he told me, "I wouldn't be playing the violin."

All this, of course, was at the height of the Troubles. People used to think I was mad to fly so often to Ireland, but I formed a warm regard for the local people, and had great respect for the work Daphne was doing. Although I did hear the occasional explosion, and there were various incidents from time to time, on the face of it people's lives seemed remarkably normal, and if anything the sense of community, in both an artistic and general sense, seemed to grow in adversity. Now and again, however, there was a stark reminder that the dangers were real enough. I used to stay the night regularly with parents of the pupils, and one family had a teenage daughter who had been out to a dance with a boy friend. He was walking back with her when two men came up to them. "Off you go home, girlie," they whispered. The boy was taken away down the dark streets and has never been seen since.

On a happier note, Easter in Scotland was marked by regular visits to Haddo House in Aberdeenshire, to lead the orchestra for a short opera season conducted by the Lady Aberdeen. Set in extensive and beautiful parkland, Haddo was the ancestral stately home of the Marquesses of Aberdeen. Behind the house itself there is a large edifice built from Canadian timber by a past Laird who was Governor General of Canada, and intended for use as a racquets court. In 1945 Lady Aberdeen and her husband David, the 4th Marquess, converted it into a concert hall and theatre, which developed into a highly successful venue for the Haddo House Choral and Operatic Society.

Until my arrival at the Academy Louis Carus had been leader, and I suspect he was reluctant to give up such an attractive engagement, so for a while we took turn about. Eventually however it became more convenient for me to take over, and I ended up playing at Haddo for about twenty years.

The Marquess died in 1974, so I never had the pleasure of meeting him. Lady Aberdeen, however, proved more than capable of keeping up the good work. As June Gordon, she had trained as a professional musician, and had a wide-ranging knowledge of choral music and opera. She quite unashamedly made full use of her influence and charm both to extract money from oil companies to fund her productions, and to persuade the great and good of the musical world to take part. Haddo's roll call over the years includes composers Ralph Vaughan Williams, Benjamin Britten, Michael Tippett and Peter Maxwell Davies, conductors Alexander Gibson and Charles Groves, and a galaxy of operatic stars like Heather Harper, Janet Baker and Pat McMahon. I played for one marvellous performance of Elgar's Gerontius with Janet Baker as the Angel, and on two occasions the annual opera was Britten's Peter Grimes, with Pat McMahon memorable in the role of Ellen.

The list of operas put on at Haddo is awesome - Turandot, Othello, Britten's Gloriana, Carmen and many more. One year the work chosen was Verdi's Macbeth, and after the last performance, in her charming speech that was always a fitting culmination to the week, June ventured to suggest that not many performances of Macbeth could have boasted the presence of the Thane of Cawdor in the audience. One less than she'd thought, as it happened - the Thane, a close neighbour, was not very musically inclined, and had gone home at the interval!

Muriel always came with me to Haddo, and helped by playing for rehearsals and coaching singers. The House was actually run by the National Trust, and June lived in just one wing, but during Opera week the whole place was commandeered. We were invariably allotted the Premier's Bedroom, an impressive chamber with a huge four-poster bed, which was situated at the far end of the building, next to the chapel and to a dressing room that was reputed to be haunted. We asked when the ghost was supposed to walk, and someone said it was usually about 3am. That night, Muriel woke up suddenly, nervously switched on the bedside lamp and glanced at the clock. It was exactly 3am! Luckily, however, my snoring was enough to deter any visitation!

It was like being honoured guests at a large and glittering house party. After opera rehearsals, all the main cast, chorus and orchestra would congregate in the enormous kitchen, where we traditionally had scrambled eggs and bacon, often cooked and served by the indefatigable June herself. She was the soul and essence of the place - many of the orchestra were well-known professionals who came up from London out of personal regard for her, although strictly speaking the terms of engagement might not have had the full approval of the Musicians' Union. This reserve of goodwill ensured that the standard of the performances was always of the highest.

It often happened that Muriel's birthday, on April 10th, fell during our stay at Haddo, and breakfast, in June's apartment with all the cast and helpers, would be a happy occasion with cards and presents. These were special times, and I miss them very much. Every Easter that comes round now reminds me of the house and its beautiful grounds, which I will always picture bathed in sunshine and awash with daffodils.

Chapter 27 - Scottish Composers

Throughout the Glasgow years Muriel and I were in close contact with a number of eminent Scottish composers. We formed a warm friendship with John McLeod and his pianist wife, Margaret. In 1982 the NYOS commissioned John to write an orchestral piece called The Gokstad Ship, which we premiered in Kirkwall, the main town of the Orkney Islands, and took on tour to the Faroe Islands, Bergen, Gothenburg and Copenhagen. During our stay in the Faroes we saw the stunning scenery of the islands at its best, with three days of uninterrupted sunshine and blue skies. Normal weather there is rain, mist and constant gloom. I chatted to a group of Faroese gentlemen, and asked if they got away on holiday very often. "Yes," they said. "Yes, we go on holiday. We go on holiday to Scotland. For the sun!"

The Gokstad Ship was inspired by the excavation of a Viking war vessel, and like all John's work was imaginative, colourful and popular with audiences. Three years later Muriel and I commissioned a violin and piano sonata from him. We also recorded a short item entitled The Song of Icarus, based on the Greek legend. By coincidence, Muriel and I had around the same time developed an interest in gliding, and spent a fortnight's holiday at the Scottish Gliding Centre near Loch Leven, by Kinross. It was great fun, but sadly we couldn't keep up our visits there due to pressures of work. Gliding is an absorbing pastime. There is nothing to equal the sensation of passing through the clouds without a sound, apart from the air in the wings and the rigging. And it's a very safe occupation - we never once looked like sharing the fate of Icarus!

We commissioned works from a number of other composers working in Scotland, and played them in both concerts and broadcasts. Frank Spedding (who succeeded David Stone as Director of Music at the Academy) wrote a Duo Elegiaco in two relatively short but intensely concentrated and concise movements. Frank was well known for his pointed wit. There was a special press conference one year at the Academy for the Scottish critics and the main Academy staff, as a prelude to the launch of an upcoming series of public recitals. One of these was to be given by the virtuoso tuba player John Fletcher (who died aged 46 in 1987), and the programme was to conclude, bizarrely enough, with an arrangement of Monti's Csárdás, the flashy gypsy violin solo that had helped get me out of the Marines. Malcom Rayment, the Glasgow Herald's music critic, looked puzzled when the piece was mentioned.

"Excuse me, could anyone please tell me - er - what IS Monti's Csárdás?"

"He's led a very sheltered life!" said Frank to me *sotto voce*.

We commissioned work from chamber music specialist David Dorward, a music producer at the BBC, and from John Purser, who is also an author and has produced a fine historical survey of the BBC Scottish Symphony Orchestra. One of John's most notable achievements was the production of a series of conjectural musical instruments and their music for the archaeological museum at Kilmartin, south of Oban on the west coast of Scotland, an area rich in prehistoric remains.

Janet Beat, a teacher at the Academy, was a composer whose work we knew well. She had a particular interest in electronic music, and although the music we played was purely acoustic, it often showed a predilection for unusual effects. The violin and piano piece we played most often was her first sonata After Reading Lessons of the War, inspired by a Wilfred Owen poem. It contains some grotesque and disturbing music, much of it very difficult to perform. Muriel, although well able to get round the more conventional passagework in the piano part, was not entirely comfortable with some of the things Janet asked her to do, which at one point included standing up and plucking the strings inside the piano.

Janet fixed us up with an unforgettable engagement playing this piece. She had a friend who taught composition in the Athens Music Conservatoire, and also ran a contemporary music festival on the volcanic Greek island of Santorini. In the summer of 1983 we were asked to give a recital there. We were paid no fee, but we did get our air fares and free accommodation for ten days on the island, which left us at liberty to enjoy a marvellous holiday once we had done the concert. The scenery was out of this world, with the core of the original volcano still smouldering, spectacular cliffs plunging into the deep blue sea, startling black volcanic beaches, and a fascinating range of ancient Aegean ruins. Janet was inspired by the place, and as well as taking some excellent photos, wrote an evocative short duo for us called Aegean Nocturne, which we broadcast on the BBC in November 1985.

The *doyen* of Scottish composers at that time was the American born Thomas Wilson, who was at the centre of the renaissance of Scottish music in the 20th century. We played his Violin Sonata on several occasions. His opera Confessions of a Justified Sinner, commissioned by Scottish Opera, was his largest work, and was a great success when premiered under the baton of Norman Del Mar. I myself conducted Tom's beautiful St Kentigern Suite, which draws to telling effect on Scottish myth and legend, both at the Academy and with the NYSOS.

Kenneth Leighton, brought up in Wakefield and a Yorkshireman like me, was another composer not born in the country whose work often explored Scottish themes. Kenneth was Professor of Music at Edinburgh University when I arrived in Glasgow, but I had already worked with him several years before in Liverpool, which he visited twice to perform his own piano concertos. Although primarily a composer, he was also a gifted pianist. He and I were once asked to play at a party together, and he suggested that we do the Elgar Sonata, which at that time I did not know well. His convincing interpretation persuaded me for the first time that the work was a masterpiece. Muriel and I often played his Metamorphosis, a set of variations for violin and piano. He also wrote an opera, Columba, which was staged at the RSAMD. The music is very fine, although somewhat lacking in dramatic continuity - it is really a set of *tableaux* illustrating different events in St Columba's life.

Contact with all these people led me into membership of the Scottish Society of Composers, which welcomed interested musicians even if they didn't actually compose. Eventually I was elected chairman, and made use of my position to encourage a greater number of my playing colleagues to join and lend the Society their support. Composers have a hard struggle to promote their work, and I was glad to help in any way possible. I was also able to exert some influence on the promotion of new music when I served a three year term on the Music Committee of the Scottish Arts Council.

Chapter 28 - Living in Scotland

A major bonus of living in Scotland was to be near our elder daughter Alison, who has made her home there since 1981, presenting us with three lovely grandchildren, all boys. Alison is the only one of our three offspring who has not gone into music. This by no means implies a lack of musical ability - she learned the piano from Muriel and the violin from me, and in home chamber music often played the viola, with a rich, natural tone quality. However, Ali was always a bit of a perfectionist, and possibly she didn't want to be compared with her Mum and Dad, either for better or for worse, so she branched out into the visual arts, where she found her own vocation.

Where her talent for this came from I have no idea - neither Muriel nor I had any gifts in this direction. My Mum used to produce charming little atmospheric water-colours when we were on holiday, and Dad used to do meticulous pen and ink drawings, but Alison has always done work showing real flair and imagination. She gained a degree from Leeds University and went on to study at the Slade School of Art and the University of Dundee. Since then she has run her own art studio and developed into an outstanding teacher. It was always a joy to visit her family on our trips up North, initially in Midlothian, then in Arbroath, and most recently at her delightful cottage in the North Fife village of Newburgh, with its idyllic views over the Tay estuary.

The year before Alison moved to Scotland we sold our Kingsborough Gardens house and bought a spacious maisonette at 2 Kew Terrace, just along from the Grosvenor Hotel opposite the Botanical Gardens on the Great Western Road. This was an elegant dwelling with well-proportioned and impressive rooms, and we were very happy in it for ten years. Constructed in the early nineteenth century, it was the upper half of a former four storey town house, with a street level entrance hall and a private stairway leading to the accommodation. The top floor had a large space that we would use as a music room, but also contained a full sized snooker table. Both Muriel and I always had a weakness for watching snooker on the television, but having a proper table to play on made us realise just how difficult and frustrating a game it is, if like us you have no talent for it!

Two related coincidences convinced me we were destined to live in Kew Terrace. The seller was a Glasgow solicitor named Lodge. When he heard we were musicians, he revealed that his father had been Herbert Lodge, conductor of the seaside orchestra at Margate and later at Worthing. I was able to tell him that in my early days as a freelance player in London, I had done late-night light music programmes with a little orchestra conducted by "Bertie" Lodge. I remembered him as a sensitive director who arranged a lot of pieces for small ensembles, including the cleverly titled Tunelandia. His band, which went under the name of the Worthing Municipal Orchestra, had broadcast regularly from 11pm to midnight on the BBC Light Programme.

Then, even more remarkably, Mr Lodge said that he had bought the premises from a musician - a violinist named Peter Gibbs.

Peter and I had more or less parallel careers. He was in the LSO and had his own quartet, while I was in the Philharmonia and doing chamber music. We never met, but I often heard about him from mutual friends. He was a little older than me, and had been a fighter pilot in the war. He had a reputation as a daredevil, and a man who called a spade a spade, and this was borne out by his playing when I heard him on the radio - forthright and direct, if slightly lacking in refinement. On my resignation from the Philharmonia in May 1955, he was offered my place and went with the orchestra that summer on their tour of the USA with Karajan. Towards the end of this trip something happened that sent shock waves through the musical universe. Obviously I was not there, but I had a detailed word-for-word account of it from Manoug, who was leading at the time. In those days all orchestral concerts were by convention preceded by the National Anthem. During the tour, Karajan had made a practice of playing just the first couple of lines of God Save the Queen, and rattling it off at a wholly inappropriate speed, which many people thought was perfunctory and disrespectful. Then one day, when the orchestra had been called for a seating rehearsal, a lone figure stood up at the 4th desk of violins as Karajan raised his baton to begin.

"Mr Karajan, before we start, I would just like to tell you that many of my colleagues and also various friends in the audiences here, take exception to the disrespectful way in which you have performed our National Anthem during this tour."

There was a stunned silence before Karajan spoke. "What does he say? I do not understand." He then stepped down from the podium and left the stage.

After several minutes, Walter Legge appeared. "Ladies and Gentlemen, I have to tell you that Maestro Karajan will not conduct tonight if that man who spoke is in the orchestra."

The reply from Dennis Brain and Gareth Morris was instantaneous. "Well, if he doesn't play, neither will we!"

I don't know the details of the negotiations that followed, but the concert went ahead, and Peter played in it. There is no doubt that this incident spelled the end of the special relationship between Karajan and the Philharmonia. People had for a long time been divided about his merits - many thought his performances, though technically excellent, lacked sincerity - and there was unrest about the fact that he had voluntarily joined the Nazi Party in Germany before the War. Indeed, it was sometimes reported that Peter finished his little speech by saying "And in any case, I used to shoot down bastards like you during the war!" Manoug assured me however that there was no truth in this mischievous rumour.

Peter was a man who took risks all his life. Rodney Friend told me he used to sit with him on the second desk of the LSO. He often gave Peter a lift to concerts, and once, on the way to an Albert Hall engagement, they hit solid southbound traffic on the north side of Hyde Park, at the height of the evening rush hour.

"God!" said Rodney. "We're going to be late!"

"Move over," said Peter. "Let me drive."

He took the wheel, crossed into the right hand carriageway, which was completely empty, sped through the Park and across Kensington

Gore with the lights at red, and parked nonchalantly outside the Artists' Entrance.

Peter was appointed leader of the BBC Scottish Symphony Orchestra during the conductorship of Norman Del Mar. None of his colleagues there who remember him can speak too highly of his ability, although I suspect Norman found him pretty difficult to handle. During this time he used his talents in property dealing to make a lot of money. He bought the Kew Terrace house and converted it into two properties, selling it only when he returned to London.

While in Glasgow he kept a small plane that he used to fly for pleasure, sometimes in the company of friends like Morrison Dunbar, a prominent businessman and a moving spirit in Glaswegian musical affairs. Morrison was a keen violinist, and at one stage owned the Alard Stradivarius violin, which I was lucky enough to be allowed to play. He accepted Peter's invitation only once. They flew from Glasgow airport over Loch Lomond and the Trossachs, and it immediately became clear that Peter was navigating solely by means of a small AA Handbook. When he got lost, he would fly down and take a quick look at the road signs!

Peter's sense of adventure was eventually to be his undoing. After he left Scotland, he came back for a visit with a girlfriend to spend Christmas on the Isle of Mull. They flew north, and landed on a small airstrip on the beach close to the hotel. Before too long he got bored, and decided one dark evening to take the plane up for a spin. He wasn't seen again until six months later, when a shepherd found his body propped up against a tree in a remote valley a few hundred yards from the shore. It was thought that he had crashed more or less straight after take off at low tide, and struggled ashore only to die of exposure. The tide had then come in and carried the plane out to sea. As recently as May 2006 I was on holiday in the Hebrides, and read in the Oban paper that the wreckage had only just then been washed ashore.

This intriguing story was the subject of a TV documentary some years ago, and we were certainly familiar with it at the time when we bought Kew Terrace. One day while we were still settling in, I was rummaging in a large dark cupboard which it seemed Mr Lodge had not fully explored, and unearthed a tin box, full of strings, violin pegs, bridges and resin - all sorts of violin paraphernalia. It gave me quite a shock - it felt as if the ghost of Peter Gibbs had come back to haunt me!

During our time in Scotland we travelled extensively around the country, both for professional reasons and on holiday. Muriel used to say with some truth that we knew more of Scotland than many native Scots, who tend not to follow the example of my Faroese friends, but to go much further south for their sun! We enjoyed motor-caravanning, and Scotland is ideal for this. We must have driven thousands of miles, from Dumfriesshire and Kirkcudbrightshire up to Cape Wrath and John of Groats, and even beyond to the Orkneys.

As far back as 1937, our family had begun a tradition of spending annual holidays in a rented hut on a tiny farm near Dalbeattie called Aikieslack, which we were told means Fairies' Glen. The farmer was Jim McLure, who had also farmed in the Falklands and had at one time been a sailor, before settling down with his wife and twin adopted daughters Mary and Martha. We had a wonderful time, bathing on the Solway coast and exploring the Galloway countryside. Visitors to Scotland often overlook this area, preferring to go straight up to Glasgow and Edinburgh before moving on to what is generally considered the real Scotland. One of my favourite novels as a teenager was set in the Solway Firth and Galloway hills - S R Crockett's The Raiders (1894), a good old-fashioned adventure story about gypsies and pirates. I must read it again.

It was in our little holiday hut that we listened to Neville Chamberlain announcing the outbreak of war with Germany on September 3rd 1939. It so happened that both my sister Kath and I had been stricken with a severe stomach bug, and had been told by the doctor that we shouldn't be moved, so for us the war started with a week of convalescence in Scotland. I was still only 15, so I had another year of school and one more summer holiday in Galloway before starting my Academy days in London. After that, I lost contact with the McLures, until almost 20 years later when I was living in Liverpool with a family of my own. Kath had kept in touch, and knew that Jim's wife and Mary had sadly died. Jim and Martha were in good health, however, and I enjoyed going back to Aikieslack to renew our acquaintance. Jim seemed little diminished by the years, and his weathered, lean visage looked exactly as I remembered it. Another 50 years have passed now, bringing their own changes. But the farm is still there, Martha still looks after it, and I still go back from time to time to rediscover one of the most magical places of my youth.

Another special relationship was with the Orkney Islands. Not that long after moving to Glasgow, we were engaged to give a recital with Irene Drummond and Frank Carroll (both members of the John Currie Singers), in the main seaport, Stromness. The reputation of the Orkney Festival of Music was growing, on the back of interest in local hero Peter Maxwell Davies, and the Scottish Arts Council had recently recognised this by installing a fine concert grand Steinway piano in the town's Museum building. In doing this they had unwittingly started a bitter controversy. Kirkwall, as the largest town in the Islands, was convinced that it should have had the piano, and Stromness, in a bid to justify the SAC's decision, had quickly instigated a series of concerts designed to showpiece the instrument in the Museum's admittedly attractive modern ambience. The piano had been chosen by Miles Coverdale, piano professor at the RSAMD, who was just about to retire. Having sold his Glasgow home, he was living in the top part of our house in Kingsborough Gardens.

Miles was invited to perform at the opening concert, and chose to give a recital with another Academy colleague, the violinist Jurgen Hess. They prepared an attractive programme and flew up on the appointed day from Glasgow, but as often happens in that part of the world, the *haar* came down. This is a thick impenetrable mist that extends down the eastern seaboard of the far north of Scotland. The mainland is not usually much affected, but the sea and the islands are totally veiled, making flying impossible, sometimes for several days at a time - I have been a victim myself on more than one occasion. Miles and Jurgen's plane circled round a few times, and was then ordered back to Glasgow. The programme had to be cancelled, and our concert a few weeks later became by default the opening ceremony, so it was Muriel who struck the first official notes on the Steinway!

We were put up for the night by a couple living in Kirkwall, Stewart and May Walker, and as sometimes happens, immediately struck up a friendship, as if we had known each other all our lives. The couple are great supporters of the Festival - they both love music, and enjoy entertaining visiting artists. That was my first trip to Orkney, but I returned there many times for various music courses and concerts, and always stayed with Stewart and May. It was thanks to them that I got to know all the famous landmarks of the Islands - the Ring of Brognar, Skara Brae, the Churchill Barrier at Scapa Flow and the extraordinary Italian Chapel, built by Italian prisoners of war out of two Nissen huts.

Actually, Muriel had been to Orkney before me, as she had done a wartime CEMA tour for the Navy, playing on battleships anchored in Scapa Flow, the natural anchorage where the German Fleet was scuttled after the World War 1 in 1919. Fortunately, Muriel was not there in the early days of World War 2, when on October 14th 1939 an enterprising U-boat commander sneaked in through the defences and sank the battleship HMS Royal Oak with the loss of over 800 lives - the first serious reverse suffered by Britain against the Nazis. Winston Churchill was then First Lord of the Admiralty, and is recorded as expressing grudging admiration of the German navy for its daring. The building of the Churchill Barriers after the event is a classic example of barring the henhouse door after the fox has been and gone.

On some of our visits to Orkney, we were able to attend events in the Music Festival. I was sorry not to be there when Isaac Stern played Maxwell Davies's Violin Concerto, but I attended many other memorable concerts in Kirkwall's beautiful St Magnus Cathedral. In 1977 I was in the audience there for the same composer's Martyrdom of St Magnus, and was so impressed that I also managed to attend the subsequent performances in Aberdeen's St Andrew's Cathedral and Glasgow Cathedral, all in the space of a week. I have not always been in complete sympathy with Maxwell Davies's music, but his dramatic works are undeniably arresting, in particular The Lighthouse, which

I heard in Kirkwall in 1979. This is based on the true story of the disappearance of three keepers from a lighthouse in the Flannan Islands in the Outer Hebrides. The three male solo singers take the parts of the keepers, and also appear as members of the Court of Enquiry in Edinburgh. The writing and orchestration are strikingly imaginative, and include a virtuoso solo horn part designed to be played from the back of the auditorium.

There must have been something about the Scottish islands that particularly resonated with Muriel and me. We were always fascinated by the Hebrides, and one of our favourite spots was the isle of Staffa, the site of Fingal's Cave, made famous by the music of Mendelssohn. Other times that linger in the mind are the moving Easter service in the Cathedral on Iona which we attended in 2002, and an "island-hopping" holiday by car and ferry which took in the whole of the Outer Hebrides.

We both loved Skye and Mull, and the very last holiday we spent together, in the spring of 2004, was on the beautiful island of Islay. I am always grateful that Muriel was able to enjoy life to the full so close to her death only a few weeks later.

She was a true Scot.

BOOK 4

Chapter 29 - Yorkshire

The time arrived when I was obliged to retire from the RSAMD. My 65th birthday fell in October 1988, but I was allowed to complete the full academic year, so my employment actually ended after the summer term of 1989. It was a reluctant parting for many reasons. Muriel and I both felt full of energy, and were happy and settled working in our different spheres. We had noticed no significant decline in our abilities, and the wealth of experience we had built up over the years had honed our professional judgement and instincts for making the right decisions. A mandatory retirement age seemed pointless to me - better, surely, to consider every case on its merits. There was however no possibility of bending the rules - they were in effect a government directive for full-time employees, and that was that.

We thought long and hard about the best thing to do. I didn't relish the thought of staying in the same environment, possibly teaching part-time and doing a bit of playing. Watching my successors taking over my duties would feel like a path of gradual decline - it would be upsetting if they didn't do it as well, and if they did it better, that might be even worse! Muriel, being entirely freelance, didn't have the same issues, but she appreciated my feelings. We both liked the idea of starting a new, final chapter of our lives in different surroundings.

Having made this decision, we had to make another choice. We could opt for a complete break, with a move to some long-admired beauty spot, perhaps to the sun of France or Spain. Or we could return to our roots and start work afresh - not as intensely as before, but with different activities to keep us motivated.

It didn't take long to make the decision. We had seen a number of friends and acquaintances take the former path, but however rosily they painted their life-style, we couldn't escape the suspicion that this concealed a feeling of frustration. We knew we would never want to give up music, no matter how attractive the surroundings.

On to the next step. My family and musical roots were in Yorkshire, and Muriel's were in Coventry. Again, it wasn't too hard to choose. Although she had been brought up in the Midland city, Muriel had never had strong musical associations with it, and the damage done during the war had left it a different place with a lot of unhappy memories. On the other hand, we had spent many holidays in Yorkshire, and Muriel had developed a passion for the Dales almost as strong as my own. I still had family in the area - my sister Kath was now settled in the North Yorkshire village of Fearby and very active in her teaching, while our son Paul was living in the pretty hamlet of Huby, near Harrogate, with his partner the cellist Carol Yeadon.

On a wild and windy day, December 20th 1988, we drove down to Yorkshire to stay with Kath and spend a few days looking around estate agents. Bingley was the first place we looked at, as Dad had been born there, but in the event we didn't finalize anything, and it was Kath who later found the comfortable Victorian terraced house in Park Road that we eventually bought. The reason I mention this specific date is that on the way south from Glasgow we passed the little town of Lockerbie, which the very next day would achieve an unwanted place in history when a terrorist bomb on Pan Am Flight 103 sent the plane crashing into the town, with the loss of 270 lives. As we drove back to Scotland for Christmas, the wreckage from the atrocity was all too visible on either side of the M74 motorway. It was a dreadful, chilling sight that I will never forget.

Over the next two months, we sold Kew Terrace and finalised the purchase of the new house in Bingley. I had to complete my year at the Academy, but Muriel preceded me and began the long job of getting things organised, while I stayed with friends in Glasgow. By the summer I was free, and we both soon settled into what was to prove a happy and fulfilling environment for the next fourteen years.

We began to build up a clientèle of private pupils, much as my parents had done in the same area. I was also asked to become Head of Strings for the Bradford Music Service, doing some peripatetic work in schools and supervising the teaching already taking place. I was reminded that it was not so very long - perhaps 20 years - since my Dad had been doing similar work, when I went for the first time to a school in nearby Baildon, entered the front office, and called out "Hello. Anyone there?"

Back came a voice from the next room. "Hello Mr Mountain."

"How did you know my name?" I asked the secretary as she came through.

"Oh, you sound just like your father!"

Muriel and I often wondered what my parents' reaction would have been had they known we would eventually take on their work. We decided they would have liked the idea, which gave us a lot of pleasure.

Although we were busy, we made sure it wasn't to the exclusion of relaxation. We travelled extensively, including visits to France, Cyprus, Italy, Spain, Jugoslavia, the USA, Canada, Egypt, and, particularly memorably, China. Most of these trips were relatively trouble free, but in retrospect there were probably undercurrents in some places that we weren't aware of at the time. In Egypt, when staying in Luxor, we joined a trip to the Temple of Queen Hatchepsut, which in 1997 was to witness the brutal massacre of 58 tourists, gunned down at point-blank range by extremists. Nowadays we are getting used to the idea that these things can happen anywhere, but it is difficult to relate our peaceful walk in bright sunshine to the horror which enveloped a very similar group of tourists just a couple of years later.

In the then country of Jugoslavia we went touring with a hired car, beginning in Lake Bled and continuing down to the Croatian coast. In the seaside town of Rovinji we had a puncture, and went to a garage for repair. The proprietor spoke good English.

"You do know you've got a car with Serbian registration?"

"Yes, we picked it up at the beginning of our holiday in Slovenia. Why do you ask?"

"Well, people from that area aren't too popular round here. Just don't leave it parked in quiet or secluded places, or there's a chance you could get your tyres slashed!"

"Oh. That sounds a bit worrying."

"No, don't worry, just take a bit of care."

"So, do you think this could erupt into real trouble?"

"No, no, it's only local prejudice. People are far too sensible to let it get out of hand."

Within eighteen months he was proved disastrously wrong, as the country plunged into a bloody conflict that would culminate in the emergence of the new Balkan states.

Chapter 30 - Teaching

I had many talented young pupils in Yorkshire, and it would not be possible to mention them all, but there are several who bear special mention. When I first started as Head of Strings in Bradford, I heard rumours of a remarkable seven year old Chinese boy who was attending a primary school in the city. I went along to hear him playing on a half size violin, and was amazed by his natural talent. His name was Yi Bo. His parents had recently arrived from Shanghai - his father was a scientist and had been awarded a fellowship to work and study at Bradford University as a chemical engineer. They had very little money, and though the boy had had lessons for two or three years in China, he desperately needed help and direction to maintain his interest and progress. Norman Wells, the then head of the Music Service, managed to have him considered as a special case, and I was able to start giving him lessons.

Yi Bo was a joy to teach, and improved at an incredible rate. He used to come along to the String School that ran on Saturday mornings in a local school. Despite his natural gifts, his reading of music was at that stage fairly elementary, so I put him at the back of the second violins in the string orchestra to gain some experience. From time to time this had a disruptive effect. If he made a slight mistake, instead of just carrying on and keeping up with the others, he would feel compelled to go back and put it right, which meant that the music was continually interrupted by this clear firm-toned contribution repeating what the others had just played!

Yi Bo's parents were charming. They had complied with the Chinese government's regulation permitting only one child per family, so Yi Bo had no brothers or sisters, but he had a very open personality and mixed easily with other children. In some ways he was a typical little boy, full of mischief. His home life, however, was firmly disciplined, and his mother, who herself played the violin, was devoted to organising his practice, and always sat in on his lessons.

In Shanghai, Yi Bo had attended one of the many so-called Children's Palaces. School time in China begins in the early morning and finishes at 1pm. In the afternoon, children attend these Palaces, where they choose from a wide variety of non-academic instruction. When we later visited Shanghai on our Chinese holiday, we were taken to see one such institution, where the classes included instrumental music, string orchestra, ballet, calligraphy and embroidery. Every room was full, and there was absolute attention to the work in hand. None of the children was at all distracted by the entry of the foreign visitors, and we were impressed to observe that although the less able pupils were not neglected, the ones with talent were allowed to shine.

The string teaching was quite mechanical, with the orchestra, all violins with a plonky piano accompaniment, rattling through a *pot pourri* of popular classical tunes, from Mozart's Eine Kleine Nachtmusik to Schubert's Marche Militaire. It was all learned by rote, so there was minimal reading ability, and the dynamics were flat and unvarying, but on the other hand they stood up well, bowed with gusto and freedom, and were getting off to a good basic start with few bad habits that might need to be eradicated later. I assumed that teachers from more advanced music schools would come round from time to time and pick out the children who showed real potential.

Yi Bo's mother told me that when in Shanghai he had been taught by a prominent violinist from the Shanghai Symphony Orchestra. It is remarkable that so soon after the repressions of the Cultural Revolution, which began to ease only in the 70s, there was such active encouragement for many art forms previously considered unsound, including Western music in all its manifestations. In 1979 the film From Mao to Mozart, starring Isaac Stern, depicted the great violinist meeting some very gifted young Chinese players, and Howard Davis, leader of the Alberni Quartet, told me how amazed they had been by the level of talent in the Music Schools on their visit to China about the same time.

Even earlier, in 1973, the LPO visited China on a ground-breaking cultural exchange, which was captured on video. The conductor was John Pritchard, and I remember watching the BBC broadcast with great interest. One sequence showed a public rehearsal in front of a large audience of officials in their uniforms and peaked caps, with John addressing them through an interpreter.

"Now, I would like you to tell the audience that we are going to play a piece of music written by a modern Chinese composer."

The translation was followed by polite applause.

"And I would like you kindly to tell them that this Orchestra has not previously played or even seen this particular work, so it will show them the incredible sight-reading ability of a great Western musical ensemble."

A rather more lengthy translation, followed by enthusiastic applause.

"Come on chaps," said John to the orchestra with a wicked smile. "Don't let me down!"

It is interesting that players of Asian origin have in relatively recent years claimed so much success as musical performers, particularly on string instruments. When I was young, it was the Jewish violinists that we all looked up to - Kreisler, Elman, Heifetz, Menuhin, Oistrakh, Milstein, Stern, the list is endless. Arthur Kaye used to say that Jewish students would always work better than Gentiles - they were less likely to be upset by criticism, and drew inspiration from the expressive singing of the Cantor in the course of religious services. To an extent this may still be true, but nowadays orchestras all over the world seem to be full of talented and attractive young Oriental ladies who have embraced the European musical tradition, and there are string soloists too numerous to mention.

What is the reason for this? For one thing, both Jewish and Asiatic children often have more disciplined and controlling family backgrounds than is usually the case in our more permissive Western society. The Suzuki method, originated by Shinichi Suzuki in Japan and now practised worldwide with its appealing subtitle Nurtured by Love, has had great success, but depends largely on parental cooperation, and is markedly less popular in the West. Secondly, I believe that many Eastern instrumentalists are favoured by the same flexible physical build and high level of physical coordination that have led Asiatic players to do well in racquet sports like squash and badminton. Thirdly, there is often a more focused and motivated approach towards whatever tasks are to be undertaken, because preconceived cultural notions are not allowed to stand in the way. Many students are daunted by requests to play in the higher positions on the violin, but Yi Bo would go up and down the fingerboard without fear. "What's the difference?" he seemed to be saying. "I can put my fingers and bow wherever I like!"

Yi Bo studied with me for about seven years. He gave a memorable performance of the Bruch G minor Concerto with my Youth Orchestra, and was an inspiration to many other students. However, it eventually became evident that he needed the stimulation of a more complete musical environment, and we arranged for him to audition for the Yehudi Menuhin Music School in Surrey. Founded in 1963, the school allows children with exceptional musical potential to attend regardless of their financial means. Yi Bo was selected, and began life as a resident there soon after.

I have always had mixed feelings about these specialised schools for talented children. On the one hand, people with a strong natural inclination for a particular activity can be frustrated by the lack of opportunity to exercise their talents in a "normal" environment. On the other, the rarefied habitat of a special school can lead to a feeling of being coerced, and some children rebel against this, the more so if they are the strong, stubborn characters that so many gifted youngsters seem to be.

I don't know how much this applied in Yi Bo's case. We kept in touch for a long time, and he often came back to stay with us. He had a successful time at the School, leading the orchestra, playing recitals and concertos, and memorably performing the Bach Concerto for Two Violins with Menuhin himself at a concert in Paris. He obtained top A Level results, going on to study Economics at Cambridge, and while he was there participated fully in musical life at the University, playing a lot of chamber music about which he often asked my advice. However, the latest I have heard from him is that he has virtually given up the violin, and is now a whizz kid in the City, where his lively mind will no doubt ensure for him a much higher financial reward than the violin ever could. Is that a good thing? I really don't know.

Another remarkable pupil I had was Rachel Higginson. With two musical parents, she was well placed to succeed in music. I taught her both the violin and the viola, on both of which she obtained distinctions in the Grade 8 Associated Board Examinations. She had obtained the same results on the flute, trumpet and piano.

"Rachel," I once asked her, "with all your musical activity, and your school work, which I understand is very good, do you have time for general reading?"

"Oh yes" she replied, "I generally manage to read a book a day!"

She must have had the same kind of ability as Lord Byron, who could apparently just glance at a page of prose and commit it instantly to his memory. Again, however, exceptional musical ability has not produced a corresponding musical career. Rachel is now a very successful dentist!

Finally, I must mention Adam Robinson. His mother Sally was a talented violinist, as well as a gifted violin maker and entrepreneur (or "fixer") who organised many local ensembles, including the Bradford Chamber Orchestra, which she invited me to lead. I first came across Adam in his primary school. He had some knowledge of the violin, but had not been strongly encouraged to develop it because he had good all round academic ability and his mother thought he shouldn't limit his future choices. When I started to teach him he was 11 years old, and a virtual beginner. That is a seriously late start for anyone aiming for professional standards on a string instrument, but Adam has the most important attribute of all, which is determination. His playing has meaning and a sense of purpose, and he also has considerable personal charm and organisational ability. It was always Adam who would fix rehearsals for quartets, make sure everyone turned up and generally keep things together. It was a pleasure to work with him, and I was delighted when he continued his studies at my old stamping ground, the RSAMD. He is now a successful professional violinist.

For several years I conducted the Bradford Youth Orchestra, giving regular concerts in various local venues. It was managed by my friend, pianist John Abbey who set up an exchange with a similar organisation in Jena. Their orchestra came to play in Bradford, and we followed this with a visit to their city, which had been part of communist East Germany. We were made very welcome, and had a most interesting time. Jena is the home of the Carl Zeiss optical works, and has a marvellous planetarium, which is open to the public. The town is pleasantly laid out, with a fine University and good municipal buildings, but while we were there practically every street was clogged with roadworks, as it had become necessary to renew all the water mains, sewers, electricity cables and gas pipes - practically the entire infrastructure - which had been completely neglected during the communist years. We walked up the hill behind the city to view the site of the Battle of Jena, fought on14th October 1806 between the forces of Napoleon Bonaparte and the Prussian Army, which was defeated with heavy casualties.

One of the places we visited nearby was Eisenach, the birthplace of J S Bach. Like many other historic German towns, this was badly damaged during the war, and no one can be certain that the immaculately restored building we were shown round is the exact one where the composer was born. It did however house a fine exhibition of the kind of instruments that Bach would have been familiar with, and we heard some short live recitals by the staff.

We also visited Weimar, well known for *inter alia* its association with Liszt, Goethe and Schiller. The two great writers are celebrated by a famous sculpture in the centre of the city. Our hosts told us that Goethe had been quite a short man, while Schiller was apparently over six feet tall. The artist, however, thought they should be remembered equally, so the two marble figures are exactly the same height!

A visit to Goethe's house highlighted a revealing contrast between German and British educational standards. German schools unsurprisingly teach their pupils about Goethe's life and works, but they also include Shakespeare in the curriculum, and evidently assume that their British counterparts return the compliment. We were treated to a lengthy dissertation about the German literary giant by a very earnest lady, to whom our party listened with admirable politeness, but not a great deal of comprehension. As we were making our escape, I overheard one of our girls muttering to another "Who is Goethe anyway?"

On a wooded hill, 8 kilometres north of the city, is a place that Goethe loved to visit for country walks, but has since achieved notoriety as the site of the Buchenwald concentration camp. We took a number of the older students there, and on the way the weather turned appropriately overcast and menacing, but the brightest sunshine would not dispel the atmosphere that still hangs over this terrible place, long after the physical evidence of the unspeakable things that were done there has been disposed of. However much you may have read about Buchenwald, it doesn't prepare you for the experience of actually standing on the ground where it happened. I still feel a chill every time I think of that afternoon, when it was so powerfully brought home to me what human beings are capable of doing to each other.

Sadly, opportunities like our visit to Jena became increasingly rare during the period I was working in Bradford. A gradual reduction in funding for school music made my work more difficult, and meant that music became less available to children from poorer families. I think this reflects badly on the Labour Government that was elected in 1997. To some extent the trend has now been reversed, but not before considerable damage was done to music education in the UK.

However, my efforts did not go entirely unappreciated. The University of Bradford was kind enough to award me an Honorary Doctorate of Literature in recognition of my work. Although Bradford doesn't have a chair of music or offer degrees in the arts, music is part of the overall educational strategy. A Fellow in Music, appointed on a two-yearly basis, is the focal point of the University's music making, and on several occasions I was consulted on who should be chosen for this post.

This is a book about a lifetime in music, about the music makers I have met during that lifetime, and the insights and ideals that have grown out of it. Although Muriel and I were blessed with three wonderful children, I cannot do justice here to the richness they have brought into our lives, with all their joys and sorrows. In the summer of 1998, however, something happened that shook life to its foundations.

Muriel and I were returning from a holiday in Russia, and in those days before everyone had a mobile phone, had been incommunicado for a fortnight. When we arrived at Gatwick, Jeanette unexpectedly met us off the plane. She had driven from her home in Newcastle to prepare us to face the shocking news that Paul was in hospital after a serious accident at his home. When we reached Leeds Infirmary, we found him barely conscious, with injuries to his head and neck and paralysed from the waist down. His life was not in danger, but the long term prognosis was not good. His spinal cord had been badly damaged, and our son, a man of 48 in his physical and professional prime, was now facing the rest of his days in a wheelchair.

So many lives are touched these days by this kind of tragedy, as a result of war, bombings, mindless acts of barbarism or as in Paul's case pure random accident, but the old cliché is true - we never think it will happen to our nearest and dearest. Paul, to his great credit, has shown remarkable courage in response to this drastic change in circumstances. His head injuries proved not too severe, and he soon recovered full command of his mental faculties. After six months of intensive and often exhausting treatment in a specialist spinal unit, he was able to return home and resume his activities as a musician. Although he has lost some sensation in his fingers and can no longer play to the same high standard, he has conducted outstanding concerts from the wheelchair in a number of venues, including Leeds Town Hall, and with the aid of a specially adapted van can get around with a high degree of independence. Throughout all this he has been fortunate to have the unwavering help and support of his partner, Carol - an example of human nature at its best, and a constant reminder to count my blessings.

Chapter 31 - Summer Schools

Coaching, teaching and conducting at summer schools are today a growing part of many professional musicians' schedules, and I have done my fair share of this over the past half century. Especially in the field of chamber music, the summer school provides an invaluable service for amateur instrumentalists throughout the country, and indeed also from abroad, who enjoy meeting in agreeable surroundings for a sociable holiday combined with music making. And the great thing is that unlike youth orchestras, these courses cater for all ages.

The Grittleton Chamber Music Course was the first summer school I took part in, back in the 1950s, and Muriel and I were involved with it for more than twenty years. Ambrose Gauntlett, with whom I played in the London Harpsichord Ensemble, had recommended me, and we had many enjoyable times together. The course was run by Viola Tucker, who was Careers Officer at the Royal College of Music in London, but spent every second of her spare time throughout the year organising the annual Grittleton fortnight. Viola had many sterling qualities, but was not noted for her diplomacy. My old colleague Peter Beavan was a regular cello coach on the course, but one year could not attend. In a panic, Viola rang us to see if we could find a substitute. We suggested our great friend Olga Hegedus, one of the finest chamber music players in London, and Olga duly accepted the engagement. At the opening meeting of the course, in her customary speech introducing all the coaches to the students, Viola concluded as follows:

"And now, I know you will all be very sorry that Peter Beavan will not be able to be with us this year due to prior engagements. I have worked very hard to try and get a replacement, and I have asked everybody with no success. However, I have finally been able to get Olga Hegedus here!"

It was all we could do to stop Olga packing her bags and going straight back to London!

The name of the course came from the Wiltshire village where it was originally held, long before my involvement. It is still running today, after migrating to many different venues. For a number of years it was held in Malvern Girls School, and I recall being there in July 1970 when we heard the news of the death of Barbirolli at the age of 71. I also know that in 1973 we were in Bexhill, thanks to a vivid memory of the breaking of the Watergate scandal and the impeachment of President Nixon!

Muriel and I often played piano trios with Ambrose at Grittleton, including very ambitiously the Tschaikovsky and the Ravel, both with minimal rehearsals. During the Ravel concert a bat got into the auditorium, and terrorised the audience with its swooping and dive-bombing. We were concentrating so hard on just staying with the music that we didn't notice a thing! Later, when Ambrose retired, he was succeeded by George Isaac. Others who joined us at various times included violinists Colin Sauer and Felix Kok, and violists Gwynn Edwards and Stanley Popperwell.

Muriel had plenty to do on these courses, playing for the tutors and for the students. She also worked with children's ensembles, because many people brought their offspring along, including ourselves. Paul, Alison and Jeanette all came with us regularly, and we found that after Grittleton they always came home full of renewed enthusiasm to keep up a proper practising schedule! One of their co-participants was Bradley Creswick, who later led the Northern Sinfonia.

Among the many students at Grittleton who became our lasting friends was Wilfred Saunders, who came as an amateur viola player with his wife Janet and family, but was professionally one of the foremost string instrument makers in the country, with a reputation that became worldwide. He made a fine copy of my Italian violin, which Paul still has, but his greatest success was with his violas, which are beautifully constructed and tonally superb. Wilfred organised comparisons between the many high quality instruments that were owned by tutors and students, in which I played each one in turn behind a screen. The resulting comments were often surprising!

It was to the Grittleton course that I was indebted for the opportunity to acquire the Guiseppe Rocca violin that became my main instrument for the rest of my playing life. It belonged to a remarkable lady, Miss Batchelor, already well into her nineties, who came to the course every year. She was unable to take part in chamber music due to failing eyesight, but always arrived having memorised a number of Kreisler violin pieces that she played every day with Muriel. She let me try the violin, and I immediately fell in love with its dark and luscious tone colour, superior to anything I had previously played. Its owner had bought it for a ridiculously small sum from Hills of London around 1898, and now that her playing days were nearly over had decided to find out what it would fetch in the open market.

I couldn't persuade her to sell it to me directly, and had to bid for it at Sotheby's famous string instruments auction sale, the most nerve-racking professional experience I have ever gone through. These sales, involving very considerable sums, happen at lightening speed, and require nerves of steel to take part in. I had borrowed money here and there, and Viola Tucker and Ambrose both came along to lend moral support. I found we were bidding against Müller, a Dutch dealer who specialised in Rocca violins, which were becoming increasingly sought after by leading players. Campoli himself played all his concertos on a Rocca, claiming that the Stradivarius he owned didn't have the same carrying quality.

So the omens were not good, and the bidding soon climbed to my pre-set limit.

"Go on," hissed Viola. "You MUST have it. I'll lend you the extra money."

I resumed bidding, but lost my nerve and stopped, thinking the bid was against me. Down came the hammer with a crash, and to my amazement the bid was with me. I couldn't believe it! Ambrose made me go straight out of the auction room and ring up my insurance company before laying a finger on the precious object. I had paid the highest sum ever achieved by a Rocca at auction, but have never once regretted it. Each time I used it was a pleasure and a thrill, and when

I eventually sold it, it proved to be an investment I'd have found it hard to better on the Stock Exchange.

Ambrose's successor George Isaac was a cellist I had not met before he first appeared at Grittleton, one year when Ambrose could not be there. Virtually his whole career was spent in Wales, playing quartets and cello sonatas for Cardiff University, and I was already familiar with his records, superb accounts of a substantial part of the cello sonata repertoire with pianists Cyril Preedy and Valerie Tryon. We took to each other right away. Virtually self-taught, George had a particularly sensitive approach to chamber music, with an exquisite sense of ensemble and of tempo. If you didn't get the speed of a piece absolutely right, he would look at you with a slightly pitying air, as if to say "Come on Peter boyo, you know that's wrong. Too slow, boy!"

George recommended Muriel and me to the Summer Orchestral Course at Harlech, which had been established before the war in the town's College for Adult Education. It was closely associated with Sir Henry Walford Davies (1869-1941), composer, academic and holder of many distinguished offices, who was well known in his time as a popular broadcaster on all things musical. I was pleased to discover that the main string tutor had been Frederick Grinke, but at that time the school was predominantly choral in character. It was disbanded during the war, and revived as an orchestral course in the early 70s. Muriel and I first took part in 1974, and continued as tutors for nearly thirty years. I became an expert at finding driving routes to Harlech, hidden behind the Welsh hills, first from Bristol, then Glasgow, and finally from Bingley!

For most of that time we had the great pleasure of working with Vilem Tausky (1910-2004). He was a fine all-round musician; the epitome of the European *Kapellmeister* with a thorough knowledge of all branches of music, and the ability and willingness to apply himself to all of them. I found it inspirational to work with someone who had not only studied with the composer Josef Suk, Dvořák's son-in-law, but as a boy had played piano accompaniments for Dvořák's daughter Magda, and had known the composer's widow. Vilem used to boast that there had been an issue of the Radio Times in which his name appeared three times on adjacent pages, for conducting Verdi's Aida at Covent Garden, the BBC Theatre Orchestra in Friday Night Is Music Night, and the music for the popular comedy show ITMA, starring Tommy Handley.

Not many people realise that Vilem was also a very accomplished composer. He wrote a lively Suite for violin and piano, dedicated to Muriel and me, and we have played it often and recorded it for the BBC. The idiom is completely his own, with an obvious nod to his native Czech roots. When I later happened to catch on the radio a recording of his Concerto for Harmonica and Orchestra, written for and played by Larry Adler, although unfamiliar with the piece I immediately guessed it must be by Vilem. I had encountered him in various ways in my earlier career. Just after the war the Marine Band did a week in Liverpool playing for factory workers, and I was able one morning to attend a rehearsal at the Philharmonic Hall. The orchestra was led by Henry Holst and conducted by Sergeant Tausky, still in his Pioneer Corps uniform - he had done his wartime service in the Corps as a Jewish refugee. Someone else I would get to know very well was the soloist in the Mendelssohn Violin Concerto, the inimitable Campoli. Vilem was for a time conductor of the BBC Northern Orchestra, and when I was leading the Phil I played several concertos under his direction in Manchester.

If the standard of playing in the early days at Harlech was a true reflection of the level of amateur music making in the UK at the time, things have certainly changed for the better. When we first arrived in 1974, there was a sizeable contingent of elderly participants who, although very pleasant and agreeable people, had limited musical aspirations. But gradually the playing improved as we attracted a growing number of young music students, and with a more balanced age spectrum in the orchestra, the course became a rewarding place to work. The surroundings, in the shadow of the medieval castle and the Snowdonian mountains, were idyllic, with good quality bathing on the beautiful beaches nearby. The social scene was lively, and the concerts themselves were great fun. Our quartet of coaches were all well-known professional musicians working in Wales, and at the tutors' concerts Muriel had the chance over the years of playing practically every known piano quintet with them.

As well as the Symphony Orchestra, there was a Chamber Orchestra that I was eventually to take over, and it was good to be able to direct some of the extensive repertoire I had learned so thoroughly in the Boyd Neel Orchestra many years before. With the coaching of the many student ensembles also keeping us busy, our annual visits to Harlech could have been accurately described as action packed.

Coaching amateur players requires the ability to combine real instruction with care not to destroy their obvious pleasure in tackling works which would test the finest musicians to their limits. On one of the many courses I did in Scotland, the St Andrews Summer Music Course, I was working one year with Willie Miller, a close personal friend and a well-known Glasgow lawyer. He was on the Board of Governors at the Academy, and did all their legal work. Willie was a passionately keen amateur violinist, and brought his own quartet of like-minded enthusiasts on many chamber music courses. On this particular occasion they were battling their way through Beethoven's Opus 131, a work well beyond their actual capabilities. I was trying to point out a few things that might be improved, without being too discouraging, when Willie interrupted me.

"Yes, that's all very well Peter, but the trouble is, with you kind of chaps; you hear what you're actually playing. I know that to you we're all making a horrible bloody noise, but we're not hearing that! We're hearing Beethoven!"

I have never grudged a moment of the time I have spent doing this kind of work. Apart from the joy of meeting so many fascinating people, it has always been hugely rewarding to be with music lovers who want to do more than just passively listen. They are the true backbone of the musical life of any community, and a vital part of the *raison d'être* of professional musicians like me.

Chapter 32 - Examining

When I first started at the RSAMD in 1975, the then Principal, Dr Kenneth Barritt, had suggested that I might like to become an examiner for the Associated Board. The idea attracted me greatly. I had been in contact with the Board as an examinee from an early age, and later entered many of my own pupils for the examinations.

My preliminary interview for a place on the Board was in front of a committee chaired by Herbert Howells, who had been influential in my appointment to the Bristol Orchestra. Howells was the most courteous and gentlemanly of characters. He was a fine composer, very much in the English tradition - not dissimilar in style to Vaughan Williams, though perhaps not quite in the same league. In Liverpool, Sargent used to include a piece of his in programmes for the Huddersfield Choir - the Missa Sabriensis for baritone chorus and orchestra. Written in 1954 for the Three Choirs Festival, it had considerable lyrical beauty, but was not without its moments of *longueur.* The title translates as Mass of the Severn, but it wasn't long before the wags in the orchestra gleefully transformed it into The Severn Bore.

After the interview and a trial period I was accepted as an examiner, and continued to serve until about 1993. Often involving a couple of weeks in unfamiliar surroundings, it was demanding work, but very rewarding. It is a great responsibility to assess what the students produce, and mark them in a way that praises their achievements while pointing out what might be improved, without needless discouragement. It also requires some skill to maintain freshness and variety over a whole day in what you say to a constant stream of young people, to whom the short duration of the exam is the culmination of months of hard work.

Whenever examiners meet there are always stories to be told - not in a spirit of disrespect to the candidates, you just can't help being amused by some of the responses you get. The younger ones especially often display a very literal logic that reminds you to be more specific in your requests. I well remember one little boy who came in to do the Grade I piano exam. He settled himself on the stool, and in my friendliest voice I tried to put him at ease.

"Well now, that's fine. Let's do the scales first, shall we?" (Scales requirements for this grade are major keys only, played with separate hands.) "Good. Play me C with your right hand."

So he did - just the one note C! Well, that was what I had asked for!

I also recall one quite forceful young lady of about 10 or 11 in Dublin, who before I even had chance to address her, turned to me and said "I hope I do very well in this exam - like I did last time!"

But the best unsolicited remark I have heard about was passed on to me by my great friend from the Liverpool days, the pianist Gordon Green. He was examining in St Annes near Blackpool, and a cheerful Lancashire lass came breezing into the room, sat down at the piano, turned round to him and said "Eee, ye'll laff when you hear my sight reading!"

Nerves in exams are always expected, and taken into consideration. Some candidates are more affected than others, but generally I found that if treated sympathetically, most managed to overcome them quite well. I do remember however one girl who began badly with several mistakes, and then suddenly burst into tears. This was most embarrassing for the poor child, who had obviously been pushed into doing the exam by either parents or teacher well before she was ready.

An examiner often has to be especially helpful to adult entrants, who may find themselves doing a Grade I piano exam which has really been designed for an 8 year old beginner. Adults are much more self-conscious than children, and an attack of nerves can turn them into physically shaking wrecks. One lady I encountered was particularly badly affected.

"Oh, Mr Mountain, I'm so sorry, I'm terribly, terribly nervous!"

"Please don't worry," I said. "Take your time. Take a deep breath. Relax. I quite understand. OK, now, whenever you're ready. Yes? Then let's hear the scales. Now, just play me G major with your right hand."

She held up her right hand, which was trembling uncontrollably, grabbed it firmly with her left hand, and forced it down onto the keys! I'm glad to say that eventually she didn't do too badly, and I was able to award her a pass.

Muriel never wanted to become an examiner. She accepted that a sense of progress kept young people motivated, and during her career put forward hundreds of children for exams, but she always tried to dissuade adults from entering. Although she loved teaching grown-ups, and appreciated the great satisfaction that many of them got from learning an instrument later in life, she was adamant that it was not good for people to feel obliged to put themselves through this ordeal. Such is the competitive instinct of the human animal, however, that many older players still insist on doing exams, and if they are prepared to take the strain, I say good luck to them!

The Associated Board is known worldwide, and although regrettably I was never able to do this because of my commitments at home, some of my colleagues undertook quite lengthy foreign tours in locations that included the Far East, Africa, Canada, Australia, New Zealand, Malaysia and Hong Kong. Apparently in some parts of the world a Grade 8 Distinction can form a valuable part of a girl's marriage dowry, and it is not unknown for examiners to be offered bribes! But a friend of mine faced an even more alarming prospect when he arrived for a four week stint at one Far Eastern Centre. What normally makes a heavy examining schedule bearable is that you have a constant variety of exam grades and different instruments to keep you alert and on your toes. Imagine my friend's feelings when he found that the entries had been arranged into their separate categories, and he was being asked to begin with an entire fortnight of nothing but Grade I Piano Exams!

Adjudicating for competitive music festivals was another activity I took part in from time to time. The main difference from examining is that you have to stand in front of an audience of competitors and (worse still!) parents, and deliver an extempore verdict, which can delight no more than a very small proportion of the listeners! The process involves listening to perhaps 30 or 40 renditions of the same short piece, writing an instant assessment of each one and giving it a mark. To protect the self-esteem of the competitors, the convention is that each child must get at least 70% just for turning up! 70% to 75% is pretty ropey, 75% to 80% is reasonable, 80% to 85% is good and 85% to 90% includes possible winners, with the odd young genius getting up to 95%. (No one can get more than that - perfection doesn't exist!)

Some people don't like the competitive element in these events, but I believe that properly run, in the right spirit, they can be good fun, and I am always in favour of anything that encourages participation. The chance to play in public is valuable for musicians, and children should be encouraged to understand that whatever level of attainment they reach, there will always be some who are not as good, but also some who are better. The important thing is to learn to accept both consolation and praise with equal grace.

After the move to Bingley I did quite a bit of coaching and direction of youth orchestras and of small amateur ensembles. Muriel and I went about three times a term to help in a chamber group run by my sister Kath in the studio of her house in Fearby. This was an admirable enterprise, because it included both her young pupils and adult amateur players from the area. There are limited opportunities these days for such players. Adult singers can often find a choir in their vicinity, but amateur orchestras are becoming increasingly thin on the ground. Many people get pleasure from playing music in their young days, but give it up to concentrate on University, jobs and family responsibility, and often don't find the chance to come back to it. This is a great shame. As well as youth orchestras there should be adult orchestras, middle-aged orchestras and even grumpy old men's and women's orchestras! I worry about our tendency to be nation of spectators. Taking part in an activity like music or sport is not only rewarding on a personal level - we need more rank and file participants to push up the standards of the top players. If more people in this country played tennis, we'd have a Wimbledon winner in no time!

I am often asked for advice about the best way and time to introduce children to music. I myself started on the piano at the age of five, and on the violin at seven. Music should be part of a child's life from the very beginning. A baby responds to little melodic fragments in a lullaby, and nursery rhymes may be sung or played on instruments for enjoyment and for comfort. However, unless a child demonstrates really precocious talent, I believe that formal music tuition should wait until there is some numeric ability, and knowledge of letters. The keyboard is the easiest way to learn about musical notation, so I would always advise a start on the piano. Many people who have never played a keyboard instrument are first rate string players, but their lack of fluency in the bass clef always to some extent compromises their general musicianship. I am OK reading the bass clef because I learned the left hand of the piano in my early days, but the alto clef requires conscious effort for me to decipher, and a spell in the viola section of a school orchestra would have been invaluable. Specialisation at too young an age is always a mistake, and it is better to develop a range of abilities and instincts in the early years when they are more easily absorbed.

The piano is an excellent - some might say essential - starting point for a musician, but it should be complemented before too long by a melodic instrument. Singing is the basic melodic skill - everyone can sing, and only instruments that play a tune can express themselves with line, colour and gradation. That is the major failing of the piano. It is essentially a percussion instrument, and can command great complexity in harmony and counterpoint, but to play it with melodic expression is much harder. Not of course impossible, but far more difficult than on, say, the violin.

It is also a lonely instrument, which was always Muriel's lament. The most sociable of people, she greatly regretted that all her early training was exclusively on the piano. Perhaps her natural talent worked against her, and it never occurred to anyone that she might benefit from lessons on another instrument. In later life she always preferred ensemble work to playing solo.

251

Chapter 33 - Balance in Music

In 2003, when I was 80, I played in my last public concert. This was with the Bradford Chamber Orchestra and was part of a festival in Saltaire, at the Victoria Hall. It was an appropriate finale, as my very first concerts that I can remember were as a young boy in the same venue. Since returning to Yorkshire I had conducted regular orchestral performances there with the Bradford Youth Orchestra, but for this last one I led the Chamber Bradford Orchestra, and the conductor was our good friend Alan Cuckston, well known as a harpsichordist and specialist in other early keyboard instruments. The programme was of English string music, including some of my favourite repertoire. After that I taught a little, but gave up that too in 2004, so now all my music is of the passive variety. For the first time in my life I am entirely audience-bound!

It is remarkable how seldom in everyday professional life someone like me attends a concert. The greatest part by far of my musical experience had been gained either playing in or leading some kind of ensemble. I would of course listen to the radio or to recordings if there was anything specific that I wanted to hear or wished to learn, but I would very rarely listen just for entertainment as many keen amateur music lovers do. After a hard day of rehearsals and often a concert as well, the idea of going home and putting on a CD of a Brahms Symphony just wouldn't have occurred to me. Martin Milner, who famously led the Hallé under Barbirolli, once told me he had been stopped in a Manchester street by a young lady who asked if he would kindly answer questions for a TV survey, and not wishing to appear churlish, had agreed:

"Thank you sir. Now, do you watch television fairly regularly?"

"Yes."

"Every evening?"

"Mostly."

"BBC or ITV?"

"ITV"

"Current affairs?"

"Just the news headlines."

"Sport"

"Yes"

"Comedy"

"Yes."

"Drama?"

"No."

"Documentaries?"

"No."

"Music?"

"No."

"Thank you Sir. Name please?"

"Martin Milner."

"Occupation please?"

"Leader of the Hallé Orchestra."

She wouldn't believe him!

Many keen amateurs have a much greater knowledge of recordings and own far more comprehensive record collections than I do. Mine is fairly substantial, but tends to be quite esoteric, involving particular performers or out of the way items that have aroused my curiosity. I doubt, for example, that I have recordings of all the Beethoven symphonies, although I know them pretty well from memory.

Most of the regular repertoire of orchestral, chamber and choral music exists in my head as heard from the first violin desk, and I am also up to speed with quite a lot of less familiar music. Like many players, I have performed Handel's Messiah more times than any other piece of music, and it is a tribute to its enduring quality that I still hold it in such high regard! It wasn't uncommon for it to crop up six or seven times over the festive season, and while I was in Liverpool we played it in numerous Northern towns whose choral societies counted on full houses for the Christmas Messiah to get them out of the red for the rest of the year. I remember much amusement being occasioned by a press cutting Gerry Macdonald put up on the orchestral notice board. It was from the Radio Times, and was the title of a talk on the BBC Third Programme by a learned professor of sociology, entitled The Cult of the Messiah in Primitive Societies!

My knowledge of the standard repertoire does contain some gaps. I regret very much never having had a regular job in an opera orchestra. I have done quite a lot of opera here and there, notably all the Mozart masterpieces, but would have liked to be more familiar with Verdi, Puccini, and of course Wagner.

Nowadays I go to quite a lot of concerts, often to the Hallé at the Bridgewater Concert Hall in Manchester, to the Northern Chamber Orchestra, and to opera at the Buxton Festival or even Glyndebourne. And the first impression I got when I started down this path was that the violins weren't loud enough! I have been used all my life to hearing violins all around me, and instinctively feel the 1st violin part to be the principal argument in most classical music. Indeed, as suggested in Chapter 15, I regard the string body and string tone quality as the main component in the development of European music since the mid 16th Century. Musical fashions have come and gone in the intervening years, but the basic format of string quartet plus bass has remained more or less constant, and features in the score to a far greater extent than other orchestral instruments. In an effort to be considerate and avoid having players hanging round unnecessarily, conductors often try to arrange rehearsals so as to work on the large ensembles first and do the smaller groups in turn later. Needless to say, it is always the strings (and especially the first fiddles with really hard passages to play) who have to stay on right to the bitter end. Not for nothing are they called the poor bloody infantry of the band! But that is just traditional orchestral grousing, and in reality no string player worth his salt would want to change places with, say, a bass trombonist, who has hundreds of bars to count and only a few moments of glory!

To be fair, my ears have now adjusted to appreciate the balance of the parts from the audience's angle, but I still feel impatient with conductors who have an obsession with getting pianissimo quality from the strings. This is fine when the balance of the music requires it, for special effects, but there are many places in ensemble music where the wind soloists can overwhelm the strings. There are two reasons for this. Firstly, wind instruments in general are not capable of extreme pianissimo. Below a certain level they simply fail to speak, whereas the strings can descend to the most exquisite *flautando* tone quality with minimal contact from the bow, producing a sound that is entrancing, but easily drowned. Secondly, many conductors have never had the experience of being in a string section themselves, having learnt their music from in front of rather than within the orchestra. When they find themselves in close proximity to a body of strings, with the wind players relatively in the background, their first reaction is to let through the wind soloists by keeping down the strings. They don't realise that the balance is different out in the hall. Also, they often don't appreciate that a subsidiary or accompanying *motif* deserves to be heard just as clearly as the main melody. Even some otherwise excellent conductors have fallen into this trap, and I have been involved in many arguments on account of it. Someone with a really good ear will study each hall, and know how to balance the sound. That is part of the conductor's job, but is regularly neglected, often by would-be superstars who prefer to go for sensational contrasts of loud and soft, forgetting that control of the overall dynamic is the secret of presenting the music clearly and audibly.

As I have touched on briefly towards the end of Chapter 8, both conductors and players often make the mistake of thinking of dynamic marks as indication of a fixed level of dynamics. In this context I must mention here Jascha Horenstein, who presided over some outstanding concerts while I was in Liverpool. Horenstein was a truly great musician with a formidable grasp of the late 19th and early 20th century repertoire, from Brahms to Bruckner and Mahler and much more. He was striking in appearance, with white flowing hair and thin almost skeletal features. Fritz Spiegel did a wicked caricature of him, with the caption Keep Death off the Roads, a parody of a road safety poster of the time.

Although in private Horenstein was witty and entertaining company, at work he was always serious. When the orchestral manager, Johnny Murphy, was talking about some publicity stunt that would raise the profile of the orchestra, the maestro said "Yes, these things are all well and good, but the only things that really improve the reputation of an orchestra are good performances." Another pronouncement of his that I have quoted many times when teaching or rehearsing was "In music there is no repetition." In other words, whenever a phrase or even a whole section appears again, it must be with a different nuance to give it added meaning.

But to return to the question of dynamics, we were rehearsing with him on one occasion when he stopped, turned to the cellos and asked them for a little more sound. Tactlessly, the leader of the cellists replied —.

"It's marked *piano,* ye know!"

Horenstein dropped his hands to his sides. He began to shake, and for a moment I feared he was going to have a fit. When he spoke, it was in a jerky staccato, with outraged and growing intensity.

"What - is - *piano*? Tell - me. What - is - *piano*? Tell - me."

When he had calmed down, the rehearsal resumed, and the point was taken. A written dynamic is not a pre-determined decibel level, but is more like an indication of mood, to be interpreted in relation to other instruments and overall musical content.

I often find myself disappointed by the sound of string soloists, whether leaders of the different sections or concerto specialists.

At least part of the problem is that we are all used to hearing concerto recordings where the solo line is given undue prominence by microphone positioning. Record producers feel they can't sell a performance unless every single note soars clearly above the orchestra, although there are passages in many concertos where the soloist plays a subsidiary part, which in concert performance may be barely distinguishable.

Anyone setting up a performance in the concert hall has to bear two principles in mind. Firstly, in the great classical and romantic string concertos, every statement by the soloist is significant, and must be audible. There is no note in the solo part of the Beethoven Violin Concerto that should be obscured. Secondly, in works where the writing and orchestration are perhaps less accomplished, a skilled conductor and soloist can work together to achieve the optimum balance. Not enough conductors pay sufficient attention to this, and not enough soloists have the required sense of projection. This does not mean just playing loudly, but the ability to imbue the sound with an inner harmonic quality and substance that will penetrate even in the softer passages. A violinist like David Oistrakh (if here ever was or ever will be a violinist like David Oistrakh!) will never be drowned, but will fill every note, from the softest to the loudest, with a richness that plays its part in achieving the blance of sound essential to a truly satisfying musical performance.

Chapter 34 - Style in Music

In music, as in all artistic endeavour, there is the style that changes, and there is the style that is universal. Something that is unstylish today, in the sense that it is tasteless, inept or inartistic, will be the same in fifty years time, and will be equally unacceptable. C P E Bach, in his essay The Art of Playing Keyboard Instruments, concludes a long discussion on rules governing ornamentation by saying that the only thing that really counts is good taste, which is as true now as it was in the 18th century.

On the other hand, some things do change, and over the sixty years of my professional career some aspects of the way music is played have altered considerably. It is easy to check this out. At the flick of a switch we can hear recordings from as far back as the beginning of the 20th century recreated on modern media. True, the very earliest records are often too distorted by primitive recording techniques, but when we use 21st century technology to enhance the electric recordings available from the 1930s, we can achieve amazingly good results. An audio engineer has assured me that the amount of information available on an old 78rpm record is actually higher than you can get from a more modern 33rpm LP. Once we have extracted it, the results will be far superior to what was possible from the original 78. So we can now have a pretty good idea of what our forebears of a couple of generations ago really sounded like.

Of course, we must remember that what survives is generally the very best of the performances of the time. We can still marvel at the artistry of the likes of Kreisler, Casals, Cortot and Gigli, but recordings of top-class performances by the artists of today are far more plentiful. The crème de la crème from both eras are probably similar in standard, but they are unquestionably different. Although we still have much to learn from the older masters, if we were to try to blindly imitate a style that was in vogue 60 years ago, we would fail miserably and invite ridicule. I remember Rodney Friend's scathing verdict on a violinist who attempted to introduce old-style *portamenti* and position changes into a Mozart concerto. "Dreadful!" he said. "Sounds like Kreisler on his death- bed!"

When I was a student, it was taken for granted that the modern style of playing was the best. We had reached the apex of correctness and artistry. Position changes must be absolutely inaudible, expressive slides were tasteless and old-fashioned, and bow changes had to be seamless. According to Rowsby Woof, the proper aspiration for a violinist was a pure, disembodied voice, with no audible imperfections. "Boy, you are growing up in a new age," he said to me once. "You will have a microphone just in front of you, and you must practise until you can produce absolute perfection."

Technical excellence is indeed an essential goal, but if that is the be all and end all, monotony soon sets in. Woof's pupil Jean Pougnet was admired for his flawless style, but the truly great players all had something in them that went beyond the bounds of mere safety. I don't agree, for instance, with today's widely held view that Jascha Heifetz was just a perfectionist. His playing was perfection plus - he went to the limits and sometimes beyond. He took risks, which usually succeeded, but even when they didn't it was still thrilling. The great pianist Vladimir Horowitz had the same almost satanic quality, and I'm sure Paganini must have had it too.

Kreisler had a wonderful humanity and warmth in his tone quality, and a sense of phrasing that we can all learn from. Not by imitating his vibrato or his slides, but by appreciating that a melodic line must express more than just a succession of perfect notes. It is the progress from note to note which gives meaning and shape to the composer's phrases. Kreisler's warm expressiveness was exceptional, but there were others at the time who came close to matching it. The American Albert Spalding (1888-1953) was one. I very much regret that I never heard him play, but I have heard many of his recordings, and have read and re-read his autobiography Rise to Follow, an entertaining look at early 20th century musical life in America and Europe.

Adolf Busch has left a treasure trove of recordings of his Chamber Group and String Quartet to inspire future generations. He often quoted the epigram that informed his approach to his profession:

"You must never think only of the beauty of your own playing, but always of the beauty of the music". Nathan Milstein is arguably the equal of Heifetz in technical and musical control, while Mischa Elman is the epitome of pure sound and instinctive phrasing, and Thibaud was Gallic elegance personified. The roll call goes on and on - Zino Francescatti, Arthur Grumiaux, Henryk Szeryng, Aaron Rosand, Ruggerio Ricci and Yehudi Menuhin, who has added a philosophical and pedagogical dimension to his musical achievements, are just a few of many iconic figures who can inspire us all with their legacy of recorded sound.

The greatest influence for change during my lifetime, however, has been the weight of research into baroque instruments and performance, and more recently a similar inquiry focused on the intervening years.

Many modern baroque players give the impression that they see themselves as the new enlightenment, rendering all previous performance ideals obsolete. Their ultimate goal is to produce performances as close as possible to those heard by the composer, or to what the composer supposedly had in mind. But why should this be our only guiding principle? In the world of literature and drama, there is no doubt merit in trying to recreate original performances, say of Shakespeare in a replica of the Globe Theatre. But no one would suggest that this excludes a variety of other approaches. Shakespeare's plays must be staged with an awareness of modern preoccupations, if they are to show that the passions and sentiments they depict are still relevant to our human condition. That is what the best theatrical directors strive to do, and surely this axiom should apply to all the performing arts. Otherwise we lay ourselves open to the criticism that we are putting the greatest creations of mankind into a dry-as-dust museum. We must allow the great artists of the past to speak to us directly, and show us that their ideas are universal and for all time, not just the mummified remains of a former age. So I am all in favour of the modern Steinway grand, symphony orchestra, concert hall and opera house, and I am sure that the great composers of bygone years, if they were born again, would love them too. It is balance that we need - to use all our knowledge and expertise to recreate great music in a way that enriches the lives of as many people as possible.

If we make the best of current opportunities, we will be living in a world where mankind has more and more time for leisure. Artists, including musicians, must do their part to ensure the best use of this valuable commodity. It cannot be done through legislation, but only through good educational practices and presentation of the arts in a form that people will accept. If my 80 plus years on this planet have taught me anything, it is that human beings, in the face of sincere artistic endeavour, will usually put aside their differences and rise to the occasion.

Vox populi, vox Deo

Selective Appendix

Sir John Barbirolli (1899-1970) Conductor – always associated with the Hallé Orchestra. Originally a cellist, he had a magical empathy with string sound. His many recordings show great individuality and warmth, enhanced by his own unique personality. I never played for him, but he was always most friendly and warm when we met. A wonderful personality.

Sir Thomas Beecham (1879-1961) Conductor. The most fascinating musician of his time. He had a magical touch with all music, but especially that of Frederick Delius. Anecdotal accounts of his wit are legion. He sometimes gave the impression of an almost dilettante approach to his work, but in reality he prepared his scores with meticulous detail to present the unique Beecham effect. He was known for his public antipathy to Sir Malcolm Sargent. One of his best- known quips is when he referred to the young Herbert von Karajan as "a kind of musical Malcolm Sargent" – thus killing two birds with one stone!

Sir Arthur Bliss (1891-1975) Composer and conductor. Born to an *English* father and *American* mother, Bliss was destined to display characteristics of both nations, his profound *romanticism* balanced by an unquenchable energy and optimism. During the *Second World War* Bliss became Director of Music at the *BBC*, and formed ideas which led to the division of music broadcasting into categories after the war, such as the present day Radios 1 and 3. In 1950 he was *knighted* and in 1953 he was appointed to succeed *Arnold Bax* as *Master of the Queen's Music*. In 1972 I played in a concert at the RAM to celebrate the 150th Anniversary of that institution, in an orchestra formed entirely by well-known past students. The conductor was Sir Arthur, and we performed his brilliant "Music For Strings". Perhaps he is best known for providing the music for the film of H.G.Wells "Things To Come".

Nadia Boulanger (1887-1979) A supreme musician who influenced nearly all the great composers and players of her day. I have written about her extensively in Book 1. It is remarkable to note that she had a sister Lili, six years younger, who was the first woman to win the much- coveted Prix de Rome for composition, and by early indication was an even greater talent than Nadia. Tragically she died in 1918 aged 25, and Nadia was so affected that she gave up composition for the rest of her life.

Sir Adrian Boult (1889-1983) Conductor. The most English of musicians. Was introduced to Elgar in his youth, and never lost his affinity with the very best of our national music. Some orchestral players disliked his disdain of meticulously detailed indications, but no-one could surpass him in his realisation of the perfect sweep and shape of the greatest masterpieces. His benign appearance concealed a tempestuous nature that could erupt if he were seriously thwarted, but he was a great colleague and always took his musicians' part. I have played under him throughout the whole of my career, always with much pleasure.

Dennis Brain (1921-1957) Superb horn virtuoso. Also a fine organist. Followed his father, Aubrey, also a great horn player. Played first horn in Philharmonia and RPO. Always in demand from the greatest conductors. Died tragically in car crash aged 36. His memory is still revered.

Rosina Buckman (1881-1948) *Prima donna* soprano with Beecham's British Opera Company. Professor of singing at the RAM. Lived in the student digs where we stayed during the War, together with her husband, Maurice d'Oisly, also an operatic singer and source of innumerable stories about Beecham.

Guido Cantelli (1920-1956) Italian conductor. Protegé of Toscanini, groomed to succeed him. Many records and concerts with Philharmonia. Died in plane crash at Orly Airport aged 36.

Arthur Catterall (1883-1943) British violinist. First leader of BBC Symphony Orchestra. Taught violin at the RAM. I played in his Chamber Orchestra and heard him play the Moeran Concerto. One of Britain's very finest soloists.

Albert Coates (1882-1953) Half Russian conductor. Excelled in Tschaikovsky and other Russian repertory. Wonderful records with

British National Orchestra made during the war; now re-issued on CD. His daughter, Tamara, a pianist, stayed at our student digs.

Benjamin Dale (1885-1943) A fine composer whose work is beginning to be re-discovered. Held post of Warden at the RAM when Muriel and I were students. Was very kind to her, and called her his unofficial niece.

Meredith Davies (1923-2005) Throughout his career, Davies was known as a champion of English music, conducting numerous works by Frederick Delius and Benjamin Britten, and premiering works by Richard Rodney Bennett, Humphrey Searle, and Lennox Berkeley. Davies' most famous association was with Britten, whose *War Requiem* he premiered in 1962 at the new Coventry Cathedral. I was friendly with him since Liverpool days and we worked together closely for three years when he was Chief Conductor of the BBC Training Orchestra. He was a true musician.

Georges Enesco (1881-1955) Roumanian violinist, composer, pianist, conductor, teacher. In all these fields Georges Enesco excelled. He was the most complete, all-round musical personality that I have ever encountered. He was teacher of Menuhin who revered him greatly. I will never forget the period when he worked with the Boyd Neel Orchestra. His memory and musical insight were both formidable. His compositions, after a period of neglect, are beginning to be properly appreciated.

Edwin Fischer (1886-1960 German pianist. Widely regarded as one of the great pianists of the 20th century, particularly in the traditional Germanic repertoire of Bach Mozart, Beethoven and Schubert. He is also regarded as one of the finest teachers of his time. Played as soloist/director with the Boyd Neel, and I also played in his cycle of Beethoven concertos with the Philharmonia, but these were less successful as he was not able to control a large orchestra. He was a fine chamber musician, and I heard him at the Lucerne Festival in his Piano Trio with Wolfgang Schneirderhan (violin) and Enrico Mainardi (cello).

Kirsten Flagstad (1895-1962) German soprano. She did several Wagner recordings with the Philharmonia, including the legendary *Tristan und Isolde* conducted by Furtwangler. Walter Legge was fascinated by her wonderful line and matchless phrasing. He even had the idiotic idea of recording her in the title role of *Dido and Aneas*, but her Wagnerian swoops were totally unsuited to Purcell, and the project was quickly abandoned after one morning session at Kingsway Hall. We continued to record with her, though age was beginning to take a toll on her voice. In some recordings the highest notes were provided by Elizabeth Schwartzkopf, anonymously!

John Francis (1908 - 1992) English flautist. Distinguished career in London orchestras and notably in the English Opera Group, with Benjamin Britten. Founded the London Harpsichord Ensemble with his wife Millicent Silver (1905 – 1986) which was very active in the post-war years. It was led by Manoug Parikian, then Olive Zorian and then by myself. It is now continued by his daughter, Sarah Francis.

Sarah Francis English oboist, Daughter of John Francis. Eminent player in orchestras and more especially in chamber music. Well known as a teacher and soloist. Continues the work of the London Harpsichord Ensemble. Muriel and I have done much chamber music with her, and have worked together at the Harlech Summer School

Wilhelm Furtwangler (1886-1954) German conductor. Thought by many to be one of the greatest conductors in history. The Philharmonia played under him several times in concerts and recordings and at the Lucerne Festival. Even *Arturo Toscanini*, usually regarded as Furtwängler's complete antithesis (and sharply critical of Furtwängler on political grounds), once said – when asked to name the world's greatest conductor apart from himself – "Furtwängler!"

Ambrose Gauntlett English cellist and gamba player. Was the first leading cello in the BBC Symphony Orchestra, and appeared on many records, notably as continuo player on Menuhin's recording of the Six Violin and Keyboard Sonatas by Bach. I worked with him for several years in the London Harpsichord Ensemble, and we coached and played together at Grittleton Summer Music School. He was an exceptionally sensitive chamber musician and I learnt much from him.

Frederick Grinke (1911-1987) British violinist of Canadian birth. A student in Winnipeg with John Waterhouse, at 16 he won a scholarship to the RAM, London, where he worked under Rowsby Woof; he later took lessons with Busch and Flesch. He played for six years with the Kutcher Quartet, and for ten was leader of the Boyd Neel Orchestra, with which he recorded solo parts in Bach's Brandenburg Concertos, Handel's concerti grossi and Vaughan Williams's *Concerto accademico*. A forthright and musicianly violinist, he gave many first performances, recorded piano trios by Bridge and Ireland, and inspired compositions by Berkeley, Gordon Jacob, Leighton and Vaughan Williams (the A minor Violin Sonata). He was a Fellow of the RAM and joined the staff there in 1944. From 1967 he acted as judge at many international competitions. He was created a CBE in 1979. My teacher after Woof died.

Sir Charles Groves (1915-1992) British conductor. Groves was born in *London*, and trained at the *Royal College of Music*. He was conductor for the *BBC Northern Orchestra (1944-1951)*, the *Bournemouth Symphony Orchestra (1951-1961)*, and the *Royal Liverpool Philharmonic Orchestra (1963-1977)*. I played with Sir Charles throughout my career, and one of the happiest periods was from 1963 to 1966 with him in Liverpool. His musicianship and great qualities as a conductor were never in doubt, and it was always a pleasure to be associated with his lovely wife Hilary and their musical family. One of Sir Charles' greatest achievements whilst in Liverpool was to be the first British conductor to perform a complete cycle of the Mahler symphonies.

Ida Haendel (1924 or 1928 -) Polish violinist. A very great player by any standard. She was an incredible child prodigy, and studied with Carl Flesch and George Enesco. During and just after the War, she was really the only world-class fiddler in Britain, and I heard her many times. When other great players began to be heard again, she was neglected to some extent and her career has not achieved the success it truly deserved. I have always admired her unreservedly; her Beethoven Concerto is supremely moving. She has a wide repertoire, playing not only the Sibelius Concerto with great authority, but also the same composer's Six Humoreskes, which are equally demanding and very fine. I have played them myself in concerts and broadcasts. Another modern work that I have played, and that Ida has performed with the greatest authority is the Benjamin Britten concerto. She has the greatest imaginable talent, and is intolerant of players who are not truly gifted, so she has taught little (except, of course, by the example of her playing!)

Jascha Heifetz (1901-1987) Russo-American violinist. The three peaks of violin playing in the 20th century could be thought of as Menuhin for emotion, Oistrakh for warmth and Heifetz for brilliance. No other player gives to me personally such a thrill. His playing is not (whatever others may say) cold. The phrasing is imaginative and inimitable, and even if not always to everyone's taste is always immaculately controlled. His personality was difficult and uncompromising, so he was not an ideal teacher, relying too much on sarcasm, and there are some recordings of his, often of very great music, where the sheer brilliance obscures the true musical line. However I have always been, and will continue to be completely fascinated by his personality and his dazzling playing. I took part in his performance of the Brahms concerto in the Festival Hall with the Philharmonia, and also attended two recitals. I remember his Drury Lane recital well. It began with the Vitali Ciacconna (not a favourite of mine) then came the Beethoven *Kreutzer* Sonata with Moiseivitch at the piano. In this, Heifetz dealt with the music peremptorily and seemed to treat the great Russian pianist as a mere accompanist. But thereafter everything was pure gold. The more virtuosic (and, it must be said, the more light-weight) the items became, the more his genius shone. But, in spite of the tumultuous applause, you could feel a sense of reserve, confronted by this austere, almost motionless figure, acknowledging their appreciation with only a slight inclination of the head. The audience seemed to feel – Is he human? The hall was packed, and rows of people were seated on the stage behind the violinist. There were many encores demanded, and suddenly for one of these, Heifetz turned round and played it especially for the people behind him. The whole hall roared in appreciation. We felt

"He knows we're here, he's human, he loves us!" It was a triumphant bit of theatre.

Leonard Hirsch (1902-1995) British violinist. As a youth in the early nineteen thirties, I used to watch Leonard Hirsch as leader of the 2nd violins in the Hallé. Subsequently he moved to London where he became the first leader of the Philharmonia, only leaving in order to devote more time to his string quartet which was then very successful. He became the first Music Director of the BBC Training Orchestra, and I took over from him in 1968. He taught at the RCM London.

Christmas Humphreys (1901-1983) Travers Christmas Humphreys *QC* was a *British barrister* who prosecuted several controversial cases in the *1940s* and *1950s* and later became a High Court *Judge*. He was also the most noted convert to *Buddhism* in Britain and founded the *Buddhist Society, London*; he wrote books on *Mahayana Buddhism*. In his private life Humphreys was a noted *Shakespearean* scholar. During the London Blitz we used to fire-watch from his lovely house in Marlborough Place, St Johns Wood.

George Hurst (1926-) Conductor. At the age of 21 he was appointed professor of composition at the Peabody Institute of Baltimore and from 1950 to 1955 was concurrently conductor of the Peabody Conservatory Orchestra and the Symphony Orchestra of York, Pennsylvania, studying during this period with Pierre Monteux. George Hurst's influence on the training of young conductors is widely acknowledged. Almost every conductor that has emerged in the UK in the last thirty years has passed through his hands at some time, either at Canford or during the trainee conductor schemes that have been active during his years in Manchester and Bournemouth. His influence was strongly felt in Liverpool and with the BBC Training Orchestra

Emanuel Hurwitz (1919- 2006) British violinist. Readers of this book will already have realised the high regard I have for "Manny" Hurwitz, and this I think I share with all my musical friends and colleagues. Manny is experienced as a chamber musician and a fine orchestral leader, but it is in the former capacity that he excels.

His tone is full and vibrant – he can pick up any instrument and it immediately sounds like Manny, though that is not to say that the beautiful Brothers Amati violin he played throughout his career did nothing to enhance his performances. Apart from the sound he has to the fullest degree of instinctive ensemble sense needed for chamber music, and he can magically transmit this to others. He is a wonderful teacher and his way of pinpointing artistic problems with acuity and wit is valued by many eminent players. I will always be grateful for my long friendship with Manny, and his lovely wife Kaye, a fine viola player and a wonderful teacher.

Ernest Irving (1878 -1953) British film conductor and composer. I never knew him personally, but played in the Philharmonia for many film sessions at Denham studios. He was a great musician, highly respected by many eminent composers. He persuaded Ralph Vaughan Williams to write the music for *Scott of the Antarctic.* This project led the composer to the formation of his Seventh Symphony *Symphony Antartica* which was dedicated to him. He had the personality as a studio conductor to inspire hard-bitten session musicians to give of their best.

Herbert von Karajan (1908-1989) Austrian conductor. Undoubtably one of the very greatest of maestros. David Oistrakh (himself a fine conductor) hailed him as the greatest of all. But there are dissenting voices. For one thing, he applied to join the Nazi Party in 1935 in order to advance his career (as did Elizabeth Schwartzkopf), which many found hard to forgive. He is probably the most recorded conductor of all time, and played an important role in the development of the compact disk about 1980. I did very many concerts and recordings under him with the Philharmonia, and the standard of playing during his time was superb. He enthusiastically embraced all new forms of audio and video recording. His performances are always immaculate, for one thing because he only worked with the very finest orchestras and soloists. However, some find his actual music-making too polished, too sleek, and ultimately lacking the human quality we find in the true greats.

Rudolf Kempe (1910-1976) German conductor. Kempe was born in *Dresden* where he studied music. He played the *oboe* in a number of orchestras before becoming conductor of the Leipzig Opera in *1937*. He directed the *Dresden Staatskapelle* from *1949* to *1952*, and the Bavarian Staatsoper in *Munich* from *1952* to *1954* (succeeding *Georg Solti*). His debut at the *Bayreuth Festspielhaus* was in *1960*. From *1961* to *1975* he was conductor of the *Royal Philharmonic Orchestra*, from *1965* to *1972* worked with the Zürich *Tonhalle Orchestra*, and from *1967* to his death conducted the *Munich Philharmonic Orchestra*. In the final months of his life, he was closely associated with the *BBC Symphony Orchestra*. He died in *Zürich*.

He is particularly remembered for his performances and recordings of *Richard Strauss* (whose complete orchestral works he recorded) and *Richard Wagner*. I played only once for him, in a concert in Liverpool on 9th December 1958 when his programme included *Trittico Botticelliano* by Respighi, Schumann Piano Concerto with Bela Siki, and Brahms 4th Symphony. That single encounter was enough to establish him as my most ideal conductor. He worked quietly, without fuss, but when it came to the concert you remembered exactly what he had said. Above all, it was his eyes. They were rather piggy looking – quite small but very intense, and everyone felt their impact. Particularly memorable at that single concert was the rhythmic lilt he imparted to the last movement of the Schumann concerto. Many colleagues felt the same about him – he was a truly remarkable man.

Eda Kersey ( ) English violinist of remarkable talent. Almost entirely self-taught. She learnt by being taken to many concerts by her father. The only contact I had with her was as a student when she judged a competition at the RAM. Muriel accompanied her in a recital and was very impressed with her playing and her personality. There is a fine recording of the Bax Violin Concerto where she is accompanied by Sir Adrian Boult.

Otto Klemperer (1885-1973) German Conductor. I have written fairly extensively about Klemperer in the text, so it is sufficient to say that he was one of the very greatest conductors of the time. He had immense authority, and it was impressive to think one was working with a musician who had collaborated closely with Mahler. Walter Legge began to use him when it became apparent that Karajan's real aim was to become conductor of the Berlin Philharmonic, but there was a less than amiable relationship between the two. When Legge announced in 1959 that he was disbanding the Philharmonia, the players themselves re-instated it as a self-governing body, the New Philharmonia, and Klemperer was invited to be its Chief Conductor, a post he held with great acclaim to the end of his life. It was said that his *tempi* became inordinately slow in later life. I went to several concerts when I had left the orchestra, and the music, if somewhat slow, still had the unmistakeable stamp of a great and profound musician. There was a story going round that Daniel Barenboim as a young conductor was criticised by Klemperer for his tempo in the Beethoven *Eroica*. "Too slow, too slow!" he said. "But, Dr. Klemperer" replied Daniel "my tempo in that performance was almost exactly the same as in your last performance". "Maybe" growled the sage "but it's too slow for *you!*"

Sascha Lasserson (1890-1979) Violin pedagogue. Pupil of Leopold Auer in St Petersburg and fellow student with Mischa Elman, Sascha was as a player equal to the best products of that fabulous Russian school. He only lacked the showman personality to make a true virtuoso and found his metier in teaching. Before and after the War when he was settled in London, practically every violinist of the day worked with him. He gained universal respect and admiration. Heifetz himself held Sascha in highest regard. Speaking personally, he helped me more than anyone else. I recommend the book "Sascha Lasserson – Portrait of a Teacher" edited by his nephew Michael Lasserson. It is both entertaining and instructive.

Walter Legge (1906-1979) Impresario and possibly the most influential person in musical Britain in the mid 20th century. He had long nurtured the idea of creating an orchestra of the highest class, using only the finest British musicians and in 1945 this came to fruition. As virtual head of EMI he was able to launch a flood of great recordings with his new band and some of the finest European conductors. He was completely ruthless in hiring and firing players. His closest collaboration was with Karajan. He was married to the soprano Elizabeth Schwartzkopf, and acted almost as a Svengali to her vocal development.

Norman Del Mar (1920-1994) Conductor. He was a horn player in the Royal Philharmonic Orchestra, which was founded in 1946 by Sir Thomas Beecham. He became Sir Thomas's assistant, and Sir Thomas arranged his debut as a conductor in 1947. Also played in the Philharmonia, where he was, as in the RPO, 2nd horn to Dennis Brain. He championed British composers at home and abroad and introduced many composers and works to Britain, including Mahler's Sixth and Ninth Symphonies, Bartok's Violin Concerto No. 1 and Prokofiev's Fourth Symphony. I worked closely with him during his three years as Chief Conductor of the BBC Training Orchestra, during which time he reluctantly oversaw its transformation into the smaller proportions of the Academy of the BBC. He was the author of an acclaimed, three-volume work on the life and music of Richard Strauss, the last volume of which appeared in 1972.

Norman Del Mar, who was professor of conducting at the Royal College of Music in London from 1972 to 1990, made more than 70 recordings, and held honorary doctorates from several universities. He was always a stimulating and tremendously knowledgeable musician.

Sir Stanley Marchant (1883-1949) English church musician, teacher and composer. In 1914 he was appointed a professor at the RAM, where he became warden in 1934 and principal in 1936. . Marchant's music, the finest of which was inspired by ceremonial occasions at St Paul's Cathedral, is well crafted, though conservative in idiom, and shows the influence of Stanford and Parry. He was in office when I was a RAM student.

Sir Neville Marriner (1924-) English conductor. Trained as a violinist, he led a similar life to mine in the free-lance world of the early fifties, playing in the LPO and leading the second violins in the LSO. In 1959 he founded the Academy of St Martin-in-the-Fields. From the concertmaster's seat in this ensemble he gravitated towards conducting. Pierre Monteux became his mentor, and the ASMF became one of the most often recorded groups in history. He now works consistently with many orchestras world-wide.

Dennis Matthews (1919-1989) British pianist. Was brought up in Leamington Spa, not far from my wife Muriel (Angela Dale) in Coventry, who was his exact contemporary, so they often competed in music festivals. He studied at the RAM with Harold Craxton and became a popular soloist with British orchestras, appearing regularly with the Liverpool Phil. He had a truly encyclopaedic knowledge of music, being able to quote at the piano anything from the symphonic or operatic repertoire at the drop of a hat. He often appeared in BBC Third Programme Quiz programmes where his prowess in this respect was only occasionally matched by the conductor Norman Del Mar. He eventually was appointed to the Chair of music professor at Newcastle University. I played a violin and piano recital of Mozart sonatas with him in the Music Department.

Yehudi Menuhin (1916-1999) Violinist and conductor. Had one of the longest and most distinguished careers of any violinist in the 20th century. A great player by any standard, it was the highly charged emotional aspect of his playing which set him apart. He was also a committed educationalist, and is particularly remembered in Britain for his foundation of the Menuhin School in 1963 for musically gifted boys and girls. I have played often for his concerts and recordings, and he played several times with the Liverpool Philharmonic during my time as leader.

Pierre Monteux (1875-1964) French conductor. Originally a viola player he played chamber music with Pablo de Sarasate. He led the violas at the Paris Opéra- Comique for the premiere of Debussy's *Pelléas et Mélisande in 1902.* Subsequently he conducted for Diaghilev's Ballets Russes, and in this capacity directed the first performances of Stravinsky's *Petrouchka* (1911) and *The Rite of Spring* (1913). I treasure the memory of his Liverpool concert in the last year of his life.

Kathleen Mountain (1927 -) My sister, and now married to George Banks, a retired farmer and one of the nicest people I know. Kath has devoted her life to music just as exclusively as I have, but although she has played widely as a free-lance cellist, she is mainly a devoted teacher of music, with a larger than life personality that endears her to her pupils. She has carried on the tradition of our parents in music teaching, and since I retired from Scotland in 1990, Muriel and I have helped run the ensemble of pupils and local amateurs which meets every few weeks in her music studio in the lovely North Yorkshire village of Fearby. Now, this work is continued by my son Paul.

Leopold Mozart (1790-1787) Father of the great Wofgang, Leopold published his Treatise on the Fundamental Principals of Violin Playing in 1756, the very year of his famous son's birth. It is the first comprehensive Violin School, and is still well worth reading in the fine translation by Editha Knocker (OUP second edition 1951). I have quoted his revealing paragraph regarding soloist and orchestral players in full.

Boyd Neel (1905-1981) Trained as a surgeon, renowned as a conductor, Boyd Neel led a richly diverse life. He founded his eponymous String Orchestra in 1933, and continued to direct it with only short wartime breaks until he left in 1953 to become Dean of the Faculty of Music at Toronto University. His influence on the growth of high class chamber orchestras in this country and abroad was immense.

David Oistrakh (1908-1974) The greatest representative of the Russian school of violin playing. Combined technical excellence with glowing warmth of tone and the most wonderful perception of the music, from classical to modern. I was privileged to take part in his recording and concert of the Khachaturian Violin Concerto with the Philharmonia, conducted by the composer

Franz Osborn (1905-1955) German pianist. Came to England as refugee from Nazis in 1933. Sonata partnership with Max Rostal. My wife had post-graduate lessons with him after leaving the Academy. She and I had several valuable coaching sessions from him on violin and piano sonatas.

Manoug Parikian (1921-1987) Violinist. Armenian, born in Turkey, lived in Cyprus as a youth. Came to England for study at Trinity College with Louis Pecskai. Quickly achieved fame as an outstanding orchestral leader, particularly of the Philharmonia Orchestra. Was very influential to me and helpful in many ways. Taught at the RCM and the RAM. A fine soloist of impeccable musicianship.

Sir John Pritchard (1921-1989) Conductor. Music Director of RLPO 1957-1963. He recommended me as Leader in 1955. Notable for Mozart performances and for opera. Closely associated with Glyndbourne from his earliest days. His quick brain and ready wit made him greatly admired by orchestras. I will always treasure the memory of our association in Liverpool and later with the LPO in Glyndebourne.

Ernest Read 1879-1965 English Music Educationalist. Aural training expert and pioneer of the Youth Orchestra movement. He was a most lively person and loved by all who knew him. It was he who first encouraged me to go to the Academy in London, and he who first said to me – "You should be an orchestral leader".

Colonel Ricketts (1881-1945) Pen name Kenneth J. Alford, writer of Colonel Bogey and many other well known marches. He was Director of the Royal Marines Plymouth Divisional Band and was my commanding officer when I first joined it in 1943. He gained the soubriquet of the English Souza.

Hugo Rignold (1905-1976) English conductor. Succeeded Sargent as conductor of the Liverpool Philharmonic but left shortly before I joined. Was then conductor of the Birmingham Orchestra, but returned to Liverpool frequently as a guest. Had suffered there because of snobbery regarding his past as a dance band violinist, but he was a highly competent musician and conductor. He was especially adept as a concerto accompanist, and I remember very well in 1954 a record he did one morning at Abbey Road studios of the Rachmaninov Paganini Variations with Moiseivitch as soloist. It was "in the can"with time to spare, and a friend and I joined the two of them afterwards for a hilarious lunch in a nearby pub. That record got top marks from the critics, and stayed in the catalogue for years!

Max Rostal (1906-1991) Violinist and teacher. Pupil of Carl Flesch he had a tremendous influence on British violin playing. Pupils include Norbert Brainin and Eric Gruenberg and many others. Publications are many, including edition of the Beethoven Violin Sonatas. Sonata partnership with Franz Osborn. I played for several of his concerto performances.

Albert Sammons (1886-1957)   Perhaps the greatest of all British violinists. To my regret I never met him, but went to his concerts and played in the orchestra for some of his concerto performances. His performances of the Elgar and Delius concertos are particularly memorable. I remember attending a recital of his in Plymouth when I was still in the Royal Marines. I sat on the very front row, within touching distance of the great man. He played the Mozart Rondo from the Haffner Serenade, arranged by Kreisler, which has almost constant spiccato running passagework, and I was horrified by the roughness and scratchiness of his bow strokes. But a friend, whose opinion I valued greatly, and was sitting further back in the hall, raved about the brilliance and clarity of the Mozart. This taught me that to project in a large auditorium you need some edginess and abrasive quality that might be objectionable close to.

Sir Malcolm Sargent (1895-1967) Conductor. Sargent tackled a wide range of repertoire (much of it he recorded) but was particularly noted for performances of choral music, most often with the Huddersfield Choral Society and the Liverpool Phil. During my term as Leader we recorded Handel's *Messiah*, Mendelssohn's *Elijah* and Walton's *Belshazzar's Feast*. He was chief conductor at the Proms from 1948 to 1966 and of the BBC Symphony Orchestra from 1955 to 1957. In 1954 I attended the first performance of Walton's opera *Troilus and Cressida* which he conducted at Covent Garden. His sometimes abrasive personality was contrasted by his many examples of kindness and charity. His conducting technique was unsurpassable. I have played with him from earliest youth onward and cannot recall any error in his performances.

Colin Sauer (1924-)   English violinist. My fellow student at the RAM with Rowsby Woof. He was a most immaculate player and was the outstanding member of Woof's class at the time. He led the Dartington String Quartet for many years with great distinction.

Elizabeth Schwartzkopf (1915-2006)   World famous soprano. Married to Walter Legge. Many records with the Philharmonia.

Famous for choosing eight of her own recordings on Desert Island Disks.

Constantin Silvestri (1913-1969) Romanian conductor. He became the principal conductor of the *Bournemouth Symphony Orchestra*, and raised their level of performance. As with another Romanian conductor, *Sergiu Celibidache,* Silvestri expected to have many hours for rehearsal, and this led to very polished, well crafted performances. A biography of Silvestri was written by musicologist *Eugen Pricope*. On his few visits to Liverpool he was most impressive and influential.

Ronald Smith (1922-2004) Virtuoso pianist and expert on the music of Alkan. Fellow student at the RAM. Many fine recordings and concerto appearances.

Walter Susskind (1913-1980) Czech conductor and pianist resident in England since 1940. I played under his baton many times in the Philharmonia, the RLPO and the BBC Training Orchestra.

Henryk Szeryng (1918-1988) Polish born Mexican violinist. Studied with Carl Flesch and studied composition with Nadia Boulanger. Was fluent in seven languages. Became a Mexican citizen and accepted a post at the university there. In 1954 he was re-discovered by the pianist Artur Rubinstein and encouraged to take up his career as a violin virtuoso that continued for the rest of his life. His musical testament is part of the era of the greatest 20th century violinists. He visited Liverpool often and I was privileged to perform the Bach two Violin Concerto with him. He gave me several invaluable lessons and shared a recital with my wife at the Walker Art Gallery.

Vilem Tausky (1910-2004) Czech conductor and composer, resident in England since 1940. I played concertos with him during his time with the BBC Northern Orchestra, and collaborated with him for many years in the Harlech Orchestral Course.

Arturo Toscanini (1867-1956) The most famous conductor of the 20th century. I played in his Brahms Cycle with the Philharmonia Orchestra in London Festival Hall in 1952.

Herbert Whone (1925-) School friend. Violinist, photographer, artist and writer. Whilst co-leader of the Scottish National Orchestra he painted many fine pictures of the Glasgow scene, including a series of the trams which have now disappeared.

Marie Wilson (1903-1983) British violinist. First woman to lead a major Symphony Orchestra (the BBC). The finest woman orchestral violinist of her day. Was a colleague of mine in the Philharmonia and the LPO and I owe much to her help and inspiration.

Sir Henry Wood (1869-1944) Founder of the Henry Wood Proms, he conducted the Senior Orchestra at the RAM in my student days. Both Muriel and I played concertos with him. He was perhaps the most highly respected and revered musician in the country.

Rowsby Woof (1883-1943) Violin professor at the RAM and my teacher. Groves Dictionary of Music and Musicians, 5th edition (1954): "b. Ironbridge Shropshire, 18/1/1883 ; d.London 31 Dec 1943 English violinist; studied RAM in London with Hans Wessely. In 1909 was appointed professor [at RAM] where his teaching proved so successful as to induce him to give up solo playing and devote his whole time to the training of students. Amongst his pupils were Paul Beard, Jean Pougnet and Sidney Griller. Woof's publications include "Technique and interpretation in violin playing", "Elementary studies", "Scale books", short pieces and arrangements of Bach and Geminiani"

Olive Zorian (1916-1965) British violinist. The Zorian Quartet was highly valued by Benjamin Britten. Was a colleague of mine in the London Harpsichord Ensemble.

Bibliography

A Treatise on the Fundamental Principles of Violin Playing

Leopold Mozart   Translated by Editha Knocker

Oxford University Press 1951

My Orchestras and Other Adventures – The Memoirs of Boyd Neel

Edited by J. David Finch

ISBN 0-8020-5674-1

Sascha Lasserson – Portrait of a Teacher

Edited by Michael Lasserson

Kahn & Averill ISBN 1 871 082 83 8

Mademoiselle – Conversations with Nadia Boulanger

Bruno Monsaignon   Translated by Robyn Marsack

Carcanet Press Limited   ISBN 0-85635-603-4

Philharmonia Orchestra – A Record of Achievement

Stephen J. Pettitt

Robert Hale ISBN   0-7090-2371-5

The New Grove Dictionary of Music and Musicians

Edited by Stanley Sadie

ISBN   1-56159-174-2

Two Centuries of Music in Liverpool

Stainton de B. Taylor

Rockliff Brothers Limited Liverpool

Talks with Emanuel Hurwitz – 82 years with the violin

Riki Gerardy

Zelia Ltd

INDEX

A

R

Rankin, Bill and Shirley 196
Rattle, Sir Simon 56, 150
Rauzzini 3
Rawlins, Mrs., Lady Superintendent 14
Rawsthorne, Alan 73, 81
Rayment, Malcom 216
Read, Ernest 11, 13, 16, 22, 129, 276
Reed, W H 123
Ricci, Ruggerio 260
Ricketts, Colonel RM 31, 33, 276
Riddle, Frederick 21
Rignold, Hugo 96, 134, 157, 276
Robinson, Adam 237
Robinson, Hilary 56–57, 71
Robinson, Sally 237
Rocca, Guiseppe 243
Rodewald Chamber Concerts 19
Rogerson, Haydn 10
Rosand, Aaron 260
Rosenheim, Sam 56
Rostal, Max 79, 275–276
Rostropovich, Mstislav 176
Rowlette, Tom 144
Royal Academy of Music, London ix, 11–12
Royal Marines ix, 30–31, 35, 276–277
Royal Scottish Academy of Music and Drama ix, x, 8, 195, 198
Rubinstein, Artur 162, 278
Ruggerius violin 5, 92

S

Sacher, Paul 60
Salpeter, Max 81, 87, 95
Sammons, Albert 10, 123–124, 277
Santorini 216
Sargent, Sir Malcolm 90, 119, 122, 156, 277
Sauer, Colin 15, 18, 242, 277
Saunders, Wilfred 242
Schaeffer, Elaine 156

Scherchen, Hermann 157
Schubert, Franz xiii, 39, 57, 154, 234, 265
Schwartzkopf, Elizabeth 84, 266, 270, 272, 277
Scott, Ernest 15, 55, 57, 81, 96, 142
Scott, John (Jock) 201
Scottish Arts Council ix, 218, 224
Scottish National Orchestra 204, 279
Scottish National Youth Orchestra 206
Scottish Society of Composers ix, 217
Sellick, Phyllis 161
Serkin, Rudolf 39
Sevcik 6
Shanghai Children's Palaces 234
Shiner, Ronald 125
Shipley 3–5, 12, 40
Sibelius, Jean 47, 75, 77, 134, 159, 205, 268
Siki, Bela 271
Silver, Millicent 102, 266
Silverstein, Joseph 136
Silvestri, Constantin 158, 278
Singapore ix, 40, 44, 46–47, 49
Smith, Cyril 161, 171
Smith, David 206
Smith, Ronald 18, 278
Solomon 160–161, 171
Sotheby's 243
Sowerbutts, J. A. 16
Spalding, Albert 259
Spedding, Frank 215
Spiegl, Fritz 147
St. George's Hall, Bradford 9
Steel, Harry and Marjory 12–13
Steinberg, William 169
Stern, Isaac 116, 225, 234
Stevenson Hall 200
Stiff, Wilfred 134
Stockholm 74–75, 86, 180
Stokowski, Leopold 185
Stone, David 203, 215
Stoner, Lieutenant RM 31, 36
Storace, Nancy 3

Printed in the United Kingdom
by Lightning Source UK Ltd.
122701UK00001B/125/A